German Ways of War

War Culture

Edited by Daniel Leonard Bernardi

Books in this series address the myriad ways in which warfare informs diverse cultural practices, as well as the way cultural practices—from cinema to social media—inform the practice of warfare. They illuminate the insights and limitations of critical theories that describe, explain, and politicize the phenomena of war culture. Traversing both national and intellectual borders, authors from a wide range of fields and disciplines collectively examine the articulation of war, its everyday practices, and its impact on individuals and societies throughout modern history.

For a list of all the titles in the series, please see the last page of the book.

German Ways of War

The Affective Geographies and Generic Transformations of German War Films

JAIMEY FISHER

Rutgers University Press
New Brunswick, Camden, and Newark, New Jersey, and London

Library of Congress Cataloging-in-Publication Data

Names: Fisher, Jaimey, author.
Title: German ways of war : the affective geographies and generic transformations of German war films / Jaimey Fisher.
Description: New Brunswick : Rutgers University Press, 2022. | Series: War culture | Includes bibliographical references and index.
Identifiers: LCCN 2021050392 | ISBN 9781978829176 (paperback) | ISBN 9781978829183 (cloth) | ISBN 9781978829190 (epub) | ISBN 9781978829206 (pdf)
Subjects: LCSH: War films—Germany—History and criticism. | Space and time in motion pictures.
Classification: LCC PN1995.9.W3 F575 2022 | DDC 791.43/658—dc23/eng/20220202
LC record available at https://lccn.loc.gov/2021050392

A British Cataloging-in-Publication record for this book is available from the British Library.

♾ The paper used in this publication meets the requirements of the American National Standard for Information Sciences—Permanence of Paper for Printed Library Materials, ANSI Z39.48-1992.

www.rutgersuniversitypress.org

Manufactured in the United States of America

An earlier version of chapter 3 appeared as Jaimey Fisher, "Landscapes of Death: Sound, Space, and Commemoration in G. W. Pabst's Westfront 1918 (1930)," in *The Many Faces of Weimar Cinema: New Approaches to Weimar Film*, ed. Christian Rogowski (Rochester, N.Y.: Camden House, 2010), 268–285.

An earlier version of chapter 5 appeared as Jaimey Fisher, "Trains, Planes, and the Occasional Car: The Rubble-Film as Demobilization Film," in *German Postwar Films: Life and Love in the Ruins*, ed. William Rasch and Wilfried Wilms (New York: Palgrave Macmillan, 2008), 175–192, reproduced with permission of Palgrave Macmillan.

For my daughter, Alexandra, who put up with travels, and travails, far and wide in support of this book

Contents

German Ways of War

1

Introduction

Two moments from the war film genre in Germany can illuminate each other across five decades. First, in the 1917/1918 *Das Tagebuch des Dr. Hart* (*The Diary of Dr. Hart*), a finely dressed doctor who has built a lucrative practice at an upper-class spa sits alone in a moving train. Then he catches a glimpse of the famed Hermannsdenkmal (Hermann's monument), near Detmold, and nods knowingly. In the very next scene, he reappears, but now he is fully clad in uniform: this private, well-to-do person has been remade for the looming war, his middle-class personhood recast in the mold of a nationally committed soldier. But this process of transformational scaling, as I shall investigate it, tellingly transpires on the move, amid panoramic landscapes viewed from a speeding train: military mobilization and its movie depiction are intimately, inextricably interwoven with modern forms of movement, especially travel, and the affects bred of them. Over forty eventful years later, in the 1959 *Rommel ruft Kairo* (*Rommel Calls Cairo*), a small group of 1942 Afrika Korps soldiers moves in a desert convoy, traversing the northeastern Sahara as part of General Erwin Rommel's famous "southern" campaigns. After spotting a British surveillance plane high above, however, they stop to discuss assuming fake identities. Within seconds, they are prying the Nazi insignia from their uniforms and lamenting "If only the führer knew . . ." Here a parallel but inverse recasting of wartime subjectivity prepares postwar Germans for the Cold War, for which Germany, in the late 1950s, was itself being remade. These sequences highlight how the genre functions spatially throughout, how war films' combat is continually contextualized by spatial, even tourist operations and their concomitant affective mechanisms.

In attending to such moments across these crucial decades, the present study addresses a surprising lacuna in German studies and in European film studies by investigating German war films from the 1914 outbreak of World War I to the building of the Berlin Wall and fading of the mainstream genre in the early 1960s. These were, of course, touchstone decades in the history of Europe, witnessing, for instance, six changes of government and even governmental forms in its largest country, Germany, largely the result of Germans' recurring wars and militarism. Given these fundamental transformations and the global afterlife of this militarism, the topic is central to German and even European culture. If militarism is the colonization by militaristic values of the broader society and polity, then it was certainly a key force in twentieth-century Germany and Europe.[1] But for various reasons examined in the present study, there is surprisingly little work on the role of narrative feature films in creating, abetting, and augmenting militarism as a cultural, social, and political force in Germany.[2] *German Ways of War* aims to address such oversights while also offering a theory of a genre that has received only modest attention in Anglo-American film studies—that is, nothing on the order of the theoretically sophisticated attention afforded to melodramas, Westerns, or horror films. In particular, *German Ways of War* explores both historical and recent theories of space, movement, and affect—approaches developed in the so-called spatial and affective turns of cultural theory—to explore how war films realize their fundamentally political projects.

German Ways of War builds on the oft mentioned linkages between cinema and warfare as they have been elaborated, for instance, in pivotal works by Paul Virilio, Samuel Weber, Rey Chow, Anton Kaes, Caren Kaplan, Tanine Allison, Roger Stahl, and so on, but it also aims to move in a different direction. Conventional links between audiovisual media and violence tend to focus on the similarities between cinematic looking and military targeting, between shooting the camera and discharging the gun. Such has been the force of Virilio's insight along these lines in his influential *War and Cinema: The Logistics of Perception* that many after him have primarily worked to unpack and elaborate.[3] But most of these studies do not illuminate other key aspects of the genre, including the spatial contexts in which the films locate their (often quite limited) combat scenes and sequences. As W. J. T. Mitchell notes, one should take a more capacious approach to the operations of images, one highlighting their imbrication in institutions, discourses, bodies, and so on.[4] For *German Ways of War*, these will be, above all, the broader spatial operations of the genre. Instead of focusing primarily on the intersection of visuality and violence, the present study argues that the films produce and then negotiate spaces, like those in *Dr. Hart* and *Cairo* mentioned above, that frame their violence in ways often more revealing (culturally, politically, socioeconomically) than their battle scenes. Looking beyond the films' battles, one can appreciate how they frame violence within specific spatio-affective operations that conjure the films' narratives, themes, and technical aspects. These spatial and affective transformations manifest themselves in the genre as simultaneously national and transnational, mapping for viewers a world beyond their own national borders as well as often being, as cultural and economic endeavors, produced abroad.

More than other film genres, these simultaneously national and transnational spaces of the war film negotiate political projects and personal subjectivities—that is, deliberately invoke their viewers as soldiers and/or citizens—and do so, I argue, largely by their production of novel spaces and affect-intensified movement through them. The direction of film studies since the dominance of psychoanalysis and screen theories through the early 1990s has been largely bifurcated between new film history and affect, often cognitive, theory, neither of which can, alone, very effectively elucidate the political character or potential of narrative audiovisual media.[5] Spatial theories as they intersect affect have the considerable advantage of foregrounding technological transformations at the core of film as a mobile medium. The affective pleasures of the war genre are, as I shall explore, based as much on travel and viewers' experiences of novel spaces as they are on violence. In this way, this study will also take the affective turn in a somewhat different direction. This affective turn has manifested a number of strains, from phenomenological to cognitive to ecomedia studies.[6] With narrative war films' particularly political projects, affect and emotion certainly play key roles in their agendas, be they for or against their characters' engagement in combat. Questions relating to the deployment of affect and emotion in large-scale political projects seem to me among the most important that we can pose in film and media studies, either theoretical or historical or both. But for war films, these affective-emotional political mechanisms prove, as I shall unfold herein, particularly spatial and emphatically mobile.

The turn to the affective-emotional function of cultural objects has also impacted the work of critical geographers in the last twenty years—indeed, I think, the well-known emphasis on affectively evocative, emotionally invested place might be seen as a trope in geography relating to the recent affective turn. But an affect-inflected geography attends to much more than emotional affinities for place. Nigel Thrift has highlighted how affect and emotion both intensify and condition attention dedicated to spaces and especially spatial distances, all of which will be key themes throughout this study.[7] It is notable, I think, that critical military studies has occasionally emphasized distance in war and wartime distance but not taken up any kind of geographical framework in a systematic way.[8] Liz Biondi, Joyce Davidson, and Mack Smith point out that acknowledging the affective-emotional in geography also means that the body as and in space is foregrounded.[9] The body, particularly as it navigates and is navigated over spatial distances, will also be a crucial theme throughout the present study. In the work of Alexa Weik von Mossner, these affective and spatial theories have also been applied to ecological texts engaging mechanisms that can elucidate war films' consistent depiction and manipulation of landscape and territory and the battlefields bred of them. As war films travel and traverse distance, landscape, and topological networks, the bodies and their affective responses become crucial means for the films' political projects. The affective-emotional responses, initially at the level of the individual body, are then, as I shall explore, carefully scaled in these films to the collective projects, pro- or contrawar, that operate at the surface of each film.

Building on this interweaving of affect theory and critical geography, *German Ways of War* explores how the war genre arose with and absorbed spatial mechanisms and operations fundamental to modernity, including specific wartime "geographical imaginations."[10] In a way not coincidentally parallel to colonial representations (a linkage explored below), war films consistently produce new spaces in which viewers can then recognize themselves as part of a collective politico-spatial project—the "imperial gaze" noted in critical military studies is always already embedded within broader spatial operations.[11] These mechanisms underscore a central insight of the kind of critical geography that the study foregrounds: thinking and understanding are always situated in the world, always presume and build on some imagination of place, especially a place of the self in a dynamically conceived and then mapped world. These films participate, in short, in what some critics have underscored as a thoroughgoing and wide-ranging process of "worlding."[12] Moreover, to produce such spaces and such citizens in them—notably, both male and female citizen-subjects—the films depict but also destroy older forms of space. In this manner, they revealingly resemble and realize the operations of modernity's capitalist economy, which also makes telling appearances in most of these films. In their economic work—and it is a genre very much based on forms of labor—the films repeatedly stage the modern "creative destruction" of older spaces and socialities inhabiting them.[13]

Such an affective-geographic approach foregrounds key aspects of the modern military as well as militaristic modernity while also offering a means to read closely the content of these cultural products. Such close reading is an undertaking I still see at the core of humanities scholarship's use value for scholars, students, and/or general audiences.[14] In this vein, I would underscore how Fredric Jameson's *The Geopolitical Aesthetic* was never really elaborated effectively at that very moment when psychoanalysis and screen theories were losing their theoretical purchase for many film scholars, at that watershed moment when new film history and affect-cognitive theory were ascendant. Some thirty years on from Jameson's declaring that to his much-cited notion of the political unconscious "must be added what I now call a geopolitical unconscious," I would submit that the promise of such an approach has gone largely unfilled.[15]

In its analysis of 1960s and 1970s political thrillers, *Geopolitical Aesthetic* has, in my opinion, two great advantages: first, it understands the spatialization of filmic narrative as crucial to how a text navigates the world it conjures—such operations and mechanisms prove revealing culturally, historically, and politically.

Second, *Geopolitical Aesthetic* argues that these spatial processes suggest how producers and viewers imagine the social: they grasp, with some futility, at social totality and, in particular, at how a text can participate in the political unconscious. For Jameson, a long series of conspiracy-minded films like *The Parallax View* (1974) and *Three Days of the Condor* (1975) attempts to come to terms with social totality through their navigation of disparate, often fragmentary yet revealing spaces. These films, says Jameson, are "more spatial" than others, especially more than those works less preoccupied with society's collective form.[16] In this way, Jameson uncovers a geopolitical aesthetic via a film genre. Genre, in Jameson's hands, traces these kinds of thoroughgoing sociocultural shifts and the remade subjectivities produced by them. Another relevant example within his study is his tracking of the emergence of the war-correspondent film out of the earlier war genre in the 1970s and 1980s, a generic transformation materializing broader changes in both politics and political subjectivities.[17] In foregoing the typologies of more traditional genre studies, I shall similarly explore the mechanisms by which new generic forms emerge out of older genres—forms of emergence that help manifest important cultural and political transformations.

At the same time, there is more to say about the spatial processes that link film-textual operations to the contexts around them. Jameson continued to write of the significance of space and spatial imagination through the 2010s, but the work on which he seems to most base such mechanisms, Kevin Lynch's *Image of the City*, is a largely phenomenological text about how people imagine their environments.[18] Throughout *German Ways of War*, I attempt to take Jameson's thinking on a geopolitical aesthetic of a genre as an inspiration—but to contribute to it more differentiated concepts of space, movement, and affect in the war genre. This would be, somewhat similarly, my stance toward Tom Conley's groundbreaking *Cartographic Cinema*, which I also regard as indelibly influential for the study herein. Both works suggest that sensitivity to space and spatial processes resonates with a work's simultaneously narrative and political mechanisms. But neither goes very far, so to say, in examining the specifically spatial processes in their genres. The war genre can, from World War I through World War II and into the two Germanys, elucidate such space-destroying and space-making processes, multiple and multifaceted operations that structure the chapters to come.

For these reasons, even as it engages with these landmark theoretical texts, *German Ways of War* elaborates upon them with recent work in geography and planning—work, as noted above, that has sustained its own affective turn in recent years.[19] The study will explore how mechanisms of space and affect are central to individual and national self-understanding and argues that, over these violently fluctuating years, such mechanisms were central to the trajectory of German history. In this investigation, I focus on moments of generic transformation, rather than on mere types or typologies of films, to comprehend how genres are interwoven and mutually illuminating with history. In these transformations of the genre, the project foregrounds the constructed characters of space, affect, and geography, including the historical rise of an aggressively expansionist "geopolitical" consciousness (that understood itself as geopolitical) in concert with the war genre. In these years and in this way, while deploying spatial and affective concepts and categories to comprehend the genre, I foreground these historical characters to chart their remarkable development throughout this period. If a geopolitical consciousness and aesthetic helped constitute the core of the historical war film genre in Germany, then the spatial imaginaries and the affective geographies they conjure proved indispensable to their selling of dubious political projects.

Throughout the chapters of this study, the production of novel spaces and evocations of new affects transform the genre as it unfolds historically. In their collective and political projects, war films consistently manipulate the movement, mobility, territory, scales, and networks with which both space and individual agency unfold, a recurring mechanism entwining narrative-generated affect and political process. Alongside this historical and influential unfolding of geography and geopolitics, *German Ways of War* works with several recent notions owing to contemporary critical geography, including the importance of landscape versus territory as well as the vectored power dynamics underpinning mapping (in chapter 2); the intersection of landscape and gender (also chapter 2); the production and manipulation of scale, which foregrounds the intersection of spatial and political levels and hierarchies (chapters 3 and 4); the recasting of distance with affectively thrilling military technologies (chapter 4); and the later centrality of dispersive networks rather than clarion hierarchy and a transition to topological rather than topographical modern spaces in the genre (chapter 6). All these mechanisms contribute to the affectively resonant geographies manifesting themselves in the genre's historical transformation through the decades—in short, to their careful cultivation and manipulation of their affective geographies.

Genre and German Film Studies

With this approach at the intersection of media, affect, and theories of space, *German Ways of War* aims to position itself within German studies, European film studies, and media theory by exploring a genre too often overlooked. In terms of German studies, major works on German cinema, unlike those in Anglo-American and French film studies, have tended to shy away from genre study. German film studies has been largely dominated by two approaches: first, a focus on specific historical periods, and second, a focus on Germany's art cinema and auteurist traditions. On the former count, the marquee events would seem to align with the radical ruptures in governmental, social, and cultural forms in the years 1914, 1918/1919, 1933, 1945, and 1989/1990, those years that most often grace the covers of these histories. Given Germany's historical vicissitudes in the twentieth century, the tendency to focus on historical periods is certainly understandable and warranted. And this approach has produced groundbreaking work, including Anton Kaes's *Shell Shock Cinema*, Eric Rentschler's *Ministry of Illusion*, Sabine Hake's *Popular Cinema of the Third Reich*, Thomas Elsaesser's *New German Cinema*, and Marco Abel's *The Counter-Cinema of the Berlin School*. This important work has also led to an abiding emphasis on conventional historical periodization in even recent analyses of German cinema, including edited volumes like Noah Isenberg's *Weimar Cinema: An Essential Guide*, Christian Rogowski's *The Many Faces of Weimar Cinema*, Hake and John Davidson's *Framing the Fifties*, and Abel and Fisher's *Berlin School and Its Global Contexts*.

This epochal approach, however, does leave something of a gap in trans-period genre criticism that *German Ways of War* attempts to address: the present study aims to take up questions of continuity and rupture among these different eras. Investigating the war genre historically entails engaging with works that were often regarded (and procedurally processed) as propaganda, including films that were also carefully censored during wartime. Neither of those aspects, however, seems a compelling reason to ignore the films, especially given how important many ended up being in the history of German culture, including in the historical relationship between culture and (conventional, self-declared) politics. For example, as Klaus Kreimeier recounts, two of Karl Ritter's films—*Urlaub auf Ehrenwort* (*Holiday on a Promise*) of 1937 and *Pour le Mérite* (*Medal of Honor*) of 1938 (the latter analyzed in detail below)—were crucial in the SS's relatively positive assessment of cinema's power and ascendancy (the SS being the Schutzstaffel) as well as in convincing Hitler of Ufa's utility to his propaganda efforts (Ufa being the Universum-Film Aktiengesellschaft).[20] For the present study, which attempts to comprehend how war films work (and work effectively), such context seems all the more reason to engage these movies. Films are virtually always collective projects that speak to numerous personal, social, political needs, and just because they might entail the work of individuals outside the conventional film industry (like political officials) does not mean they have had less impact. Indeed, if one wants to consider the role of culture in political projects mobilizing both resources and psychologies, it seems time to reexamine such works (see chapter 4, on cinema under the Nazis). Such a reexamination seems all the more occasioned by the increasingly sophisticated understanding of military culture in the recent wave of critical military studies discussed throughout this study.

As Timothy Corrigan and Patricia White observe in their massive anthology-overview of film theory, there has hardly been a concept more central to both film theory and history than genre.[21] Yet in German film studies (with a few intriguing exceptions, like Johannes von Moltke's *No Place like Home* and Laura Heins's *Nazi Film Melodrama*), even in works that consider film pitched at a popular market, there is a general neglect of substantial scholarship on the history and theory of film genres, something that the present volume aims to address.[22] There are a few other exceptions, like Karsten Witte's important work on the Nazi period or Michael Wedel's on operettas, but they are still in the decided minority compared to the previously mentioned, usually periodized studies. And, as noted above, investigating the histories of genre should not focus solely on popular cinema but rather reconceptualize film history in a way that can pertain to both popular and art cinema. As with its approach to conventional periodization, this volume deploys theories of genre to reconsider and refigure foundational notions about German film history. In these ways, this work aims to offer a fundamental reconsideration of where German film studies has been and where it will now go.[23]

In Anglo-American film studies, work on war films (e.g., Jeanine Basinger, J. David Slocum, Douglas A. Cunningham and John Nelson, Allison, and Stahl) has tended to focus on questions of character, objectives, and plots.[24] Another important set of studies has engaged the pressing yet still-elusive question of violence,[25] but *German Ways of War* explores the implications of new theories of space and affect for the war genre, even as studies of (non-wartime) space and travel in cinema have begun to appear in the last ten years (Jeffrey Ruoff and Alexandra Schneider, Jennifer Lynn Peterson, Julia Hallam and Les Roberts, and Lynne Kirby, all to be discussed below).[26] Exploring war and combat cinema—the cornerstone of the modern military-entertainment industrial complex, now much discussed in critical military studies (Timothy Lenoir and Luke Caldwell)[27]—allows European and German film studies to contribute to media studies more generally. Germany helped pioneer the war film as nationalist propaganda during World War I; witnessed the sustained, often war-critical production trend of the late 1920s / early 1930s; then, infamously, further refined wartime propaganda before and during World War II; and, finally, demonstrated an abiding commitment to the genre even after World War II—in the late 1940s and into the 1950s, when it remained one of West Germany's most popular genres. Given this important history of the German (cultural) ways of war, this is an area where Germany's meandering cinematic Sonderweg (particular/special path) can contribute to media and critical military studies in general.

Genre and/as Film History

By exploring film culture across conventional historical caesurae, *German Ways of War* attempts something new: to open new pathways to comprehending German film history. In the field of history, for instance, some have reconsidered conventional periodization, particularly Konrad Jarausch and Michael Geyer.[28] In rethinking and revising this sort of conventional periodization, *German Ways of War* is not in any way a- or anti-historical but rather intends to open up film history in new ways: it indexes and tracks such history via continuities as well as vicissitudes within an abiding genre. A transperiod film history affords the opportunity to register that history in different ways, to highlight both fundamental transformations and suspect continuities. Second, tracing genres past these conventional caesurae of German history aims to show how German cinema has been, from its earliest stages, intriguing even in its popular cinema. German cinema is also, fundamentally, a cinema of genres, and art cinema (as I shall suggest in chapters 3 and 7) can and, indeed, should be seen in the larger context of such popular and genre cinema. Third, foregrounding generic transformations across the conventional breaks in German history, as I have argued in the anthology *Generic Histories*, allows us to more fully attend to the context and institutions around cinema, for example, to better comprehend its industry and production trends while also folding such contextual information into readings of the films themselves.[29] Finally, by tracing generic transformations across the traditional periods of German history, from the 1910s to the early 1960s, I aim to illuminate anew canonical objects from more conventional film histories. Analyzed in isolation as they often are, such films, like the 1930 *Westfront 1918* or the 1959 *Die Brücke* (*The Bridge*), appear quite different once located within longer-term genre histories.

With what critical conceptual tools should one trace such a winding transformation of a genre? While *German Ways of War* is engaged with recent media theories of space, movement, and affect, my generic approach also follows the recent turn in film studies to more historically based research. The proposed shift herein from violent combat per se to the spatio-affective contextualization of such violence occasions a careful investigation of that context. In seeking generic transformations in the historical archive of both document and film, it is important to acknowledge the constituent aspects of any fiction film. Rick Altman is probably the most influential contemporary theorist of film genre and has offered much-cited linguistic analogies for genre. For instance, a genre's semantics refer to "shared plots, key scenes, character types, familiar objects or recognizable shots and sounds" and thereby seem quite close to conventional iconographic theories of genre.[30] Altman suggests that one can judge a film's semantics in part through still images from the film, an assertion underscoring its relationship to mise-en-scène and, in certain genres, space. On the other hand, a genre's syntax refers to the "building blocks" of a genre like "plot structure, character relationships, or image and sound montage."[31] Certain genres will operate more by a semantic approach, some more by syntax, but both semantics and syntax operate simultaneously. The war film, indeed, has relied on both, although in various ways at different moments in its history—a variety that will elucidate the vagaries of that history herein.

Altman's second key contribution to genre study, the notion of genrification, underscores shifts from mere typologies of genre to the historical dimensions of these semantics and syntax.[32] If Altman's notion of generic semantics and syntax builds on older iconographic and narrative analyses, genrification hints at what has largely replaced earlier understandings of genre—namely, a historical-discursive approach. This interest in the historical character of genres and their transformations can also be seen as a reaction to structuralism, which both Steve Neale and Altman (two of the leading proponents of the historical-discursive approach) criticize for its tendency to dehistoricize genre.[33] Tracing genre via its historical transformations will be at the core of the present project—the historical conditioning of generic syntax and semantics tells us not only about the films in question but also, I will argue, about that history. Rather than focusing on typologies or the categorization of films, as in many traditional genre studies, the focus herein will be on case studies, with close readings of films that transformed the genre. In this way, the goal is not to classify films by types imposed from above but to comprehend how the generic processes and historical transformations are manifest in particular works. Thus above all, Altman emphasizes the process character of genrification, a charting of its ongoing unfolding.[34] Genrification, in effect, helped open up genre study to the new film history of the 1990s. Foregoing and rethinking the conventional typologies of genre studies, Altman underscores how these processes do not produce a linear up or down of genre but rather require the tracking of its unpredictable vicissitudes, unanticipated turns, and unforeseen twists.

In a parallel fashion, Neale has foregrounded and popularized a now much-cited phrase: genre as "inter-textual relay."[35] Altman's and Neale's analyses are both full of citations to distributors' advertisements, studio memos, and critics' reviews contemporary to the films and their reception. Such a discursive analysis of a film's genre reveals, for instance, that many marketing campaigns avoid associating a film with a single genre even as critics regularly do (something that Janet Staiger has influentially investigated).[36] Such marketing materials might emphasize the overlap of the war with comedies or romances, for example, and highlight in the latter case broader gender appeal that I shall also investigate throughout this study. Foregrounding generic hybridity underscores how studios constantly experiment with product differentiation until a new genre gains commercial and critical purchase—at which time they often innovate again, to renewed commercial advantage. These concepts, genrification and intertextual relay, not least unto generic innovation and hybridization, resonate with the focus of the present volume—namely, a historical-discursive approach to the transformation of the war genre in Germany. This tracking of the dynamic, diachronic balance of both generic semantics and generic syntax—the constant shifts in the balance between iconographic and narrative aspects of films of the genre—will reveal how images and sounds of various, variegated spaces cut repeatedly across the scarred face of the abiding genre.

One caveat about the sort of historical-generic investigation that *German Ways of War* aims to undertake is this: because the current study attempts to use a genre to explore broader cultural history across the conventional caesurae of German history—because it covers so many decades—it will not attempt a comprehensive history of the genre in each and every period. For example, as noted above, it will not attempt a typology approach to genre, of the sort offered in more traditional genre studies, not least because a typology of the genre across five decades is simply beyond the scope of the present study (or any single study, I would suspect). Moreover, I would question the utility of such typologies, which, as Andrew Tudor argues, frequently manifest the categories of the examiner more than anything—indeed, the works of Staiger and Altman on the hybridity of genre call into question stable generic categories at all.[37] Instead, following the groundbreaking work of Witte, von Moltke, and Heins, *German Ways of War* will offer case studies of watershed or especially revealing films that manifest the key transformations of the genre—films that innovated and transformed the genre historically, not least because so many of the multifaceted currents that Altman emphasizes flow through them.

Violence, Affect, and Geographies of the War Film

With these notions of genres ever unfolding in mind, I can turn back to the specifics of the war genre. The genrification of war films highlights, I argue herein, how central the transformations of a nation's affective geographies are to the syntax and semantics of the genre. In foregrounding spatial processes and practices, the present investigation aims to address the relative theoretical neglect of the war genre cited above. Even if there has been recent scholarly attention paid to military/militaristic perception and targeting in fictional and nonfiction media, the narrative genre has not been afforded the same degree of theorization because, I suspect, it is quite difficult to analyze narrativized violence per se.[38] This would be the first of my counterintuitive insights about the genre: that, theoretically speaking, violence ipso facto does not have much to tell us about the war genre of fictional features films. Certainly, violence plays a key role in the fictional genre, although, it should be noted, it is probably not the "indefinable X" that Andrew Tudor points to (as a problem) in what he calls the "empiricist dilemma."[39] For example, violence, even in the form of a battle of two groups, is shared by many genres, especially by horror and action thrillers. In that way, violence per se would likely not be the key "narrative image" that Steve Neale cites:[40] violence is doubtlessly important, but one suspects that the narrative image at the core of the genre foregrounds soldiers in uniform within theaters of war—thus other aspects of mise-en-scène (uniforms, weapons, their settings) are as important as the narrative development of violence. This is, for instance, true of the film *D III 88* (1939), which does not have two opposing sides engaged in combat so much as extended military training, so physical endeavors and affects qualify it, per the contemporaneous reviews, as a war film. As uniforms imply, the violence of the war genre has to be scaled, a process distinguishing its violence from that of the horror and action genres. This process of scaling has become a central notion of contemporary critical geography to describe and chart fundamental spatio-social processes and subjectivities, and I shall develop this core aspect of the evolving genre in the third and subsequent chapters.

While violence and anticipation of it help generate the affective charge of the genre—film, as Steven Shaviro notes, is a "machine for generating affect" and genre particularly so[41]—it is also worth noting, I think, that violence (likely also due to the production costs associated with making it convincing) rarely takes up anything like the majority of a feature film's plotting. This insight resonates with one of the recurring critiques of affect theory: the abstractness and transience of its effects. I would highlight herein that one needs to better comprehend how such affects can function as longer-lasting phenomena. In fact, I shall argue that the affective mechanisms of the genre are consistently siphoned off into political and social modalities in the films—amid the films' carefully cultivated geographies, the ephemeral affects are carefully converted into what Carl Plantinga terms *construal-based concerns* at the root of more sustained emotions in the films.[42] Emotions as sustained construal-based concerns prove central to the films' core transformation of viewers into soldier-citizens and/or their supporters. Such deliberate conversion of generic affects into longer-lasting emotions happens to a large degree through corporeal movement and subsequent spatial transformations—the "affective atmospheres" that Lauren Berlant has described are, I will argue herein, spatially conjured and manipulated.[43] Violence is carefully contextualized, fundamentally framed, within territorial operations that reveal a given film's political agenda, often more than the violence itself. Part of the challenge in locating wartime violence at the core of the popular fictional genre would be that not many people know what such violence feels like, whereas modern spaces (including travel, particularly traversing landscape at speed) have been experienced by the majority of people in increasingly industrialized societies.[44] And even if violence did become more present for wartime Germans, the later films seem geared to exploit the positive effects of a war-bound culture rather than the decidedly double-edged promise of violence (perhaps exhilarating for some but also problematic for many). War films thus regularly mine familiar experiences for their marketable affective effects—something almost all genres do—even if they conclude with violence. The use of the so-called expansive body of positive, exhilarating affects is especially pronounced in films promoting wars, one that contravenes the constrictive body of much combat violence.[45] These affective manipulations of an expansive and constrictive body will also become crucial in chapter 3, in the first wave of critical war films I examine amid the late 1920s and early 1930s production trend.

Linked to the relatively limited plot role for violence is the notable narrative lack of details about the enemy. In war film plotting, it is remarkable how little narrative exposition the enemy receives, even if the enemy is vaguely present as a threat. It is more often the case that the dramatic conflict featured in the fictional emplotment is conflict arising from the good and bad of the same nation/side, often within the same military unit (and sometimes within the same person). This finding corresponds to something that historian Alexander Watson notes in his magisterial studies of World War I: that propaganda for the war (in his account, in numerous noncinematic institutions) attempted to convince the population to fight the war through love—love of family and friends, of neighbors and colleagues, of region and country—much more than through hatred toward an enemy.[46] Of course, this is not a zero-sum game, a Manichean dichotomy of love of country versus fear of enemy—both can be, and often are, in operation. But analyses of war films, including in Paul Cooke and Marc Silberman's otherwise excellent collection *Screening War*, have addressed too little of the latter, of the genre's affectively positive effects—for example, those to be found in movement and travel. Travel, with its numerous pleasures and its gratifying transformations of space, frames the violence and reveals the genre's politics. Such spatio-affective pleasures and transformations are at least constituents of the genre's positive value proposition to viewers as violence or the enemy.

Recent years have seen considerable scholarship and work around both a "spatial turn" and a "mobility turn" across cultural fields, work that very much informs the present project.[47] In approaching cinema with these so-called turns, it is notable that Jameson and others have characterized certain films as especially spatial, and I would extend this to certain genres that rely, fundamentally, on the mise-en-scène of intensified settings and locations. If melodramas, as have been widely discussed, tend to deploy domestic mise-en-scènes (costumes, props, and sets) in an especially powerful manner, other genres, like Westerns, rely on both costumes and location settings—certainly the recurring landscapes contribute to what Neale would consider the narrative image of Westerns. For the war film, I shall highlight a different aspect of what Jameson calls a cinematic "spatialization of the narrative," especially how war films locate at their center certain modern spatial practices, arguably even more than road movies:[48] in turning to story making around war and combat, these films invariably invoke travel and other forms of movement and, through them, subtler transformations of spaces local, national, and inter-/transnational.

In Anglo-U.S. film studies, these various spatial/mobility turns have started to bear notable theoretical fruit. These phenomena—the repeated invocations of travel and mobility—were crucial in the earliest phases of the medium with the popular travel or travelogue films of the sort Jeffrey Ruoff and Alexandra Schneider as well as Jennifer Lynn Peterson discuss.[49] As Ruoff and Schneider have pointed out in their influential anthology *Virtual Voyages*, travelogues and moving images to document journeys—to traverse distances virtually—were among the first and most popular aspects of cinema in its earlier phases. In fact, Ruoff and Schneider see the travelogue dominating early cinema between 1895 and 1905 and then having a considerable, though unexamined, afterlife thereafter, particularly as it was absorbed by long-form feature films. Following the groundbreaking work of Charles Musser in the 1980s, Tom Gunning has also underscored the importance of travel to early cinema, which is not surprising, he observes, given that travel images—such as photographs of distant places, postcards, panoramas, and so on—were key aspects of modernity.[50] The films that were available in the years with which I start this study, 1913–1917—those works listed in catalogs, by distributors, and so on—confirm the centrality of travel films of various sorts, foreign views, and so on to the film market as well as to Germany's struggle to maintain the genre as imports were increasingly controlled, limited, and banned (as discussed in chapter 2). In that chapter, I explore how the onset of World War I transformed German film genre due to the international film market and sudden obstacles to it. These changes transpired at the same time that long-form narrative cinema was consolidating, and among these changes (and key to its genrification) was the war film's redeployment of travelogue syntax and semantics. Confirming the above observations about the relative scholarly neglect of war/combat cinema, however, Ruoff and Schneider's and Peterson's works offer no chapter or even section on war cinema, which certainly seems, perhaps next to the road movie, the genre that would most build on the affective potential of travelogue and/or travel footage. A similar lack of engagement with the war genre amid the spatial turn can be found in John David Rhodes and Elena Gorfinkel's collection *Taking Place: Location and the Moving Image*, in which the spatial fallout of wars is everywhere without addressing the filmic genre of war itself.[51]

Geographical Imaginations and Spatial Transformations: Homogenizing and Fragmenting Place and Space

The present study will argue that war films aim, foundationally, to refigure citizens' feel for the world by remaking their sense of space—they conjure an entirely second, affectively resonant geography for their viewers, one often close at hand but usually neglected.[52] In fact, the discourse around the war genre—central, as noted above, to the films' historical genrification as "war films"—refers repeatedly to the import of geographical and geopolitical understanding for the efficacy of the films' messages. This is an especially telling link because in these years of war film genrification, new forms of geography and geopolitics changed the intellectual landscape of Germany. If Jameson has pointed to how the paranoid political thrillers of the 1970s cultivated "the" geopolitical aesthetic, war films in these years were interwoven with the emergence of a multifaceted geographical and geopolitical consciousness throughout German society and polity—many different geographies became entwined with militaristic tendencies. I agree with Jameson's sense of a spatial and specifically geopolitical consciousness in certain genres, but at least in the Germany of these decades (1910s–1960s) and this genre, it is important to historicize geography and these geopolitics themselves.

National(ist) impulses long manifested themselves in interest in German landscape and topography, as they did famously in the work of Johann Gottfried Herder.[53] By the late nineteenth century, the dual impact of the 1871 unification and colonialism helped drive a new wave of German geography and its rapid institutionalization in both universities and academic journals.[54] It was no accident that, as I detail below, the most influential thinkers of classical geopolitics emerged in this geographically minded period, when the European powers jostled and jousted with one another over both local territories and overseas colonies.[55] Among the key thinkers of this late nineteenth-century growth in geography was Friedrich Ratzel, holder of a chair in geography at the University of Leipzig, who developed overtly organic metaphors for political states and their territorial tendencies. For instance, he likened the state to a tree that has its roots in nearby soil but also requires adequate space for arboreal, aka territorial, expansion. Ratzel influenced other well-known geographers around this time, including the English Halford Mackinder, who had studied zoology before switching to geography. It was Mackinder who developed the influential notion of a crucial "heartland" in eastern Europe-Russia on which the balance of European power would putatively pivot, an interpretation anticipating the territorial agenda to acquire formerly Ottoman and Austro-Hungarian holdings as those centuries-old empires withered. These geographical links to colonialism and its territorial ambitions (not least in "the East") are especially intriguing because they highlight how what Henri Lefebvre calls "representations of space"[56]—that is, the spaces conjured by specialists like geographers—may go, at the very least, hand in hand with political and military projects. As I shall argue, this kind of expansionist geographical imagination was juxtaposed not only to the military objectives of World War I but to genrification of the early war film.

After World War I, with the loss of German colonies and the restructuring of European borders, a more pointed, soon more disturbing version of geography became increasingly influential—namely, geopolitics. The term *geopolitics* was coined by Swedish (but Germanophile) Rudolf Kjellén, who adopted some of Ratzel's ideas more explicitly to the political arena: he used metaphors of the body for the state and saw it as an organism unfolding in geographical space.[57] For Kjellén, then, the spatial expression of a state would, as for a body, be a key to its success. Such an organic and even corporeal framework would only amplify the affective resonances of such speculations. Geopolitics was then probably most importantly invoked and institutionalized by a World War I general-turned-academic geographer, Karl Haushofer, professor at the Ludwig-Maximilians-Universität in Munich and chief editor of the influential *Zeitschrift für Geopolitik*. Under Haushofer's guidance, geopolitics firmed up its conceptual position as a more emphatic embrace of the intersection of spatial and political orders—of space and power. Geopolitics served, fundamentally, as simultaneous "practices and representations of territorial strategies."[58] It yielded self-serving hierarchies and, ultimately, helped justify expansion and empire.[59]

While some now dispute how much geography and geopolitics influenced the Nazis' radically racist and murderous agenda, there is certainly evidence of its ideas being part of the broader 1920s–1930s intellectual context, swirling around not least in the heads of leading Nazi officials like Rudolf Hess and even Hitler.[60] Hess, in fact, became a research assistant of Haushofer's and was close friends with Haushofer's son Albrecht—for example, Haushofer was in the Hess wedding party in 1927. When Hess was imprisoned with Hitler in Landsberg after the attempted 1923 coup, Haushofer visited the pair frequently to read scholarly literature with them, including the classics of German geography. While it is impossible to prove any kind of conceptual causality, of course, it is difficult to imagine that Haushofer's geopolitical ideas were not familiar to Hess and Hitler. Perhaps the most identifiable influence comes in one of the key notions of Nazi political strategy and probably its key spatial concept—namely, Lebensraum (living space). Lebensraum traces to Ratzel, who in turn influenced Kjellén and, through him, Haushofer. One historian of German imperialism and colonialism, from Bismarck to Hitler, suggests that in Hitler's "imagining, Ratzel's neologism, *Lebensraum*, the geographical space that peoples required for their continued health, became the central, academically legitimated justification during the 1920s for the imperialist displacement of Slavic and Jewish populations of the east."[61] The trajectory from geography to justification for imperialism and colonialism is revealing. In this way, it seems, geography and geopolitics did indeed become certain ways of seeing the world that migrated from academic to political and military contexts—from representations of space to spatial practice, as Lefebvre would emphasize.[62] In the much-quoted words of Donna J. Haraway, the practices and representations of geopolitics have relied upon "a view from nowhere," a conveniently self-serving nowhere that could serve as the basis for aggressive and affectively arresting expansion.[63]

These geographers highlight the potential for spatial transformations in both politics and society, spatial transformations that I locate at the core of the war genre's vicissitudes.[64] These kinds of transformations, as understood at the end of the nineteenth and beginning of the twentieth centuries, foreground the operations of modernity in and on space, including the remaking of older spaces and the importance of travel and movement in general, as with the railroad or aircraft (both foregrounded in the geopolitical literature at the time). The war genre exploits the affective potential of images, particularly of affectively charged movement, but it also scales these mobile experiences to the broader society and polity, much as the geographers above do. To confirm the importance of such specifically militaristic spaces in modernity, one might start with the changing import of fortifications and forts to modernity, modern space, and warfare. Attending to such fortifications underscores, above all, the spatial refigurations of modernity and its relationship to both mobility and warfare. For an early example of this spatial transformation, one of the first developers of the hot-air balloon speculated immediately on its implication for breaching fortress walls.[65] Then, in breathtaking fashion, technological advances in artillery rendered conventional fortifications near irrelevant after millennia of architectural refinement, fundamentally recasting both rural landscapes and cities' topographies. Many scholars have noted that artillery—rather than gas or airpower—was the most consequential modern feature of World War I, its most defining difference from what came before, and I would underscore how much this development impacted the longer-term arc of the space and history of cities.[66] It, in effect, refigured distance itself and thereby remade the violence at the heart of war. If for thousands of years military strategists, civilian architects, and city planners had worked to devise defensible structures both for military-minded commanders and for lay populations, then the advance of artillery accelerated the removal of such walls and their replacement.

Such a development in defensive architecture remade both urban geography and the geography of war. What replaced cities' and towns' walls and fortifications in such short order was telling: largely, it was roads. For a famous example, the Ringstraße of Vienna, where so much of European modernism was minted, replaced Vienna's much-older walled fortifications.[67] This remarkable replacement of ubiquitous walls—structures explicitly (if now hopelessly) designed to interrupt the free movement of enemy forces—by roads geared to facilitate mobility elucidates one of the fundamental processes of modernity and one at the core of the war genre: the relentless, modern homogenization and then integration of space. Such homogenization of space is linked fundamentally to how modern economy and society transform space via a thoroughgoing abstraction. When David Harvey (paraphrasing and elaborating Marx) famously describes the annihilation of space and the constant remaking of it under capitalism, he is emphasizing not only the literal destruction or "compression" of distance along with it but rather what it becomes in the wake of capital. What he describes in the rendering of space (more) frictionless for the purposes of capital circulation and accumulation is a thoroughgoing and wide-ranging homogenization and integration of it. The destruction of place makes space more homogeneous, more segmented, and therefore more predictable—thus more abstract and like capital itself.[68] In these assertions, Harvey is following his acknowledged forebear Henri Lefebvre, who himself moved spatial processes near the core of his peculiar Marxism. Such abstracting and homogenizing of space, rendering it frictionless for movement and mobilization, will be central mechanisms of the genre through the German decades.

Modern homogenization and abstraction are, however, always dialectically balanced by countervailing forces. The homogenizing recasting of space along the lines of the above—that is, toward geopolitical expansion—has a contradictory, negative side, as Harvey has underscored. As soon as space was homogenized and "democratized," he writes, it also had to contend with concomitant fragmentation and exclusivity (and here he cites Lefebvre explicitly): "But there is a contradiction in this [revolutionary homogenization of land]. The homogeneity of space is achieved through its total 'pulverization' into freely alienable parts of private property, to be bought and traded at will upon the market (Lefebvre 1974, 385). The result is a permanent tension between the appropriation and use of space for individual and social purposes and the domination of space through private property, the state, and other forms of class and social power (Lefebvre 1974, 471). This tension underlies the further fragmentation of otherwise homogenous space."[69] At the very moment, Harvey writes, that the homogenizing modern city as a "place of encounter" was at its "apogee" (a sociospatial phenomenon examined chapter 6), it also became a "fragmented terrain held down and together under all manner of forces of class, racial, and sexual domination."[70] A contemporary symptom of this modern, contradictory homogenization and fragmentation of space would be the recent debates about borders and the walls to allegedly enforce them. Modernity's contradictory remaking of space continues apace: city fortifications might have fallen and movements risen in the late nineteenth and twentieth centuries, but borders have become discursively and physically intensified. As spaces of simultaneous conflict and flow, borders will figure centrally throughout the genre.

Such is modernity's underlying dialectical entwinement of spatial homogenization/expansion and its simultaneous fragmentation/exclusivity. *German Ways of War* will attend to these complex processes as core elements of war films as it traces the spatial transformations and their affective pleasures of the genre across the traditional periods of German film history. The historical study begins with chapter 2, which examines the genrification of the Kriegsdrama (war drama) shortly before and during World War I, laying the groundwork for the war film's syntax and semantics later on. During World War I, Germany is regarded as having pioneered state-commissioned film propaganda with some of the earliest and most effective war films. These early war films are remarkable because they often contravene the familiar hero-group-mission syntax of war film plotting, as Jeanine Basinger has described it, but nonetheless develop spatial and affective mechanisms marking later works. In the years 1914–1918, the consolidation of the genre intersects with the fundamental transformation of narrative cinema and the programs in which they were shown. The most important aspect of these sundry transformations for my analysis of the war genre, spatially inclined as it is, was the impact of the war on popular travelogues (Reisebilder and the related Kulturaufnahmen [cultural documentaries, literally "cultural images" or "cultural recordings"]) and their subsequent absorption by the Kriegsdrama. This absorption of the early genre gave war films one of their crucial affective engines—that of travel and other forms of movement—but also demonstrates how such effects could be recast, with their affect siphoned off into longer-lasting emotion, in a geographical and increasingly geopolitical mode.

For my historical and theoretical investigation of the war film's genrification, these early generic developments reveal many of the basic spatial mechanisms of the genre. For example, not only travel and its transformation of mobile subjectivities but also landscape and its thematization function in an increasingly geographical and territorializing lens. Paul Leni's *Das Tagebuch des Dr. Hart* (*The Diary of Dr. Hart*, 1917/1918), for instance, transforms traditional spatial assemblages, especially landscape and the conventionally contemplative subjectivity associated with it, in covering the telltale distance to the fighting front.[71] Leni, who would go on to be one of the most celebrated directors of the Weimar era, had a background in design and art history, and *Dr. Hart* demonstrates longer-term trends in landscape imaging and its transformation. Against *Dr. Hart*'s transformations of conventional landscape and bourgeois subjectivities linked to it, Georg Jacoby's *Unsühnbar* (*Inexpiable*, 1917) underscores another key theme of this work: the link of the war genre to depictions of work and economy. Both works highlight the constitutive intersection of space and gender in the wartime spatial ensemble of the early genre. In both films, female characters play a central role in the spatial mechanisms of the genre, a role that I will track throughout the project.

Chapter 3, "Landscapes of Death and Memories of the Human: Distance, Scale, and the Double Map of the First 'War-Sound-Film,'" examines how, some ten years after World War I, there was a remarkable production trend of works revisiting the war experience in a memorial mode. This was not a coincidence, given the degenerating political context of the late 1920s and early 1930s. While detailing how such a production trend can alter an ongoing genre, the chapter takes a different approach from chapter 2 by examining films (G. W. Pabst's *Westfront 1918* and *Kameradschaft* [*Camaraderie*]) that have had a long critical tradition. But the chapter argues that these art cinema classics have not been adequately analyzed in terms of their genre operations, as has been the case generally with the celebrated cinema of the Weimar period. This is the only chapter to take up such canonical films and aims to demonstrate how the project's generic approach can elucidate even fairly familiar objects from conventional film history. In *Westfront*, Pabst deploys the notion of transformative landscape to dismantle and critique its use in films like Leni's *Dr. Hart*. In *Camaraderie*, Pabst engages another central spatial mechanism of films in a geopolitical context—the dynamic evocation of the border and national other—to rework the affective geographies common to most war films. The chapter explores in both films the operations of (geographic) scale as central to the genre's narrative mechanisms, be the films self-consciously pro- or antiwar.

Chapter 4, "Combat Films and Their Aerial Spaces under the Nazi Regime," highlights distance, modes of travel, and the associated subjectivities in the genre, underscoring one of the central changes to war films of this period—namely, the role of air travel and airpower. In Karl Ritter's *Pour le Mérite* (*Medal of Honor*, 1938), the affective pleasures of air travel are imbricated within a broader network of airports and airfields for a Luftwaffe squadron during World War I and World War II. Ritter rewrites recent history through the affective thrill of flying then mapped deliberately over a series of airports that unfold that history in a definitive direction. The other most famous filmmaker of the retooled Luftwaffe films was himself a famous flyer, Hans Bertram, whose *Kampfgeschwader Lützow* (*Squadron Lützow*, 1941) demonstrates the ability of the genre to conjure new spaces for the war's many refugees. Finally, Ritter's *Über alles in der Welt* (*Above Everything in the World*, 1941) uses an episodic structure in his trademark Zeitfilm style to remake the practices of a prewar cosmopolitanism. Polyglot cosmopolitanism is depicted as an affliction to be overcome by the likewise border-crossing but also very different Luftwaffe. These films register the transformation of the war genre as technologies of mobility shifted while also manifesting the political trajectory of the regime as it moved (figuratively, literally) to total war.

In the late 1940s aftermath of Germany's unconditional surrender, addressed in chapter 5, the so-called rubble films revisited the war by taking up the genre in very skeptical ways—including explicit, critical references to those very popular films of the Nazi period. Chapter 5, "Out of the War Mode: Demobilizing the War Genre in the Postwar Rubble Film," registers a couple of important revisions to the current scholarship on the rubble film—above all, the uncomfortable continuities from (extremely popular) cinema under the Nazis to postwar films. This includes two of the most popular films made during the Nazi regime that sketch how the war genre became a mode operating across a wider range of films. *Wunschkonzert* (*Request Concert*, 1940) and *Die große Liebe* (*The Great Love*, 1942)—both very popular films—are mobilization melodramas because they absorb and normalize the war genre within a broader narrative of romantic love and loss. With the war mode within various genres, one can see in postwar rubble films how there was no Stunde Null (zero hour), an insight now accepted in sundry historical fields though not yet elaborated in film history. Second, the chapter reconsiders one of the most cited tropes of the rubble film genre—the Heimkehrer (soldier returning home)—and contextualizes the Heimkehrer in the context of the citizen-soldiers the genre has been producing since *Dr. Hart* and World War I. There have been remarkably few specific investigations underscoring how the Heimkehrer was a former soldier, an individual militarily conditioned and experienced, returning from a war that required a specifically mobilized and scaled psychology. In light of the preceding chapters, one can appreciate the ways in which rubble films were meant explicitly as *demobilization* films, films directed against the militaristic mobilities, scales, and spaces that the Nazis had exploited during the war years.

Chapter 6, "War in the Reconstructive 1950s: Genre, Espionage, and Cold War Subjectivities in the War Film," analyzes the West German war film of the 1950s, the era's second most popular genre that nostalgically revisits war experiences while also deliberately negotiating the rapid remilitarization of postwar West Germany. In this mobilization for the Cold War, the chapter examines a revealing late-genre hybridity of the war film—namely, the nesting within it of the emergent postwar espionage genre. Films like *Canaris* (1955), *Fuchs von Paris* (*The Fox of Paris*, 1957), and *Rommel ruft Kairo* (*Rommel Calls Cairo*, 1959) open with the familiar accoutrements of the war genre (decorated officers, war plans, battle maps), but their plots shift to young protagonists abruptly becoming spies, unfolding a novel form of soldierly subjectivity fitting their Cold War and democratic moment. These war-spy films explore foreign cities with a tourist gaze that exploits the wartime travel pleasures that *German Ways of War* traces from the genre's earliest moments. They also forge a new, topologically driven subjectivity fitting the democratically minded postwar period. The earlier scaling of soldier-unit-nation fades in favor of what David Harvey has termed the (individual) *body as a strategy of accumulation*.[72] The topological, urban subjectivity underscores the ever-changing spaces of the genre, here manifesting the sort of networked flows that Manuel Castells has sketched in the postwar city.[73]

These late 1950s films underscore how genres are always unfolding historically from and even contributing to the politics of cinema of the sort so celebrated in the multiple new waves of the 1960s and 1970s and beyond. In fact, the conclusion expands on the postwar arc of the war genre by discussing films of the 1980s and post-2000 eras. Those films, including works that are among the most popular German films ever abroad, both extend and negate aspects of the genre charted above. Films like *Das Boot* (*The Boat*, 1981) and *Der Untergang* (*Downfall*, 2004) elaborate on many of the historical spatial and affective operations of the genre while surrendering other territorial ambitions. In those two films, space continues to parallel the scalar mechanisms central to the genre but in ways that navigate the complexity of postwar guilt. With such works, the generic mechanisms continue to register the cultural-historical changes of the postwar and even post-Wende eras. Those more recent eras continue to highlight how film genre and its transformations over time seismically register the wider culture, with both processes of scale and the production of affective geographies central to media's collective projects and their broader impacts.

2

Land into Landscape, Landscape into Territory: Transformations of Space in German War Cinema, 1914–1918

(*The Diary of Dr. Hart*, 1917/1918; *Sword and Hearth*, 1916; *Inexpiable*, 1917)

In mid-1915, the *Lichtbild-Bühne*, then one of Germany's key trade journals for cinema, surveyed recent publications on the direction of the war film (Kriegsfilm). It considered a recent newspaper piece by Dr. W. Warstat important enough to reprint it almost wholly—in fact, of the articles the *Lichtbild-Bühne* surveyed, Warstat's was the first, the longest, and the only one it quoted in its near entirety.[1] In his article, originally appearing in the *Frankfurter Zeitung*, Warstat criticizes at length the kinds of motion pictures that had hitherto been produced about the war in which Germany and so much of Europe were engaged. He observes that the widespread "aktuellen Aufnahmen" (early documentaries/newsreels) of the war merely aim to satisfy the curiosity of those on the home front. Instead of and against those early sorts of documentaries—modern documentary had not yet emerged—Warstat advocates for better-informed and thoughtful fiction films. His suggestions for how to make fiction about the very real war, made in an important newspaper and then in a leading industry trade journal, emphasize how both the public and professionals debated the shape of wartime genres very specifically. Even this early in film history, such debates underscore the interplay of industry, audience, and critique—what Steve Neale calls the "inter-textual relay"[2]—at the heart of genrification and generic adjustments that will be the topic of this chapter on war films during World War I.

Warstat's advocacy for fiction films against an (early) documentary approach is both surprising and revealing: after all, from the 1914 commencement of hostilities, there had been, in fact, a good number of fiction films foregrounding the war. In autumn 1914, in the first productions after fighting commenced, a number of German films addressed the onset of the war and aimed primarily at overcoming domestic differences and divisions. Films like *Ich kenne keine Parteien mehr* (*I Do Not Know Any Parties Anymore*, 1914) and *Das ganze Deutschland soll es sein* (*It Should Be All of Germany*, 1914) prioritize the much-discussed Burgfrieden (peace among the factions), while by Christmas 1914, the wartime divisions that the films address are those between the combat and home fronts (in the so-called Christmas films like *Weihnachtsglocken* [*Christmas Bells*, 1914]).[3] When Warstat was writing in spring 1915, however, initial expectations for the war's imminent end were fading. The war was settling in longer than anyone had expected and would, Warstat concludes, require recalibrating the war genre.

At this crucial 1915 moment of the war—as it became clear that the highly touted Schlieffen Plan had failed, then Chief of the General Staff Erich von Falkenhayn even suggested positioning for peace negotiations as early as winter 1914–1915—Warstat was posing fundamental questions of how to depict the war for the general population. His article regards merely documenting present, real events as inadequate to the now considerable task. This advocating for a deliberate departure from documentary signals a notable change in strategy that anticipates the subsequent emphases of the 1916 BUFA (Bild- und Filmamt [Image- and Film Office]) and then 1917 Ufa.[4] For Warstat, and increasingly for others as well, storytelling—including selecting, interpreting, and embellishing, as storytelling must—is required for a more edifying and moving understanding by the population.[5] At this 1915 point, Warstat's emphasis on developing long-form storytelling coincides with the often-cited consolidation of narrative cinema, against the earlier and sometimes-chaotic myriad of different lengths and formats that dominated early films.[6]

In addition to his general advocacy for storytelling about the war, however, Warstat also offers specific suggestions for cinematic tropes for the retooled war film. In a sudden but revealing turn of logic, he observes that for any substantive understanding of the struggles of Germany's troops, certain geographical knowledge is essential. In fact, observes Warstat, the "form and peculiarity"

(Gestaltung und Eigenart) of the battles are determined by geographical facts with which wide swaths of the population are unfamiliar. Would it really be so difficult, he muses, to foreground the "geographische Eigenart" (geographical characteristics/specificity) of the particular battlefields and so to illuminate geography's influence on the form of each battle and direction of the war in general?[7] As we know with hindsight, Germany's geographical "peculiarity" did help determine its "destiny" in its multifront wars. But I want to explore how Warstat's particular turn to fiction stories—a turn and transformation indicative of the wider consolidation of narrative cinema at the time—demands a deliberate and, indeed, affective geography. Such a turn indicates a tendency in the wide range of war representations but especially in war films, one that has been curiously overlooked in the literature in German studies and on the war genre generally—namely, the importance of geography and its constitutive spatial practices that underpin these depictions and their cultural resonances. As discussed in the introduction, "geography" itself is a contingent series of discourses and mechanisms, a historically conditioned set of practices and processes realized through the production of knowledge around space. This production unto geographic practices and processes is itself symptomatic of modern conceptualizations of space and humans' place in it. As Warstat indicates and as I shall explore below, the war film genre increasingly offered a self-consciously geographical aesthetic, one that foregrounds the affective pleasures around both movement and the territorial transformations of space.[8]

The Outbreak of the War and Generic Transformations

July and August 1914 witnessed not only the outbreak of histrionic hotheadedness and then the "fateful" hostilities but also, at least in the film industry, a distinct sense of crisis, even panic. Certainly, there were to be found, per the well-known bellicose stereotypes, jingoistic calls to arms in the swelling "Spirit of 1914." But there were also, particularly in the trade journals where matters had to be pragmatically minded, stark signs of alarm. Perhaps because those in the film industry were not merely reaching for pen and paper but also had soon-to-be-drafted employees and soon-to-be-requisitioned resources, they were very, and fearfully, aware of the cultural-industrial implications. For one telling instance, a late August 1914 piece suggests that the war and its changes to the cinematic system highlight how Germany's film industry success had everything to do with its ability to effectively import and export. There is much evidence of the importance of imported products to what was running on German screens and to what was so effectively lining exhibitors' pockets.[9] Various articles from July to August 1914 make clear—as the economic consequences of the war came into painful focus—that due to the very transnational nature of the film industry in the years preceding, the war would mean a complete shock to its foundations.[10]

It is widely accepted, however, that after this initial shock of radical industrial change (initially plummeting attendance, new taxes, import and export controls), the war helped the German film industry by way of forced independence.[11] As Philipp Stiasny observes, it was not only the changes to the film industry that favored emergent autonomy and growing success but also the shift away from other entertainments like theater, variety shows, or even Rummelplätze (fairs/carnivals), all of which demanded more direct labor from trained personnel. Less personnel-intensive cinema had clear advantages when, as I shall discuss below, workers were being mass mobilized for the war effort.[12] German films reached not only new leisure-time markets within Germany but also new regions through its Feldkinos (field cinemas) and general expansion into the occupied areas, including into the territories of what we now understand as Poland, a key subject of *Das Tagebuch des Dr. Hart* (*The Diary of Dr. Hart*) to be discussed below.[13] This seeming contradiction—utter panic at the beginning of the war but a more mature industry by the end of it—begs the question of the adaptive adjustments that were made, the key transformations realized.[14]

Beyond these concerns about labor and capital shortages at the war's outbreak, the industry was anticipating a debilitating lack of material in both cinematic content and film stock. So many trade articles from the time, after assuring their anxious readership that the industry would survive these tough times, propose prospective substitutes.[15] These proposals for helping the film industry through this time make clear, like Warstat's article, that the transformation of the industry outlined above—from a crisis to a fortified national cinema—would require adjustments to its dominant genres. Such adjustments became necessary because, as Jennifer Lynn Peterson notes, the international markets for certain genres tended to be dominated by particular countries whose exports to Germany would plummet.[16] For the most relevant example, the market for travelogues was flooded by French firms, which meant programming French travelogue films became more difficult and eventually a virtual impossibility for German screens. This was true even before the actual import/export controls just because, as pieces from that complex time recount, exhibitors worried about audience anger at seeing French products on the home-front screens.[17] This kind of industry adjustment is confirmed by distributors' offerings in the German market, which saw French producers and their travelogues dry up almost immediately. Some U.S. travelogues continued to be on offer, at least in the interim, given the U.S.'s neutrality earlier in the war.[18]

One of the key industry adjustments made after this 1914/1915 crisis was the intensified development of the war genre—the so-called Kriegsfilm, or Kriegsdrama. This genre was overtly, soon propagandistically pro-war, but that does not diminish either the ambivalence it would often manifest or the influence it would definitively demonstrate for the more famous Weimar era.[19] Moreover, because of when and where World War I fell in film history—that is, on the cusp of the consolidation of long-form narrative cinema, usually dated 1913–1917—the war film manifests important trends in the lengthier, multireel narrative films and their genres. In light of the widely acknowledged advances in German genre during World War I, it is curious how little sustained attention these early stages of the genre have garnered, a lacuna only fairly recently addressed in studies like Stiasny's and, to a lesser degree, Bernadette Kester's.[20] The present work, however, takes an approach diverging from their primarily historical perspectives. Although I shall make recourse to the archive central to new film history, I also want to explore the war genre more theoretically as it unfolded over the decades, especially how its spatial and affective aspects serve the genre. Such an approach aims to add to our understanding of how genre can function across the familiar caesurae of German cinema history (1918/1919, 1933, 1945, 1949, etc.).

If, as Rick Altman describes, genres are always evolving, being perpetually rethought and retooled by audience-minded directors and success-sensitive producers, this was an era of unprecedented generic adaptation. A crucial but neglected dimension of the evolving war genre, I argue, was its emphasis on the images and themes associated with the travelogue, including traditional landscapes and the modern mobilities deployed to experience them. As outlined by Jeffrey Ruoff and Alexandra Schneider as well as Peterson, the absorption of the travelogue by long-form narrative cinema counts as a central development of 1910s and 1920s U.S. cinema, although they oddly, like most, do not mention the clear links to war films.[21] In the German context, these trends and transformations were similarly operative. For example, a prewar article from late 1913 entitled "Landschaftskinematographie" (Landscape cinematography) traces these changes in filmed landscapes as they parallel the emergence of long-form cinema. The article opens by confirming for German markets what Ruoff and Schneider as well as Peterson claim for the United States: that for "over ten years," thus back to at least 1903, images of landscape and travel had been central attractions within film programs. According to this cover article in *Der Kinematograph*, even as one looks back to the era of cinema Kisten (boxes) at the Jahrmarkt (fair)—so well before more modern genres had emerged—travel and the accompanying landscapes were central features of the multifaceted film programs.[22] As long-form cinema emerged in the early 1910s, the article recounts, images of travel and shots of nature, especially landscape, contributed indelibly to cinema's "higher" purpose, with these aspects coming evermore to the foreground as the films grew more sophisticated. In a direct foreshadow of Warstat's advocacy for the war film (mentioned above), the 1913 article proposes that German filmmakers should incorporate more landscapes and the geography around them, all while answering one of cinema's putatively highest callings—namely, educating viewers about foreign lands.[23]

If this prewar article anticipates Warstat's retooled war film—landscape and geography rolled into one even before the war started—assorted industry professionals proposed similar directions to navigate the crises of summer 1914 and fall 1915. Given the abrupt changes in available films, including much of the most popular genres, these articles address how to fill the sudden film-content void.[24] One *Der Kinematograph* piece, "Krieg und Kino," from as early as August 5, 1914, two days after Germany declared war on France, acknowledges the looming crisis in available films and suggests looking for inspiration in foreign products that will soon disappear from the market.[25] From such foreign products and the now necessary mixture of old and new materials, it deduces the relevance of both comedies (to lighten the mood) and military scenes that incorporate landscape (to serve the Vaterland, or "fatherland").[26] In a similar direction a few days later, the article "Kinematographie in Kriegszeiten" (Kinematography in wartimes) proposes a number of genres that could be developed out of older material, including images of medical procedures, modern transportation, and notably, geographical subjects.[27] In early September 1914, another article, "Zeitgemässe Kinobetriebe" (Film industry appropriate for the times), extends this argument in greater detail, proposing the recycling of surgical films as well as "cinematic trips" through the "places, cities, and lands" that the troops will visit, perhaps best delivered in a kind of panoramic presentation familiar from the Kaiserpanorama of the sort recalled so vividly by Walter Benjamin in his fin de siècle *Berliner Childhood around 1900*.[28] In fact, this intersection of the medicine of the modern hospital, the geography of distant landscapes, and the wartime transformation of both is precisely that which will structure *Dr. Hart*. A slightly later piece from about a year into the war continues to affirm these links: although ostensibly about landscapes and how to shoot them—one should always seek vibrant colors and show the minimum number of bystanders, apparently—the article also lobbies for incorporating travel images into those about war. Central to the effective representation of cinematic landscape, the piece suggests, is movement: a cinematic landscape without movement would be "like an artillerist throwing stones."[29] It recommends incorporating this movement amid scenic landscapes via trains, likewise crucial to the early narrative of *Dr. Hart*, confirming the absorption of the generic syntax and semantics of the German travelogue (Reisebilder) by the evolving Kriegsdrama.

The Diary of Dr. Hart: Travel, Landscape, Territory in the Emergent War Genre

As the directorial debut of Paul Leni, who became an important director in the Weimar period, *Das Tagebuch des Dr. Hart* (*The Diary of Dr. Hart*, 1917/1918) addresses the spectators foregrounded by Warstat and the others above.[30] Warstat's geographically sophisticated war film posits specific spectators: viewers lacking the geography requisite for comprehending wartime events but also interested in and even susceptible to the genre's geopolitical approach. One could pick any number of the many war films cited throughout this book, but

Dr. Hart seems a telling case study for the genrification detailed above. The film follows the eponymous doctor as he is mobilized from a privileged private life as a physician in a spa town to military duty on the eastern front, where he serves as a field doctor on Polish territory. The few, more extended readings of *Dr. Hart* confirm the import of the geographical content in the film: they focus on its deliberate negotiation of Poland as an emerging political entity.[31] When the film declares at about fifteen minutes into its circa seventy-minute running time, via intertitle, "Polen!" (figure 2.1), it invokes a complex geographical history in which territory, sovereignty, and spatial contestation had played a central role for centuries.[32]

At this historical point—in either mid-1914, when the film is set, or early 1918, when it was released—there was no actual Poland, no single sovereign territory for Polish people. The intertitle is a filmic speech act, a fantastical invocation not so much of an imagined community (the community of Poles was already being imagined) but rather of an imaginary and intensified space. *Dr. Hart*'s depictions reconstruct a time when the Central Powers' commitments to Poland looked more promising—that is, when they liberated many Poles from the Russian dominion of Russian Poland and the Russian army's early invasions of Austro-Hungarian and Prussian Poland.[33] So the film seems, pace Warstat, a clear geographical and therefore geopolitical invocation and intervention—but what exactly are the larger spatial practices that deliver to viewers this sort of geographical intervention? And what do they contribute to our understanding of combat films as genre-spanning multiple historical moments and even epochs?

In its production of an imaginary Polish territory, *Dr. Hart* demonstrates three tendencies that became crucial in the spatial and affective practices of the genre more generally: the significance of travel in imaging war and its psychological mechanisms, the centrality of landscape, and the deliberate deployment of space-destroying and space-creating mapping to conjure but also to remake the intensified spaces of war. The first section of *Dr. Hart* underscores how spatially oriented the narrativization of combat proves in the genre. What I am terming, following Fredric Jameson, the *spatialization of the narrative* builds on an important tendency at the heart of many war films: their tendency to stage, dramatize, spectacularize travel and the affectively intensified movement to realize it.[34] At a fundamental level, the film will chart—and later map—the fantastical wartime transformation of Polish landscape and the subsequent conjuring of complex territory. Revealingly, however, it opens with the travel of its eponymous protagonist in a nonwar, tourist mode.

Hart is courting Ursula von Hohenau—a pursuit that requires him to travel back and forth from his home/practice in Baden-Oos, near Baden-Baden, to her home in Saxony, thus traversing much of the German nation. As I noted in the introduction, the recent wave of work on the travelogue and travel genres in early U.S. cinema (Ruoff/Schneider, Peterson, and Tom Gunning,

FIG. 2.1 Territorial intertitle as a speech act in *Dr. Hart* (1917/1918). Digital frame enlargement.

following the earlier insights of Charles Musser[35]) underscores the importance, even centrality, of travel-oriented genres for the world market of early cinema. Some work has explored how, with the consolidation of narrative cinema in the early to mid-1910s, travelogues were absorbed into the multireel feature films that came to dominate. Surprisingly, however, none of these scholars takes up how the emergent war genre would absorb these images of distant places and the mobility required to get there—and do so at the very moment that the French-dominated travelogue would have been disappearing from the German film market. It is curious to me, both in this work on the travelogue and in the literature on war films, that no one has investigated such spatial practices as central aspects of the emerging war genre. Travel images, as kinds of cinematic tourism, tip the hand of many of these intensified spatial practices of the (place-destroying, space-producing) war film.[36]

Dr. Hart is particularly useful for tracking the transformation of the genre because it creates a plot whose narrative trajectory—in its dramatic conflicts and character arcs—is thoroughly interwoven with a whole array of spatial practices, including not only travel but also landscape, mobility based on it, and the territorial transformations of each. It furthermore underscores one of the recurring tendencies of war films that I highlight throughout: that what many assume to be the core of the war genre, violence, is carefully contextualized—fundamentally framed—within deliberate spatial operations that reveal a film's political agenda more than the violence itself. Part of the challenge in locating war violence at the core of the popular genre would be that not many people know, affectively speaking, what it feels like (at least at the time of World War I). Modern mobility, on the other hand, has been experienced by the majority of people in these increasingly industrialized societies—and mobile experience can yield what Julian Hanich calls an affectively activated "expansive body" more consistently than violence.[37] Recent film theory has focused on the affective operations of audiovisual media, and many war films aim to mine familiar experiences for their marketably affective experiences. The opening act of *Dr. Hart* proves particularly illuminating for these spatial purposes. It not only anticipates the colonial transformation of contested Polish landscape into German territory but also foregrounds the imaging of space in the visual arts—perhaps not a surprise given Leni's artistic and design background.[38] *Dr. Hart*'s first act of travel takes up space by engaging the precinematic traditions of spatial representation around landscape and then recasting them: it underscores the centrality of landscape and the affectively arresting and changing images of it in the war film's territorial operations.

Recent, more critical understandings of landscape have brought to the fore this linkage between traditional landscapes and territorial ambitions. In *Landscape and Power*, W. J. T. Mitchell intriguingly ties the "rise" of landscape depiction in Europe to the territorial ambitions of Western imperialism and colonialism. Landscapes are, for Mitchell, "central to the national imaginary, a part of daily life that imprinted public, collective fantasies on places."[39] But these often-sentimental cultural artifacts are no simple, romantic depictions of nature. Rather, these collective fantasies in the rise of landscape are, territorially speaking, very specific: landscape painting and sensibility came to serve, writes Mitchell, the "sacred, silent language" of territorial aggression and organization, thus part and parcel of the spatial integration I am highlighting.[40] Landscape was both a language expressing the territorial mechanisms of imperialism and a mode of perception of, especially of looking at, space unto such integration. Landscape is coconstitutively entwined with what Mitchell calls "imperial vision," with that vision helping conjure the romanticism of landscape painting while also being reinforced by such landscapes.[41]

Artistic visions of empire concerned images of spatial homogenization, movement, and integration often more than images of the violent subjugation of others. One is reminded of paintings of ships amid faraway seas and then trains among exotic landscapes. Although Mitchell regards landscape not merely as a genre of painting but rather as a broader cultural medium of a historically conditioned spatial imaginary, he has admitted that his much-cited volume does not elaborate enough on cinema.[42] Indeed, the travel-oriented works of both Ruoff/Schneider and Peterson also acknowledge that landscape has not been adequately analyzed in cinema, with the possible exception of Westerns. But as the debates above on the wartime genre suggest, landscape and travel prove highly relevant to generic thinking about cinema. Moreover, the neglected links drawn between landscape and territorial aggression/integration illuminate how *Dr. Hart* initially offers an aesthetic idiom resonant with older landscapes but then stages their fundamental transformation. Here, too, depicted "nature" is deployed in the imagination, legitimation, and creation of a certain territorially driven modernity—mechanisms confirmed by recent ecocriticism of cinema.[43]

In his work on landscape in early cinema, Tom Gunning traces the trajectory from painterly landscapes in the nineteenth century that Mitchell discusses through a series of technologies, visual and otherwise. Landscapes, according to Gunning, were remade over the course of the nineteenth century first by the train,[44] by photography,[45] by the panorama,[46] and then, perhaps ultimately, by cinema.[47] What Gunning is tracing (and Peterson and Urry have also confirmed[48]) is, fundamentally, a transformation in how landscape was deployed in a series of modern visual technologies, technologies that became increasingly industrialized over the course of the nineteenth century. Gunning locates this transformation above all in the technologically conditioned frames of landscape and in the experiential sensations surrounding them, confirming historically what affect theory has recently emphasized about cinema. To return to my central theme of distance—how it is depicted and deployed in cinema foregrounding movement and mobility—earlier viewers of landscape remain at a deliberate and contemplative distance. But with the technological changes associated with industrialization, this distanced viewing arcs toward literal and experiential proximity. One finds, as I explore below, this trajectory deliberately staged in *Dr. Hart*, although, as with the train and map, it unfolds within broader spatial practices and pleasures relating to territorial transformations and acquisition.

In act 1 of *Dr. Hart*—its introductory fifteen minutes—the film's subjective and territorial transformations are anticipated through a careful reframing and then remaking of landscape images. These landscape views initially look back to earlier traditions of travelogues (Reisebilder, Tonbilder, and Naturfilme in the German tradition) but also look forward to the war genre unfolding during the war. And these spatial changes anticipate changes to citizen-soldier subjectivity of the film's eponymous protagonist: wartime subjectivity, with its affectively arresting experiences, is spatialized in specific ways, as it had been in travelogues. Revealingly, the film's narrative opens by weaving space, movement, and landscape into a specific spatial assemblage, as Nigel Thrift has termed it, before the war. The film opens in a large, even majestic orphanage where the supervisor, Ursula von Hohenau, entertains her male caller, Hart. Although von Hohenau's home, located in Saxony, largely drops away as a relevant setting, it does allow Hart to undertake a carefully staged trip back to his home in Baden-Oos (near, and altogether like, Baden-Baden), affording spectators abrupt and revealing views of the German countryside (figure 2.2).

The lovely scenery here corresponds to what Peterson and Giorgio Bertellini have (separately) investigated as the picturesqueness in early cinema, which they

FIG. 2.2 Early landscapes in *Dr. Hart.* Digital frame enlargement.

both see unfolding especially in landscapes of the pre-1914 travelogue.[49] With its wide-angled but deep-space images of the broad countryside and gently rolling hills, Leni's war film takes up this tradition of the landscape as soothingly picturesque (as opposed to the nineteenth-century romantic sublime).[50] Even the staging of the image highlights the links to conventional landscape depiction, with the trees framing the scenery behind and Hart as a foreground figure. In that placid vein, *Dr. Hart*'s initial images of landscape come via a horse-drawn carriage: this carriage-borne point of view evokes Wolfgang Schivelbusch's panoramic gaze but in an antiquated form predating the railroad. If Schivelbusch claims that it was the train that irrevocably changed landscapes with its panoramic gaze, *Dr. Hart* establishes longer-term links to the depiction of landscape via older mobile media.[51]

With these opening images of formal courtship, traditional architectural spaces, and broad vistas, Leni's film commences a spatial assemblage belonging to an entirely different era.[52] These early external views and antiquated transportation could be either late eighteenth or early nineteenth century, when such landscape depictions began to proliferate and, as Gunning observes, began to be mass reproduced.[53] The images reinforce a few aspects of the affective geography these depictions invoke: first, the solitude of the doctor coincides with the privatized, interiorized subjectivity of the middle class that drove modern secularization and subsequent ascendance of landscape, as Malcolm Andrew has outlined.[54] Such solitude intensifies the embodied experience of these spaces in *Dr. Hart*—of bumping along in the carriage and watching them pass by. Second, and certainly resonating with the production of a certain war-relevant subjectivity, *Dr. Hart*'s opening also suggests the contiguity of landscape views and the male gaze that Gillian Rose has foregrounded in her feminist critique of landscape.[55] The film's opening narrative gambit of exchanging a courtship visit for picturesque views enacts a sentimental substitute for von Hohenau, an erotic-spatial fort/da game to be replayed later in the film. Finally, these artificially out-of-time images in the first minutes of *Dr. Hart* invoke what Mitchell terms the "indeterminacy of affect" relating to painted scenery.[56] With such an effect, viewers are not directed to look at any particular aspect of the imaged space but rather invited to allow the pictured space and its misty distance to wash over them in an open-ended affective experience. Of course, as Mitchell also observes, such indeterminacy of affect in appreciating landscape is poised on the privilege that underscores Hart's perspectival command of the imaged space. His movement carries him seamlessly between his happy courtship in Saxony and his professional practice back in Baden-Oos, a successful physician traversing and thereby integrating the space in between for his own (subjective) contemplation and (private) reveries.

Such middle-class will and agency express themselves even more definitively in the destination of Hart's carriage trip—namely, the film's next setting of the spa town where he has his practice. In linking the carriage's panoramic landscapes to Hart's hometown spa, the narrative invokes another nineteenth-century spatial assemblage and its ancillary subjectivity that the film will soon transform. The Baden-Oos spa is revealingly used to introduce the other lead characters from other nations, including Polish Count Bransky, Russian Count Bronislaw Krascinsky, and Hart's second love interest, the Polish Jadwiga. The film stages the subterfuge of spa flirtation and then jealousy in a love triangle among Jadwiga, Hart, and Bronislaw Krascinsky, a plot bespeaking a bygone, border-busting cosmopolitanism that the film will soon renounce in its nationalist remapping.[57] This cosmopolitan setting and its transnational romance—along with cinematic spectacles recalling early cinema visual attractions (fireworks!)—return to an era when most of what appeared on German screens was not German. And even the content that had been produced locally tended to downplay nationality in favor of export potential.

Dr. Hart's tourist-like views of the spa town Baden-Oos—especially looking back to 1914 from later in the war—invoke this earlier spatial assemblage of aristocrats and their old-world cosmopolitanism. Such an assemblage offers the plot amorous intrigues the film associates with traditional views of landscape. But the phantom of war haunts the good doctor and these comforting settings: a postman bearing a newspaper announcing the 1914 Austro-Hungarian ultimatum to Serbia appears on von Hohenau's doorstep. When full mobilization is subsequently declared shortly thereafter, Hart suspends his spa town practice and embarks again—a historical watershed the film chooses to stage by (literally) reframing the travel and the landscape it opened with. The familiar images of departure give away to Hart once again on the move, against the backdrop of rural images, though now in a refigured mobile mode. This time, however, Hart rides in a train that tellingly moves in the opposite direction of the earlier horse-drawn carriage, from right to left. In his compartment, the viewers see the protagonist again contemplating landscape but now from a speeding train that anticipates the modernity of mobility so central to the war. The carriage has become the affectively resonant train, and the landscape and his private subjectivity—both carefully depicted in an earlier, prewar spatial assemblage—are effectively transformed by the war.

With this new mode of rail-based travel, the landscape itself has been revealingly remade via a new kind of embodied movement—by mechanical mobility, as Urry has charted.[58] Here guided by Hart's perspective, viewers catch a glimpse of a monument amid the rolling hills, the Hermannsdenkmal (figure 2.3).

The Hermannsdenkmal and its surrounding landscape were woven into the longer history of German national consciousness as revealed in the Teutoburger Wald.[59] At least since the nineteenth-century rediscovery of Tacitus's *Germania* (ca. AD 98) and its account of Hermann/Arminius's defeat of the Romans there, one of Germany's most "heroic" deeds had been associated with hilly forests in general and this forest in particular. It is a sylvan-set history whose allure stretches from the Grimms to contemporary artist Anselm Kiefer.[60] For centuries, if not millennia, the Teutoburger Wald remained a central, fantastical locus for national consciousness, even as its location had to be recalculated and moved numerous times—a dislocation and disjuncture highlighting the self-serving "nature" of national mythmaking and its spatial manipulations. For German-minded thinkers from Luther to Kleist, the misnamed Hermann (his name was probably closer to Armin) became a potent symbol for the struggles against southern and western, allegedly "civilizing" oppressors.

By the late nineteenth century and the rise of the modern German nation in/after 1871, this long-term national myth manifested itself in the monument that *Dr. Hart* offers as a narrative turning point. As Simon Schama recounts, "German patriotic enthusiasts from Chicago to Buckingham Palace . . . had dutifully made contributions" to the erection of this monument and its memorable statue.[61] The neoclassical statue and pedestal invoke Hermann's ambiguous relationship to imperial legacies. His victory was, at the least, substantively aided by his initial training and adoption by the Romans, before he turned on them in what the Romans certainly regarded as treason. Any lingering questions about Hermann's loyalty were quickly forgotten, however, and the statue was inaugurated in 1875, four years after war-forged German unification. The festive celebration included an elaborate imperial procession led by the then emperor Wilhelm I, who had visited the studio of the sculptor, Joseph Ernst von Bandel, in Hannover in 1869 to lend the project his royal imprimatur as well as financial support. The dedication ceremony even included a playacted battle with the Romans, underlining the association of the young German nation with its belligerent past.

As Hart glimpses the monument from his train window, he nods (literally) to the historical and psychological interpellation emanating from the statue, monument, and surrounding landscape. Steeped as a designer in the traditions of Western visual culture, Leni has recast the contemplative distance of the opening, very nineteenth-century landscape: viewers now see, from the perspective of the newly train-riding protagonist, a distant landscape deliberately nationalized through Germany's mythological battles. This is a notable revision of the kind of landscape imaged in the opening sequences. The film's

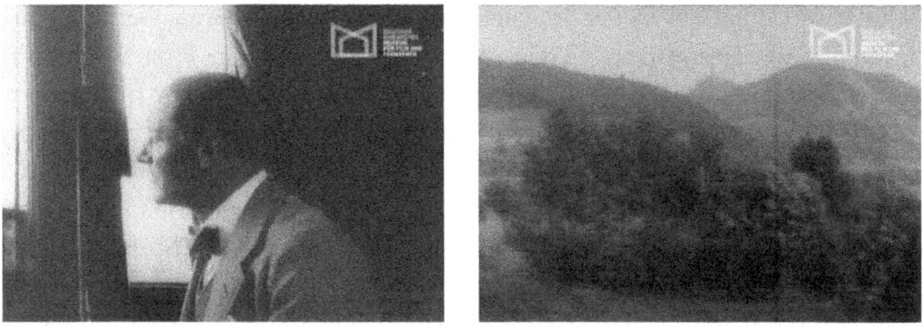

FIG. 2.3 Hart mobilized and inspired by the remade landscape. Digital frame enlargement.

earlier landscape highlights Mitchell's indeterminacy of affect, not least via a view aesthetic lacking the so-called serpentine path to guide the gaze of the viewer.[62] Leni's transformed landscape works differently with the travelogue's telltale depth of the image. Now in a more framed and fostered fashion, viewers look to a character's view, through a window, and onto a landscape remade with a national monument. It is a more guided gaze and affect reframed by a national memory and objective. Hart's train homogenizes the landscape, permits affect-intensifying movement through it, and then—transformed into national(ist) memory—is integrated into the consciousness of the changed citizen-soldier. Notably, it is the sort of landscape image that one would find later in the nineteenth and twentieth centuries among postcards and other staged views that commodified an emphatically national landscape, including those adorned with national monuments, that proliferated after Germany's war-forged unification (cf. Berlin's Victory Column).[63] National landscapes were commercialized in the new market of visual media, one thoroughly interwoven with new modes of mobility and the embodied movement they afford. When Hart arrives and celebrates the mobilization with his comrades, he is imaged at a considerable distance in the same pose as Hermann, with Hart rallying his comrades not with a sword but with words. Long before any shots are fired, this remade movement has refigured the landscape, with the protagonist's formerly private-professional subjectivity now a transformed public-political one.

Landscape Rendered into Territory: Mapping the National Future

The reframing and remaking of the view-aesthetic landscape yield Hart's memorable mobilization. Landscape is homogenized, sped through, and then integrated by the emergent soldier-subject. It also anticipates the way that the film finally, about one-third of its way through, transitions to the front, which it introduces abruptly with the intertitle "Polen!" To today's viewer, it might be surprising that a film featuring Baden-Oos/Baden-Baden in its first reel chooses to foreground the First World War's eastern front, particularly since most scholarship on the war—be it Anglo-American, French, even German—has favored the western front.[64] The popular perception of the First World War as an intractable trench war comes primarily from the western front, where the basic battle lines and trenches to maintain them were more or less set by midautumn 1914. But such stereotypes about the trenches highlight, I think, why Hans Brennert and Leni (along with many of the first German war films) feature the eastern front, even if it is all too often "forgotten."[65] The eastern front offered significant territorial acquisition and therefore more troop mobility, thus making it more cinematic for the fundamentally spatially driven genre. It also helped that German atrocities during the eastern occupation were less documented and politically consequential in contrast to the much-reported atrocities in neutral Belgium.[66] Cast against the relative spatial stasis in the west, the eastern front saw significant territorial back-and-forths for the first couple of years of the war as well as, for spectacular examples, the Tannenberg and Gorlice-Tarnów victories that rendered Paul von Hindenburg and Erich Ludendorff so central to German hopes about the war.

In my spatial analysis of the genre, war films' transition to the front always relates the combat spaces to society: as they reveal how the film remade its citizen-soldiers, they mediate distance between society and the front. As Gunning and Urry suggest, such distance in landscape was central to the modern remaking of space in nineteenth-century and early twentieth-century visual media.[67] Relevant are both the literal distance of the combat front from home and the psychological distance the would-be warrior has to travel. *Dr. Hart* stages this distance as many war films would later: as a literal and metaphorical journey of spatial, psychological, and social transformation. In line with the view aesthetic, and after the abrupt "Polen!" intertitle, audiences might well expect some kind of establishing shot of the Polish countryside. But rather than offering a bucolic landscape indexing the distance covered, the next shot is an amazing image of what viewers are, apparently, to understand as Poland (figure 2.4). The first image following the declarative "Polen!" is territorializing but in a very specific way. Rather than a distance-affirming, meandering depth of field one might expect from the landscape tradition invoked earlier in the film, viewers are subjected to a much closer up, vertically staged hillside remade by the sophisticated command-control structure of Germany's army. The depth of field of the earlier landscapes (standard in travelogues) has been abruptly foreshortened, the distances compressed: no longer at a detached distanced perspective—rather thrust right in viewers' faces—are the complexity and hierarchy of the military machine.

Dispensing with the open landscapes, or even the nationalizing panorama from the mobilizing train, "Polish" territory is now an assemblage of coordinated German military mechanisms, a perceiving and communicating machine geared to integrate and colonize space. Although the scene would seem to confirm Paul Virilio's assertion that in modern warfare, a "watching machine"

FIG. 2.4 Poland as the command-control hillside in Dr. Hart. Digital frame enlargement.

emerged next to the "war machine"—that is, that modern war is built on new modes of technologized vision—it also underscores, I argue, how this watching machine must be analyzed within broader spatial mechanisms.[68] Part of the impression such a scene leaves derives from the film's remaking of earlier spaces and production of new ones. Replacing earlier, Germanic landscapes is a communications system that was seen as an important innovation in warfare. Shortly before the war, Alfred von Schlieffen himself emphasized, in his private writings and published analyses, that command and control would increasingly shift from the traditional personal presence of the commander on the field to a "distant, highly-centralized, and control system" with "wire and wireless telegraphy, telephones, and signal apparatus" that would allow the commander to manipulate the fighting from afar. In other words, the commander's distance from the front and communications to it would become operational and, indeed, indispensable.[69] Leni realizes this shift visually by replacing the middle-class contemplation by Hart, with its linear movement and leisurely travel, with what Bruno Latour has called "circulating entities."[70] Initially, the view aesthetic's perspective on landscape was that of Hart in a horse-drawn carriage, then that of Hart in a train, both of which are now replaced by a militarized point of view built into a constantly moving, circulating assemblage. It is into this militarized assemblage that conventional landscape depictions and traditional view aesthetic are inputted, processed, and ultimately integrated.

This transformation of the film's opening landscape underscores one of the key spatial mechanisms of the genre: the repeated conversion of distanced land(scape) into proximate, affectively evocative territory via a territorializing gaze. This transformation grounds and hosts the violence so often presumed to be the pumping heart of the genre, as it frames the violence to reveal the sociospatial politics underlying it. The film's earlier landscapes—in the first instance, aiding and abetting middle-class subjectivity via contemplation during private courtship, and in the second, nationalized psychology in a public monument—are definitively recast as territory to be conquered. What is territory as defined against landscape and subjugated by this territorializing gaze? It is land, or space more generally, whose vectors of power, as geographer Doreen

Massey would put it, are foregrounded in the perceptions of that land.[71] Territory emphasizes how apparently open and/or empty space is simultaneously a forum for sovereignty and struggle around it. In fact, theorists of geography and international relations define sovereignty and territory coconstitutively, each defining the other.[72] The territory imaged here highlights who controls space and who struggles over this control: the hillside's depicted circulating entities highlight the many-vectored contestations that constitute territory. The perceiving and communicating machine on the hill is staffed by no one viewers have met. Its impersonal operations replace the view aesthetic and landscape that had grounded the earlier, private subjectivity of Hart. On this militarized hillside, spatial mastery, control, and integration yield very different affects than the interweaving of sentiment and landscape earlier in the film. A similarly stark contrast to the earlier landscapes is the verticality of the hillside in the frame, which emphasizes the hierarchy of the circulating entities.[73] Such hierarchies are central to the controlling and integrating mechanisms of the territorializing gaze, since they underscore the ordering of the vectors above. At the top are the commanders with binoculars and telescopes; in the middle are those with maps relating the perceived space to the conceived space, as Henri Lefebvre might have put it; and then finally, there is the communications facility to encode and impart the space as a reified, conveyable object.[74]

This territorializing gaze and transformation of a distant space realize what Lefebvre would term *abstract space* or David Harvey, following Lefebvre, would emphasize as *homogenized space*.[75] Rather than being admired for its natural features, this old-fashioned, distant landscape is processed with visual technologies, plotted on a map, and then conveyed amid circulating entities via communication—this is a space, once processed and rendered proximate, ripe for conquering and appropriation. Indeed, the very next image that viewers see includes the declaration "Vormarsch!" (Advance!) and a column of soldiers attended to by now "Feldartzt" Hart (figure 2.5). The film's formerly distanced landscape is now homogenized, rendered open to (troop) movement that definitively territorializes it.

The formerly private subject has been refashioned into a citizen-soldier, similarly subjected to the new vectors within this spatial transformation. With this marching column tended by the good doctor, the landscape now has, visually speaking, its clear serpentine path—it is a distance that is no longer to be contemplated but to be overcome with a disciplined military deployment. This remade landscape and view aesthetic now feature, amid the horizontal countryside, the spectacle of troop deployments that guides the audience through its spatial expanse rather than the indeterminacy of affect of the film's earlier landscape. As with the conversion of the carriage-based views of the passing landscape into those of the train, the film achieves a higher degree of homogenized mobility and integration of its open spaces.

FIG. 2.5 The landscape remade in Dr. Hart. Digital frame enlargement.

The film's second act extends this homogenizing and abstracting of space but does so more via character—it emphasizes how Hart himself partakes of these territorial lessons. Soon, an alarm is dramatically raised, and the troops are redeployed eastward. Hart removes a map from his satchel, a move that then drives the narrative forward into the final act's territory. The contrast between the landscape and the map is, for the genre, highly revealing. As Tom Conley has demonstrated in his *Cartographic Cinema* (2007), it is essential to understand mapping within the larger-scale spatial processes of modernity, especially the transformation of older spaces by the homogenization of space common to (affirmative) war films.[76] Conley, however, limits his study to the narrative intervention of mapped reality in films' diegeses. But Hart's point of view shot on the map underscores how the crude, diagram-like map does not so much link the film to a world outside as much as initiate the protagonist into geographical spatial processes occasioned by the war. A map early in a plot functions differently, as it situates the narrative by anticipating future events in spaces that already exist for viewers. But the midway appearance of a map in *Dr. Hart* links elements already at work in the narrative, homogenizing and abstracting them in new ways. The map materializes the training of Hart in the production of newer, increasingly abstract and homogenized spaces. Hart's map is part of a wider arc of geographical transformations symptomatic of the war film.

For viewers, Hart's map further intensifies the film's spatial aspects, especially on the key remaining spaces of the film: the makeshift medical facility that Hart commands (Verbandsplatz), the stately castle that bespeaks the earlier spatial assemblage of the aristocratic estate ("Schloß Bransky"), and a traditional windmill past which the German soldiers march. Conley notes another important effect of a map is it "heightens [viewer] perception" of the film's spaces.[77] This is certainly true here, as the seemingly innocuous windmill soon emerges as a key obstacle to reaching the castle. Both the castle and the windmill belong to an antiquated spatial assemblage, and both will, as Hart's map makes clear, have to be transformed as part of the film's genre-specific scheme. First, the arrows on the map indicating troop advancement are telling. They emphasize vectored space that both newly sought territory and its mapping underscore. As Lefebvre reminds us, any space is always already a terrain for struggle—and thus any map simultaneously reflects that territorial complexity while reframing it for its own deceptive purposes. This concomitant complexity and its reduction include the map's deliberately homogenizing and emptying of spaces, producing spaces that underscore the potential purview for human agency.[78] Every map is, in effect, some kind of geographical creative-destructive lie.[79] Hart's map depicts this self-serving emptiness filled with the vectors of both literal and metaphorical movement. The troops will recast the windmill, the castle, and the socio-spatial assemblage that underpins them, much like the militarized hillside mentioned above recasts the traditional landscape by way of homogenization, abstraction, and territorial integration. Hart's newly learned map system and epistemology based on it triumph over both landscape and the bucolic windmill that charmingly embellishes it.

Wartime Space Remade: Of the Castle, Hospitals, and Medicinal Trains

When the windmill is demolished in a spectacular explosion, the German troops' route to Castle Bransky is also cleared—homogenizing the place, conjuring the seamless route of abstract space. Soon they attack the Polish estate to wrest it from Russian forces. This conquering of the castle ushers in the film's most extended battle sequence: most of *Dr. Hart*'s second act (and third reel), roughly from the thirtieth-second through the forty-ninth minute of the seventy-minute film, offers extensive, if stuttering, combat. Before the German troops conquer the castle, however, viewers see in it a surprisingly familiar cast of characters: Hart's erstwhile Polish love interest, Jadwiga; her father, Count Bransky; and the Russian Count Bronislaw—the very same eastern European aristocrats who cavorted with Hart back at the spa in Baden-Oos. How the (war) times have changed. Bronislaw is now a Russian officer charged with defending the castle, Hart is part of the German attacking force, and Jadwiga and her father are, like Poland itself, stuck between them. The aged Bransky is shot in Expressionist tones—underlit face, histrionic expression, chiaroscuro makeup—and ominously announces that he will not flee, that he will instead await the Germans in his castle.

Bransky's historic castle becomes the key locus for the spatial transformations that the film realizes after the geographic integration and affectively intensified mobilization charted above. As with the carefully staged transformation of travel images in its first act—landscapes, spas, trains into national monuments, territories, command-control systems—the transformation itself seems the point: the conversion of older social spaces (the windmill, the castle) into modern military assemblages. Completing the transformation of the antiquated castle—and claiming it definitively as German territory—is a new sort of train that arrives, set to remake the frivolity of the prewar economy, with its rollicking spa and carefree courtship. This train, however, sports not weaponry but rather the latest in medical technologies. It speeds to the front with not rifle-cocked soldiers but bandage-bearing nurses. And one of these nurses is Ursula von Hohenau, Hart's original distant love object—such that the war and its transformed trains fulfill private desires via its public fighting.

Von Hohenau's departure from Germany invokes the familiar stereotypes of a mobilizing soldier: sporting a uniform at the train station, boarding with determination, and waving a happy goodbye to the cheering crowd. Given my argument about the centrality of distance and how it is handled in war films—the centrality of such imaging to the genre's syntax—the details of her mobilization are as revealing as the film's violence. By conspicuously mobilizing the central female character to meet up with the wound-tending protagonist—by paralleling his mobilization with hers—the film makes an overt appeal to early cinema's female viewers, especially as *Dr. Hart* was likely to be screened at home to audiences that had become composed of even more female during the war.[80] Von Hohenau's fidelity to both Hart and her country, now realized in this parallel mobilization, will be rewarded by Hart's ultimate choice of her over the Polish Jadwiga. After von Hohenau boards her train for the front, the camera focuses on the special features of the railcars: their compartments rendered to medical beds, gleaming white washbasins, and crisply folded linens, all the latest medical technologies crammed into the confined but highly mobile spaces. The surprising world inside the normal-looking train cars renders them revealing heterotopic spaces in the Foucauldian mode, an entire, unexpected world that dazzles the viewer.[81] As heterotopic spaces—places simultaneously present and near yet elsewhere and faraway—these infirmary trains, like the war itself, integrate apparently disparate and distant spaces into politics. Once so dramatically introduced, the train's journey is intercut with the German troops' later stages of the assault on the castle, together creating a suspensefully crosscut sequence of the sort that D. W. Griffith is usually credited for innovating around the time. The (cross)cuts between the medical train speeding to the castle and the ongoing attack underscore how the war, particularly its use of travel and travel technology, fostered the simultaneity of time-place as well as the advanced editing and storytelling of filmmaking. Such crosscutting was a specifically cinematic—and war genre—way of handling temporal and spatial distances of wartime.

The deus ex machina medical train that races the narrative into its final and concluding act returns us to Warstat's article with which this chapter commenced. In addition to advocating generally for a geographically informed war film, Warstat cites a number of specific topics that war films ought to explore—with just such new medical technologies prominent among them.[82] Other pieces similarly exhorted Germans to flaunt their nation's advanced medical facilities and health-care prowess in such films as well. Such exhortations are logical, given the exponentially increased demand for medical services in the wake of a much-longer and more devastating war than had been presumed.[83] Featuring Germany's medical facilities (more than merely battles) would address anxiety on the parts of both male and female audiences as well as advertise Germany's comparatively advanced medical technologies. Shortly after the advanced medical train arrives at the castle, the film shows, in short order, motorized ambulances delivering more patients as well as comfortable and bright hospital beds. Easing these transitions is the arrival of the train and von Hohenau in Poland, reaffirming the initial prewar private desire and the later one of the public war.

Sword and Hearth and *Inexpiable*: The Economy and Fragmentary Spaces of the Home Front

Dr. Hart is a Ständesmelodrama (melodrama among classes) that converts older landscapes into territory as it remakes those same Stände (classes) of the aristocracy and middle class. Tellingly, there are multiple conversions realized via new modes of mobility even more than with violence. Other high-profile war films from the time also forge new spatio-social ensembles. In these films, one finds combat selectively deployed within a larger agenda of dismantling older sociospatial forms and assembling new ones. In Georg Victor Mendel's *Schwert und Herd* (*Sword and Hearth*, 1916), both battles and land are similarly transformed in the "forgotten" east of the war, ultimately to recast what the characters understand as Heimat. While the eastern-front Castle Bransky and its aristocracy are conclusively recast in *Dr. Hart*, *Sword and Hearth* similarly depicts the war as "creatively destroying" older eastern spaces, including the spatio-social assemblages of Heimat. But the self-proclaimed Kriegsdrama also manifests a narrative pattern that proves important for the syntax of subsequent war films—namely, the multiple-protagonist plot.[84] Many later war films offer multiple protagonists in order to explore the grisly effects of violence on some of the central characters, although here the multiple protagonists are deployed to explore the different classes in the Ständesmelodrama.[85] If *Dr. Hart*'s single-protagonist Ständesmelodrama unfolds between the cosmopolitan aristocracy and the middle-class Hart on the move, then *Sword and Hearth* develops a more complex, spatialized social triad: the declining old-world estate owners, the university-educated middle class, and the rising working class.[86] Moreover, *Sword and Hearth* extends the generic syntax of *Dr. Hart*, particularly the war film as a spatial transformation, to a different thematic constellation—namely, that of disabilities resulting from the war. These disabled veterans are nonetheless deployed to modernize the social spaces the film has been investigating from its opening.

To a degree greater than in *Dr. Hart*, one can see in *Sword and Hearth* the importance of the economy in the war genre—especially the economy as it underpins the genre's constitutive spatial mechanisms. The (literal) changing fortunes of the film's three featured families are explored not so much through a romance (as in *Dr. Hart*) but through the boyhood friendship of two young men, Wilhelm Trautmann (Carl de Vogt) and Paul Marwitz (Kurt Vespermann), both drafted into the war. Such camaraderie had already become a standard means to establish multiple protagonists, for instance, in the so-called Christmas film *Weihnachtsglocken* (*Christmas Bells*, 1914), although here the boyhood friends are contrasted to estate holders, the Krafft family, in marked economic decline. Just completing his vocational training in his father's trade, Wilhelm is the son of a successful blacksmith in a small town, while Paul, son of a middle-class pastor, is just finishing up his university studies. Wilhelm is engaged to Emma (Wilma von Mayburg), while Paul secretly courts the daughter of the estate-owning Kraffts, Erika (Elfriede Heisler). *Sword and Hearth* traces the wartime fate of Wilhelm and Paul against the falling fortunes of the Krafft estate, with all figures' trajectories unfolding different social backgrounds and future prospects—prospects that then diverge radically due to the war.

The wartime modernization of the Krafft estate is one of the film's primary plot points, evident from the film's earliest scenes. Paul, who has been away in a larger town studying, pines to return to the rural setting of his childhood, coded early and emphatically in the plot as Heimat (act 1, scene 3). But as Johannes von Moltke argues in *No Place like Home*, this turns out to be a Heimat very much in the crucible of modernity. Even as Paul longs to return from university and marry the estate owner's daughter, Erika, the estate in its traditional form is proving untenable. As von Moltke proposes, Heimat doesn't turn out to be an unalloyed idyll of rural homeland but rather is already entwined with its ostensible others—with the modern, the urban, and their complex social dynamics. The challenging economics of maintaining a rural estate transform at the same moment that Paul longs for it: the elder Krafft is depicted early on as selling off livestock, both cattle and even Erika's beloved horse—with the latter sale a foreshadow of his more sinister plan to arrange an economically advantageous marriage for Erika. Needless to say, a middle-class pastor's son is not in his plan to save the family estate.

By the fifth scene of act 1, Paul reiterates to his father that, despite his completed university studies, he longs to return to this complex Heimat. He insists he cannot remain in the city and wants to return home to a rural lifestyle of a Landwirt (farmer). Paul's father, initially distraught, promises to discuss his son's future with estate-patriarch Krafft (act 1, scene 5). The war, however, intercedes, modernizing as it unfolds. A carefully staged tableau and its repetition demonstrate how the war will immediately transform the spaces of the Heimat: the film initially images a rural street and gate, with the ritualized procession of the estate owners underscoring the interweaving of social structures and their coconstitutive spaces—or, as Lefebvre puts it, the "production of social space."[87] Once the war starts, however, the film revisits this tableau-establishing shot to underscore how the war transforms such traditional spaces and their social forms. The military parade brings together the different Stände (classes) in a Burgfrieden (truce, literally "castle peace") that begins to remake the complex social spaces the film has established in its first two acts. Revealingly, if the middle-class elder Marwitz has long had a sense of a looming war (act 2, scene 9)—and is mocked for his geopolitical foreboding—the subsequent battles eventually kill the landowning Krafft. Before the outbreak of war, the estate was already in decline, with the elder Krafft even considering selling some of it off to Wilhelm's successful blacksmith father. But the war resolves these class tensions conclusively, highlighting its modernizing potential and longer-lasting consequences.

The recurring multiple protagonists of the later war genre also allow for the diverging fates of the main characters: Paul continues with his professional success, while Wilhelm sustains a life-changing disability when he loses his arm in combat. The film's theme of disability was much trumpeted in the trade journals and even marketing of the film. Such a theme also highlights the affectively intensified embodiment of war films, though with a different affective register altogether. Although *Sword and Hearth* makes a positive case for the war and the regime running it, the theme of veteran disability and its intersection with gendered desire anticipate Weimar-era antiwar films, post–World War II 1940s rubble films, and postconflict classics of U.S. cinema like *The Best Years of Our Lives* (1946) and even *Coming Home* (1978). By the end, Wilhelm inhabits a new house with a new love interest, Lise, and works in a new workshop space with new technologies to compensate for his disability, an economically productive "settlement" (Ansiedlung, as the various news media call it) for the disabled unfolded in the divided-up, formerly Krafft estate. The camera draws back at the end over a remade landscape as Heimat, the spatial transformation registering the resolution of this midwar Kriegsdrama.

In covering the 1916 heralded premiere of *Sword and Hearth*, the press trumpeted a number of celebrity attendees, above all the much-loved field marshal Hindenburg.[88] The old but increasingly celebrated field marshal, however, proved an even more important presence for the 1917 *Unsühnbar* (*Inexpiable*). The film's title was, in fact, drawn from Hindenburg's widely reprinted letter to the head of the Kriegsamt, General Wilhelm Groener, about unrest on the home front.[89] That titular invocation manifests the film's downbeat approach. Stiasny regards *Inexpiable* as signaling a new, darker direction for the war film, one warning of, and ultimately blaming, the home front for combat failures.[90] Contextualizing the film in the April 1917 strikes, Stiasny finds that the film links its fictional strikers to actual radical labor groups like that of the Spartacus League, which agitated publicly for the April strikes.[91] In this way, Stiasny suggests, *Inexpiable* anticipates the emergent stabbed-in-the-back myth (Dolchstoßlegende) that would be crucial after the war, a myth asserting that certain (especially "foreign") elements on the home front proved fatal to Germany's war effort. Stiasny argues that this admonishing, more negative approach to propagandistically propping up the war rendered *Inexpiable* a watershed, not least for its calculated garnering of official approval, critical praise, and audience popularity.[92]

For our purposes, the crucial question is how *Inexpiable*'s more sober tone about the war is cinematically depicted, what spaces and spatial assemblages the innovative film contributes to the genre. *Inexpiable* narrativizes and spatializes war differently than *Dr. Hart* or *Sword and Hearth*. Rather than converting land(scape) into territory via a territorializing gaze that integrates it into the war effort, it stages the paranoid threat of spatial fragmentation. Both Lefebvre and Harvey regard modernity as a dialectic of the homogenizing and fragmenting forces around space. With *Inexpiable*, the war's fragmentation of such spatial ensembles moves into the troubled foreground. If *Dr. Hart* transformed older spaces by homogenizing and integrating them into the war, then *Inexpiable* explores the flip sides of wartime spaces for the emerging genre. Spaces are riven apart and, ultimately, remain unintegrated into the war effort. Like *Dr. Hart* and *Sword and Hearth*, *Inexpiable* introduces new spaces for the genre, but these new spaces drive a narrative wedge between the home front and the combat front, with the distance between them remaining unbridgeable. In this way, *Inexpiable*, though not an antiwar film, anticipates anxiety and skepticism about the war and its sundry transformations to society. Foreshadowing the openly antiwar war films of the 1920s, *Inexpiable* suggests different spatial relations at the core of the genre: those tending to the threat of fragmentation as the war rolls on and stress and duress grow. And it helps establish this telling fragmentation and abiding distances by deploying other fundamental aspects of the genre, including gender as well as war's intersection with the economy.

Inexpiable might now be considered a home-front film, as the majority of it unfolds in the hometown of its key soldier. But the film was regarded as a Kriegsdrama at the time, not a surprise given its familiar scenes from the war genre, including images of a soldier's departure from his family, his travel to the front, and a narratively climactic combat scene.[93] It is revealing that *Inexpiable* opens, like *Dr. Hart* and many other war films, with its principals in transit—in this instance, with the departure of a train. The small-town family at the heart of *Inexpiable*'s plot (a mother and her two sons) is gathered at the station to bid farewell to the uniformed older son—he is returning to the front after home leave. These images of a hometown train station establish the familiar wartime spatial ensemble at the film's outset (trains coming and going, soldiers in uniform posted to depart, tearful relatives bidding farewell). With this assemblage, the film invokes the war genre but also immediately varies it, not least because it commences with, rather than builds to, this moment of mobilization. I noted above how many war films slowly negotiate the distance from home to the combat front, often building (narratively and spatially) on both the challenges and the excitement of mobilizing from civilian life and integrating the combat front into it. For example, *Dr. Hart* achieves, in transitioning to its third and final reel, a spectacular double mobilization of its romantic couple, such that both are integrated into the combat front.

By opening with a mobilizing farewell, *Inexpiable* tellingly takes its first fateful turn against the war. The same transit space that dispatches the soldier also introduces a new character, the Fremde (stranger and/or outsider). *Inexpiable* signals from its opening that it will engage the familiar spatial ensemble (home, transit space, and front, populated by a soldier and his family around him) but innovatively investigates the potential perils of this modern, mobilizing ensemble. If *Dr. Hart*'s hillside modernizes conventional landscapes with the complex but controlled circulation of military command, *Inexpiable* is hinting that such circulation of modern transit spaces can also prove pernicious. While the transit space offers the integration of the home into the front, it can similarly mobilize "foreign" elements to invade the home—a mobilization thus exacerbating, rather than overcoming, fragmentation. *Inexpiable* images the train station not just as the mobilizing mediator of the hometown to the combat front, to overcome the various distances therein, but as a potentially problematic circuit of circulation. Such dubious features of modern transit spaces will emerge especially after World War II, as we shall see.

With this insidious side of modern circulation in the arrival of the Fremde—at the very moment the hero-soldier mobilizes to the front—the film recalls a less-discussed aspect of Germany's transit systems during the war: the "civilian draft" and internal mobilization. Both of these phrases were codes for the military control of labor and the wider economy during the later phases of World War I. Ludendorff and Hindenburg proposed this so-called civilian draft shortly after being named supreme commanders of the army in late summer 1916, the moment that the Battle of the Somme had confirmed (after Verdun) how important the Materialschlacht (material battle) would be in the war. Since the economy was simultaneously reduced and coordinated to war-essential industries, domestic labor was brought under military control and mobilized accordingly. The much-cited subsequent Hindenburg Program sought, per Ludendorff's vision for "total war," to realize his militarist vision for all German society and economy, and the Reichstag had, in 1916, approved this civilian draft to mirror the military one.[94] Civilians could thus be drafted and mobilized to war-essential industries, especially to the munitions manufacturing that anchors the plot of *Inexpiable*. In this identification, mobilization, and utilization of civilian human resources, this second draft created, as Roger Chickering notes, another burden for the already struggling train system with which *Inexpiable* opens.[95]

In these ways, the opening train station arrival of the Fremde parallels, in a downbeat mode, *Dr. Hart*'s and *Sword and Hearth*'s modernizing of key social spaces—the very narrative event of an encounter with a racially coded stranger (with an imaginary Jewish subtext), in fact, materializes the homogenizing/

fragmenting forces of modern space, as Harvey has described. Harvey explores how the modern remaking of space—in both homogenization (e.g., in ever-expanding transportation systems) and fragmentation (e.g., in ever-increasing individuation of living spaces)—renders the chance encounter with the stranger a more frequent and formative phenomenon in modern society.[96] Harvey locates these spatial processes that facilitate the encounter in the city, something to which Walter Benjamin is certainly attuned in his critical engagement with Charles Baudelaire and the figure of the flaneur.[97] But in *Inexpiable*, the family's fateful encounter with the Fremde—the plot-conjuring encounter—transpires in a train station in the countryside.

The countryside of *Inexpiable* also offers a notably different sort of landscape than *Dr. Hart*'s opening. In *Dr. Hart*, the opening picturesque landscape was nationalized and then increasingly modernized and integrated into the war effort. Here the conventionally imaged planting fields highlight a central question of the war: that of the relationship of the civilian economy, especially farm-grown food, to the war effort. The German countryside and its agricultural industry assumed enormous importance during the war, for both the military and the government recognized that Germany would require the full participation of farmers. In this era of both the British blockade and the burgeoning black market, *Inexpiable* seems geared to acknowledge the central place of farmers in the war economy.[98] The difficult, so-called turnip winter of 1916–1917 and the increased quotas and control through the Hindenburg Program meant heightened tensions between the authorities and farmers, tensions that morphed, as Robert Moeller has observed, into a "sharpening conflict between city and countryside" that was "one of the most noticeable and distressing manifestations of the war."[99] Whereas, despite its rural settings, *Dr. Hart* dispenses with images of the civilian economy after its first-act mobilization and modernization, *Inexpiable* foregrounds throughout how hometown production of both food and munitions—underpins the dubious destiny of the soldier just mobilized.

Beyond the home front that mobilizes the wartime economy, *Inexpiable*'s farmland setting establishes two more central themes of the film from its outset. First, "Mother" (as she is called throughout) is the one pushing the plow, not her sons: due to demographic shifts on the home front—men were called up to the war or mobilized to "essential" work elsewhere by the civilian draft—many farms were left in the hands of women (Alexander Watson recounts how, by 1916, half of Germany's farms were run by women[100]). Mother's operating the plow highlights the heavy physical labor this era demanded, particularly in a context where horses were also increasingly requisitioned to the front.[101] The next scene, to drive the gendered point home, offers the intertitle "Frauen die siegen helfen" (women who contribute to victory), emphasizing (not least for the many female audience members) female contributions to the war effort but also, as the film suggests from this early moment, dividing up women into those who help and those who do not. To wit, a peripheral female member of the family who resides with them, the Magd (maidservant), ends up falling prey to the seductive charms of the Fremde, emphasizing how the film aims, like *Dr. Hart*, to condition female behavior as much as male. With Mother, however, the Fremde admires her hard work in the fields, asking, impressed, "At your age . . . ?" which introduces another of the film's recurring themes, that of age and the war's growing generational divide. Generations' diverging responses to the war become increasingly important in the film's next carefully depicted economic space, that of the factory.

The Fremde foregoes helping the earth-hugging matriarch, ostensibly because, as outlined in a letter of employment resembling a draft notice, he is scheduled to begin work at the local munitions factory. The film contrasts him to the earthy endeavors of Mother, highlighting the Jewish-coded (wandering) outsider who has only an attenuated connection to both land and traditional, now essential, economy. The film cuts directly from the field to this factory, a crucial setting for the rest of the film and foregrounding, in parallel fashion to the farm fields, Germany's domestic economy for the war. Like the train station and the field, the factory, especially a munitions factory, was a thoroughly overdetermined space in this period generally and at this 1916–1917 moment in particular. German industry had, of course, powered the nation's rising profile in Europe, with its share of world industrial production rising fourfold between 1860 and 1913 (while Britain's sank by one-third) and its output between 1895 and 1913 shooting up 150 percent, with metal production up 300 percent and coal 200 percent[102]—all gains that had exacerbated the fierce competition among nations that would manifest itself in World War I. Smooth-running munitions manufacturing is important to any war, but as noted above, modern artillery was probably the key technological innovation of World War I. For example, on each day at the 1914 First Battle of the Marne, Germany expended more munitions than it had for the entire Franco-Prussian War.[103] Moreover, the devastating battles of 1916, especially Verdun and the Somme, had underscored how important material resources would be to this particular war, running at that point both much broader and longer than expected. To an unprecedented degree, civilians working in home-front factories would be as important to this war as soldiers, something not lost on military leaders like Hindenburg and Ludendorff, who increasingly asserted their power over the home-front economy featured in *Inexpiable*.

As Hindenburg and Ludendorff replaced Falkenhayn in the wake of Verdun and the beginning of the Somme—a midconflict promotion that Chickering regards as bringing "epochal changes" to the war[104]—they aimed to double munitions production by May 1917, the precise period in which *Inexpiable* was written and then shot. These ambitious, likely impossible goals were announced as the army had to replenish its rapidly thinning ranks because the Allied blockade had more and more dire consequences. Additional demands on German labor had workers earning, in real salary, only 60 percent of their prewar wages while the work week had increased from its already rigorous prewar fifty-seven-hours/week![105] *Inexpiable* focuses not only on these economics of factory labor but also, unfolding from its farm setting, on the intersection of these harsh realities with increasingly rationed food supplies and the social tensions it would yield. In light of what turned out to be fantastical production quotas—Ludendorff later claimed that he set them so high to "boost morale"[106]—the Hindenburg Program granted the "heaviest workers" (including, first and foremost, male munitions workers) additional bread and potato rations. Hindenburg himself called for additional rations for these heaviest workers, and they sometimes ended up with as many as two thousand calories per day more than the meager, regular rations.[107]

Given the importance of such munitions factories and the tensions surrounding them in 1916–1917—tensions including but not limited to the April 1917 strikes—it is no surprise that labor relations would play a central role in a war film from that time, highlighting how such Kriegsdramen consistently engage with their broader social contexts. And these social contexts so engaged are spatialized in very specific ways. When the Fremde meets his notably older supervisor in front of the factory, the film spatializes These economic and labor issues "in front of the munitions works" (vorm Munitionswerk), as the intertitle puts it. The Fremde meets his soon-to-be supervisor and joins the labor force in front of the factory, between the factory door and the town street, the latter becoming an increasingly contested site of protest. In good cinematic repetition and variation style, the film revisits this image of the factory entrance set on the street to register the degenerating relations between the workers and their supervisors. The recurring invocation of this borderline space—transitioning from work to personal transit and freedom—recalls Kevin Lynch's emphasis on so-called interface or edge spaces in people's cognitive maps of their environment. In his study of cognitive mapping—which Jameson cites extensively—Lynch highlights how important such interface spaces are to people as they think and navigate the spaces of their lives.[108]

At this point in German film history, the image of a factory's interface with a street had, in fact, already appeared in films about labor unrest—for example, in the 1911 *Tragödie eines Streiks* (*Tragedy of a Strike*), which likewise admonishes willful workers to stay on the job (at that 1911 point, the film depicts striking as threatening workers' own children, not Germany's fortunes in war). And as Harun Farocki memorably explores in his film *Workers Leaving the Factory* (1995), the image of workers in abeyance in this in-between space—outside the factory but not quite free of it—is one of the Ur-scenes of cinema in general, recalling the Lumières' *Workers Leaving the Ciotat Factory* (1895) and then revisited throughout cinema history. For our wartime purposes, not only Inexpiable but also *Sword and Hearth* repeatedly evokes the revealing spatial image, with the latter's disabled veteran depicted in a factory doorway where he can still contribute to the war economy. The doorway to the factory spatializes the sundry emancipations associated with the factory, be they tending to the economic inside or out.

In *Inexpiable*, however, the factory's unstable interface with the street materializes the fragmentary state of the 1916–1917 war. As Watson notes, winter 1916–1917 seemed to be a turning point for unrest building to public protest.[109] Although initially the Fremde seems happy to assume his workplace in the factory, at a workbench depicted in deliberate deep-space shots that highlight the ordered efficiency of the munitions industry, he soon sets out to sow discord and disrupt production: the same deep-space images of farm fields and then of the factory are reframed and fragmented by the Fremde's subsequent agitation. For example, he and his newly minted minion, the above-mentioned Magd, have their first assignation amid (and even literally on) farming machinery imaged in such deep-space framing, highlighting again how the Fremde's very presence signals labor idleness, even destructive indolence.

The political materials then propagated by the Fremde and Magd underline the economic constellation sketched above: their agitating fliers claim that the government is actually denying bread to the munitions workers. In the scene following the Fremde's seduction of the Magd to his cause, the posters/flyers first appear in front of the factory, in the same in-between space where the Fremde and Magd now prowl, one now politicized in an altogether different direction. This form of agitation draws the workers out to the street, spilling and spreading discontent of the factory. The very same in-between space that inaugurated and initiated the Fremde to the workplace now disgorges the mobilized mass on to the town. This kind of politicizing mobilization to the street has been noted in Weimar-era cinema, as Bastian Heinsohn and Todd Herzog have emphasized.[110] But *Inexpiable* demonstrates how the street was already a highly contested and political space by the midwar, a pointed refiguring of public space after years of successful Burgfrieden (peace among the factions).

This initial, poster-inspired mobilization is defused when the workers return to the factory after some coaxing. But the lingering unrest soon produces an entirely new space for the film, a highly vectored space in Massey's sense, one that becomes important for the war film in general—namely, the packed pub as an unruly, even anarchic public sphere.[111] Like many cultural venues (theaters, cinemas), pubs and coffeehouses became contested spaces during the war, a home-front battlefield for wartime social decorum. Some cities, as Chickering has traced, even banned live music and dancing in pubs, toeing the line of earnest, ascetic bourgeois cultural norms during the war.[112] Containing the social effects of such spaces suggests an awareness of how important they were for public sentiment and even politics, something that Jürgen Habermas highlights in *Structural Transformation of the Public Sphere.* That work outlines a fundamentally spatial trajectory in modern democracy, from the monarchical authoritarianism of the audience chamber to the protodemocratic public sphere of coffeehouses, pubs, and theaters that foreshadowed parliamentary debate.[113] *Inexpiable,* however, contrasts its politicized pub visually, via shallow-space images full of circles and circular motions, to the economically productive deep spaces of the farm, factory, and even front.

In a very deliberately contrastive crosscut sequence of five scenes, the pub is intercut with the faraway front, where an attack on the German positions commences without necessary provisions being delivered—soldiers' discussion of the missing food cuts back to oblivious drinking and dancing in the Fremde-invaded home-front pub. The construction and handling of distance in the war film prove again revealing. Here the crosscut distances between the home front and the combat front are not reduced and ultimately traversed, as in *Dr. Hart,* by modern transportation but instead deployed by the film's editing to point to the perils posed by the home front to the distant combat front. Here crosscutting, so important to war films' homogenization and integration of disparate spaces, fails to cohere—it remains fragmented and dispersive. The (protest) public sphere of the pub contravenes the front, be it the home or combat front, and provides an abiding, threatening space of the war film, one that underscores its potential to fragment amid war's putatively homogenized spaces.

The pub scenes also confirm another vector of this fragmentary spatial ensemble—namely, generational tensions. As the Fremde climbs up on a chair to exhort the workers to strike, an intertitle underscores a generational aspect to this rollicking agitation: "The young workers try to convince the older ones to strike" (Die jungen Arbeiter suchen die Alten zum Streik zu bewegen). The film revealingly cuts to a different angle of the Fremde amid the pub crowd, one shot from the perspective of older workers looking through a window at him, with this intertitle: "Go to your work, do your duty!" (Geht an Eure Arbeit, tut Eure Pflicht!). As noted above, the demographics of the war, with many adult men drafted or moved for work elsewhere, meant that workplaces filled with both younger and older workers (25 percent of farmworkers were under sixteen, for instance, with 12 percent over sixty).[114] This sort of generational polarization provided for the kind of generational panic that would be seen throughout the 1920s–1940s.[115] The young's increased participation in the work economy afforded them more disposable income, which gained them increasing admission to the culturally controversial spaces above, including pubs and coffeehouses, from which they were subsequently often banned.[116] In *Inexpiable*'s riotous pub, the Fremde ignores the admonitions of the older workers: soon, he has climbed up on a table with his agitating posters, with the young son's generational solidarity clear in his conspicuous support. The youth panic here includes the abiding anxiety about the susceptibility of "Germany's young" to the "Jewish" organizer and agitator (cf. *Hitlerjunge Quex* [*Hitler Youth Quex*], 1933). Soon, the Fremde-led workers march on the street, eventually invading the factory interface with the street and idling the machines.

This long sequence, the dramatic and cinematic high point of the Kriegsdrama that offers remarkably little combat, crosscuts from the raucous pub not only to the faltering front but also to the now quiet home of the film's key family. Mother likewise underscores these generational tensions: she visits the pub briefly to convince her younger son to return home (now coded "feminine"), but he refuses. This refusal to return home and to obey his generational elder underscores how the long crosscut sequence depicts its multiple spaces as fragmentary rather than homogenized and integrated, as in *Dr. Hart*. The events in the pub detract from the factory, the front, and the private home, which remain isolated from one another, with the war film's telling crosscutting contrasting rather than integrating. After returning to her private domicile, Mother sits tired and defeated to read the newspaper. But in a memorable deus ex machina, in the newspaper—and thus in the officially approved public sphere—she encounters the famous lines from Hindenburg's letter to Groener that provide the film its title and key theme: that any idleness on the home front is "inexpiable." When the pub mob then leads to another street march and protest, she confronts them with this article, her officially censored and mandated public sphere facing off with the fragmented, grassroots public sphere the Fremde has produced. The protesters predictably ignore her, and it is not until the police come to arrest the Fremde that the younger son and the other workers desist. By this point, however, the crosscutting has turned fatal: back at the front, the lack of food and then munitions has led to the older son's inability to defend himself in the face of the enemy attack, and he is killed on the edge of a crater, a void symptomatic of the film's larger downbeat strategy.[117]

Mother's confrontation with the Fremde underscores how Hindenburg, as a charismatic monarchical ersatz, was supposed to integrate the fragmentary spaces both of the pub and of the street—that is, integrate by closing them down as police frequently did at that historical moment. Such was Hindenburg's charisma and popularity that the kaiser was sensitive about competition with him.[118] Habermas emphasizes how, long before democracy transformed the public spheres of coffeehouses and pubs into protoparliaments, the bodies of monarchs had served to spatialize state authority for the polity. After his early victories in the east at Tannenberg and Gorlice-Tarnów, Hindenburg's body was, indeed, deployed throughout German public spaces to garner support for the war effort, perhaps most famously in the twelve-meter-tall wooden Hindenburg statue at the Siegessäule (Victory Column) in the Berlin Tiergarten, to which people would nail coins, thereby donating much-needed funds to the depleting war effort. The statue confirms how the charismatic body serves to unify and organize the dispersive fragments of modern space and economy. On its inaugural day in September 1915—right after the victories in the east depicted in *Dr. Hart*—a reported twenty thousand people climbed up it to hammer coins onto the commanding, colossal body of the old general.[119]

This Hindenburg colossus actually did appear in films at the time—for instance, in the war-bond propaganda film *Der feldgraue Groschen* (*The Field Gray Dime*, 1917), in which the same actress playing *Inexpiable*'s Mother is pictured with the "Iron Hindenburg." In the fragmentary diegesis of *Inexpiable*, however, the real Hindenburg merely hovers over the film from the opening title sequence, when viewers first see his quote and name: he never actually materializes, underscoring the decline of conventional authority over the uproarious street. *Inexpiable*'s image of Mother's facing off with street protesters highlights how war films offer not only a cartography of new territory to be conquered (as I argued in *Dr. Hart* or *Sword and Hearth*) but also a hometown street map to be followed. If war films' images are always already political—insofar as they address how a society is to expend its resources, inanimate and living—*Inexpiable*'s approach to this hometown map is nonetheless unusually economic in depicting the relations among the farm, the factory, and the front. It is, as noted above, a map that proves revealingly gendered and generational, manifesting the home-front divergences in demographics of the time. Although the climactic cross-cut sequence connects these sundry economic spaces, the linkages offered by its maps fail to cohere as they do in *Dr. Hart* or *Sword and Hearth*: the Fremde is arrested, the older son is killed, the younger son enlists, and Mother is left alone and desperately lonely. The film leaves its wartime map of the economy broken, dispersive, even failing. In stark contrast to *Dr. Hart*'s mobilization and the final-act integration of the home and distant eastern fronts, *Inexpiable* as a war film offers instead a prescient foreshadowing of the Russian revolution that year and the German surrender the next that would finally end the war.

3

Landscapes of Death and Memories of the Human: Distance, Scale, and the Double Map of the First "War-Sound-Film"

(*Westfront 1918,* 1930; *Camaraderie,* 1931)

When *Der Film* put the festive premiere of *Westfront 1918* on its cover on May 24, 1930, it declared G. W. Pabst's film the "first war-sound-film" (Kriegs-Ton-film), underscoring both the pioneering momentousness of the production and the continuing genrification swirling around war films.[1] As I explored in chapter 2, the Kriegsfilm had consolidated into a recognized genre by the end of World War I; and in the mid- to late 1920s, there was more and more talk of the importance of Tonfilm (sound film) for the industry, but *Der Film* revealingly used the premiere of Pabst's film to merge these two discourses. Such a declaration suggests how even those films that we now celebrate as groundbreaking art cinema negotiated existing genres. I shall have more to say about the novel audio aspects that *Westfront* brought to the war film—aspects that did, indeed, transform the genre and its spaces—but the reviews also suggest that Pabst's war-sound-film would be different from what had come before in other ways. For example, *Der Film* declares that with *Westfront,* "we have the first pacifist film, that is, a war film [Kriegsfilm] that serves the peace."[2] Such a statement underscores the relevance of the conventional genre as films cross over into antiwar films. This film, the review goes on to observe, manages to avoid clichéd themes like "suffering on the homefront" and "the stabbed-in-the-back legend"[3]—the invocation of these much-evoked controversies highlights how the film, even as it negotiates the existing genre, is also weighing in on the many contestations around memories of the war, some ten years after its official conclusion. The wave of late 1920s and early 1930s war films, of which *Westfront* was part, suggests, indeed, not only how the genre continued developing but how war films often intersect the multifaceted mechanisms of collective memory.

As the particular war that the films depict faded further into the past, it had to be recollected in new but no less political ways. As Francis A. Yates's *The Art of Memory* has famously outlined, space and memory have long been entwined in efforts to comprehend and even manipulate mnemonic phenomena. More recently, Pierre Nora has foregrounded "sites of memory" (lieux de memoire) in his multivolume studies of memory practices, including monuments, exhibitions, commemorations, and so on. Such practices help ground the collective memories of social groups and contribute to mnemonically conditioned group identities (notably, by both remembering and forgetting in a process of "commemorative vigilance").[4] Spatially seen, however, the common, and near mis-, translation of *lieu/x de memoire* seems to me telling. Although Nora's phrase is usually translated as "site/s of memory," *lieu* is, of course, also (with *endroit*) one of the quotidian French terms for "place." This alternative translation of Nora's much-cited term underscores, I think, that Nora is charting, fundamentally, the spatialization of a mental phenomenon, the concretization in space of psychological mechanisms that help constitute a culture. While "site" shifts its semantic emphasis to human activity and deliberate labor—as in its most common usages in phrases like *construction site* and *archeological site*—"place" focuses on space itself and our affective investment in it.

Place is a central aspect of an affective geography that people develop, knowingly or not, to negotiate the world. Of course, one of the key contemporary places for such a spatialization of collective memory would be in and through the modern mass media, something that Alison Landsberg has famously traced in her *Prosthetic Memory*. Likewise, in Nora's spatial direction, Landsberg argues that media like film or comics create "transferential spaces" that foster consumers' prosthetic memories that they did not experience firsthand.[5] Landsberg also highlights the importance of affect and its manipulation to memory. Although she, in various ways, maintains the importance of space for comprehending memory, the concept has been somewhat evacuated in her overly general understanding of the above media. Narrative cinema, I have been arguing, engages specific spatial and affective mechanisms, many of which can be, and frequently are, deployed to invoke and manipulate multifaceted memory. Filmic memories—perhaps particularly as they intersect marquee histories, for example, as of wars—are always constructed and mediated phenomena that the specific spaces of those memories can illuminate.

Westfront, as that review in *Der Film* hints, sets out to suggest a kind of countermemory, one deliberately sketched against the prevailing nationalist interpretation of the fateful defeat and events of 1918/1919. In his work on memory practices and the "shadow of the war," Jay Winter has highlighted how the "multivocal" character of remembrance can counter the dominant modes of commemoration,[6] and in this vein, Michael Geisler has emphasized how Pabst's film responds to the way in which nationalistic readings of World War I had dominated the early, crisis-ridden years of the republic.[7] Other scholars of war and its aftermath, like Bernd Hüppauf, have also emphasized precisely these kinds of discursive contestations that straddle both history and memory.[8] In considering the generic spaces of *Westfront* within this study's longer history of cinema about war, I would suggest that the Pabst classic innovates the war film in important ways by exploring how personal memories may fragment the war genre's collective project. Here I depart from Anton Kaes's groundbreaking *Shell Shock Cinema*, which explores memories of the war in the Weimar era as trauma, as the return of the repressed, in primarily noncombat films.[9] Instead, I highlight how the war genre itself in this period self-consciously took up memory. Jeffrey Olick has highlighted this transition from personal to collective memory, a trajectory that proves central in *Westfront* in both plot and technique.[10] In fact, as I shall argue, the film constructs its individualistic, affect-intensified countermemory to detach soldiers from the national scale normatively achieved in most war films. The operations of scale, explored below, are central to the politics of virtually all war films—a politics of scale, as I am arguing throughout this study, that unfolds spatially. For just one eponymous example of this phenomenon, the film's spatially and temporally specific title (*Westfront 1918*)—one that alters that of the novel on which it was based—seems directed against the vague, romantic, even abstracting shibboleths, like the Spirit of 1914, still ubiquitously rolled out in the 1920s. The title localizes the narrative as a memorable place, ultimately descaling from the nebulous nationalist vagueness of the "Spirit of 1914" via a specifying spatialization.

Despite Pabst's reputation as one of the great directors of Weimar cinema, *Westfront*'s generic operations—especially its approach to the key spaces of the war genre charted in chapters 1 and 2—underscore the particularities and power of the film. This chapter will explore how the now canonical film, with its countercommemorative practices, deliberately reinstalls the landscapes and reestablishes the distances that more conventional war films like *Dr. Hart* or *Sword and Hearth* homogenize and overcome. In this way, Pabst's approach is thoroughly interwoven with the genre to which it belongs, even as it undertakes a fundamental critique of the genre's syntax, a fragmenting of its usual homogenization and integration of landscape. If chapter 2 argues that the 1910s war genre absorbed the ubiquitous travelogue (Reisebilder or Kulturaufnahmen) in its foundational overcoming of distance, *Westfront* spends much of its plot reestablishing and problematizing such constructed distances. These core elements of the film come into sharp focus if one compares *Westfront* to the novel from which it was adapted. In its first hour, the film's plot foregrounds two unusual journeys and their dissonance with the conventional genre. *Westfront*'s intensified travel is geared not so much toward homogenizing mobility as toward fragmenting the spatial assemblage of the conventional genre. These fragments underscore the genre's regular destruction of older spatial ensembles and creation of more open, homogenized, frictionless space: the breaking apart of the genre's homogenized space lays bare the two maps (personal and national) that the genre usually integrates. Such severing of the genre's double maps uncovers and contravenes what I sketch as the "scaling" processes inherent in war films' assiduous travels. If chapter 2 aims to demonstrate how distance and its traversal function centrally in the genre's affective geography, here I explore another fundamental operation of the genre's spaces—namely, their scales' relationality as they negotiate between personal and collective memory ten years after the war.

The Scales of Memory and of War (Films)

In probably the most cited work on the war film, Jeanine Basinger has located the soldier/unit/mission triad at the heart of the narrative syntax of the war film.[11] I argue how *Westfront* highlights another central aspect of the genre—namely, its continuous production of what geographers have termed *scale*. The notion of scale has moved to center stage in the spatial turn to explain how spaces resonate not only in different places but also at different orders of spatial-social magnitude. In later spatial theories (many influenced by Henri Lefebvre's *Production of Space*), these different magnitudes have come to be known as the different "scales" at which spatial understanding and social practice operate.[12] For critical geography, such scales concretize the underlying intersection of spatial and social forms and practices. It is not only, however, that different scales (of, for instance, the personal, the local, the regional, the national, the international) exist but that they are also constantly constructed, negotiated, and interwoven in very political ways.[13] While the conventional understanding of scale is, in fact, based on the concept of a fixed scale for a map, theorists like geographer Neil Smith have emphasized how societies are constantly producing and reproducing varying scales for their myriad spaces, constantly and self-servingly relating individuals and their spaces to other scales of society. The deliberate production and negotiation of spatio-social scale, it seems to me, count as fundamental features of the war film. Such mechanisms distinguish it from other but related genres like melodrama (likewise full of sacrifice, suffering, and loss), action/adventure (similarly full of movement), or horror (also full of violence). Such scaling points, in fact, to the war genre's foundational entwinement of space and politics as well as space and economics.

In order to construct and negotiate such multiple scales, societies may, at the intersection of space and social forces, undertake myriad processes like the following: deploy and manipulate symbolic representations (such as war films), organize and undertake social actions (such as actual mobilization), and stage and execute scale-negotiating events (such as battles). These would be upscaling mechanisms that, like a map and its scale, relate the individual to larger orders of spatial-social magnitude. On the other hand, such scalar operations might also deliberately delimit the impact of certain actions—for example, containing the scale of political activism at a more local level, as in Neil Smith's groundbreaking work or, as I showed in chapter 2, in the local containment of strikers in *Inexpiable* (1917).[14] It seems, however, that war films upscale individual efforts to the level of the national and then international: in fact, like these theorists' models of the production of scale, war films interweave different levels of political, social, and economic hierarchy with the different scales of space they explore. The levels of the individual (and its private space) are sublated by the collective (and its shared spaces) as well as subsequently related to the national, the international, and sometimes the transnational. War films consistently elaborate and deploy certain spaces, but an awareness of scale elucidates the organized, hierarchical, and politicizing fashion in which they do so.

Sallie A. Marston, J. P. Jones III, and K. Woodward's later call to abandon the term *scale* altogether does raise the question of its fundamental analytic utility.[15] I would argue, however, that periods of increased space-time compression (including during wartime) intensify the operations, and awareness, of scale: the headiness of sudden leaps spatially and temporally encourages an epistemological adjustment of scale, I think, as demonstrated by the ubiquity of discussion of scale in our information technology economy. As information technology and its ancillary businesses have compressed space-time in ways hitherto unimaginable, there has burgeoned ever more discourse about the level at which a product is "scaled," how subsequently ready it is "to scale," and how effectively it will operate "at scale," with the specific meanings of scale in each case defined by the product in question. Even as one acknowledges the relevance of scale to spatial and social conceptualization and practices, Marston's point is well taken that one should not reify such scales—that is, not regard them as stable "containers" or (as often imagined) simple concentric circles.[16] To address the perils of this sort of reification, I would cite Lefebvre, who offers critical insight into the concept by historicizing scalar operations.[17] He suggests that each geographical scale undergoes three entwined moments, including their historical emergence, their always partial and provisional stabilization, and finally, their disappearance, be it by withering away, transformation, or even bursting apart. Certainly, scales are important to how people imagine space and themselves as actors in it, but as Marston and Lefebvre observe, such scales are never stable or predictable and, above all, not fixed for all of history. This very contingent history of scalar imaginaries is that which intersects a genre like that of the war film.

In considering such scales in cultural products like a film genre, I would emphasize Marston's critique of scales as too often (as on a map) reified but also underscore that many cultural products, especially those geared to politics, locate citizen-subjects at a specific, if imaginary, scale—this is a crucial part of their geographic and geopolitical operations and aesthetic, in Jameson's sense.[18] And following Lefebvre, I would emphasize that there is a history to these scales, the magnitude and place at which these products understand themselves and their audience to function. As I shall aim to show below, scale allows, in a more dynamic way than Basinger's soldier/unit/mission triad, one to comprehend and conceptualize a genre's negotiation of the tensions and politics between individuals and the collective. This would be particularly true in the 1920s, as the cultural and political context shifted, per the above, to remembering the war. The scales of war were to be renegotiated in a memory mode. In fact, personal memory's fragmenting the putatively collective war allows for a critical descaling of the generic elements that were tightly integrated and hierarchized in the 1910s genre—not least by the new technology of sound.

Sound and the Scaled Double Maps of War Films

To track the scaling performed by Pabst's innovative use of sound, it is useful first to consider how *Westfront* establishes and negotiates its basic spatial aspects—aspects like setting, its various locations, and their distances from one another that I am highlighting as fundamental to the genre. The film's narrative breaks down into three main spaces that suggest the sundry scales at which the film operates: first, private spaces set behind the front; second, the eponymous western front lines of trench warfare; and in the film's final sequences, the more open battlefield and then the improvised field hospital in a Christian church. As I noted in chapters 1 and 2, central to the genre and the workings of these films is the narratively staged distance to the front, including how it is covered in the films' constructed affective geography. Narratively speaking, the first hour of the film revealingly oscillates between the first two types of place: it opens in an interior, a French Ruhequartier (billet) near but behind the front where a few German infantrymen are enjoying themselves, but then quickly returns them to the front. In this first quasi-private space, the youngest (der Student) of the "four from the infantry" (Vier von der Infantrie; the title of the novel by Ernst Johannsen on which the film is based) falls in love with a French woman, Yvette/Jacqueline.[19] The film's second half hour negotiates, in deliberately parallel fashion, between the front lines and another private terrain of desire: the home in Germany of Karl, another of the eponymous four from the infantry. With the subsequent death of the student, the evacuation of Yvette/Jacqueline from her home, and the return of Karl at around one hour, the film's final half hour unfolds between the latter two of the film's three types of space, between the front lines of the film's climactic battle scene (especially the appearance of tanks on the French side) and the hospital/church turned infirmary that has largely replaced the mildly more upbeat affective geography with which the film opened.

In this way, the film traces a basic spatial trajectory from, in its first hour, private plus public spaces to, in the last half hour, the increasingly fragmentary public spaces of a failed war (the dugout, the battlefield, the field hospital). This trajectory itself suggests a narrative-spatial arc that overlaps with but also counteracts most war films, a genre that, I am arguing, carefully produces and integrates sundry spaces and scales among them. Here, however, instead of traversing the distance from the home to the front and scaling the private individual to the nationalist public (as in *Dr. Hart* or *Sword and Hearth*), the extended, detailed journeys covering distance are back toward home and/or civilian spaces. Such scaling reconstruction of space relates to the affective geography of the genre and reconstitutes the war film's foundational distances, fragmenting the scales that are, normally, interwoven as distances are compressed. It is a descaling that reestablishes distances that had been self-servingly (and politically) compressed in most of the genre.

Fredric Jameson posits that some films—and genres—are particularly spatial, and my investigation herein suggests the war film as just such a genre.[20] In analyzing the political thrillers on which he focuses, Jameson unfolds a double mapping that rests at the heart of the films' narratives and plotting: there is the map of the explicit diegesis (the film's obvious fictional world), usually understood without much difficulty by both the protagonist and the audience, and then there is a secret second map that often determines the narrative trajectory of the first map: "This promise of a deeper inside view is the hermeneutic content of the conspiracy thriller in general, although its spatialization in [*Three Days of the*] *Condor* seems somehow more alarming than the imaginary networks of the usual suspects: the representational confirmation that telephone cables and lines and their interchanges follow us everywhere, doubling the streets and buildings of the visible social world with a secondary secret underground world, is a vivid, if paranoid, cognitive map."[21] Rather atypically and in contrast to many thrillers (e.g., of Hitchcock), viewer knowledge of the unfolding of the secret second map rarely surpasses that of the protagonist. The metaphorical and mental dimensions, key landmarks, and accessible routes of this second map remain covert, or at least obscured, for both the protagonist and the viewer, creating an epistemological challenge. There reigns, for both the protagonist and the viewer, an epistemological confusion in its very structure, resulting in perplexing paranoia in the face of both the political context and the emerging global totality. Gaps open up between the two maps, and confusion and paranoia come to haunt characters and viewers alike.

The mobilization kernel of war films typically manifests, as Jameson suggests in the above passage, a kind of narrative double mapping, one more legible but still nonetheless challenging for the characters. In war films, I would suggest, there is typically, especially toward the beginning, a map of the characters' private lives (usually desires and attachments in romance, family, and/or the local community), and then there emerges a second map of nationalized public spaces of mobilization and, eventually, combat—and the distance between them is telling. Such double mapping matches the deliberate parallel civilian and military geography of even the home front that both John Keegan and Caren Kaplan describe, in different contexts.[22] Many war films' affective geographies offer locations—both places and faraway spaces—that chart the characters' psychological investment in them as they shift to the second military map, rather like *Dr. Hart*'s opening journey to the spa town Baden-Oos versus the subsequently cleared attack vectors to Castle Bransky. But in war films, the two maps require some kind of mobility between them, mobility and the subsequent negotiation of scale (scaling to the global conspiracy, as in Jameson, and to the national war, as in most war films). Of course, both of these maps in the war film are much more comprehensible than the inscrutable secondary mapping that Jameson describes in *Geopolitical Aesthetic*. In fact, the syntactical operation that the film achieves, usually via mobilization, is the transformation and upscaling of the first map to the second map. For example, *Dr. Hart*'s private cosmopolitanism in Baden-Oos is scaled to the nationalized, militarized cosmopolitanism of the concluding, conquered castle. But even with such scales, there are still, as in the films Jameson analyzes, considerable tensions between the two maps, tensions of distance and struggle with scale that help structure the narrative, narrative suspense, and ultimate resolution.

The gratification or dissonance associated with that resolution depends on the given film's approach to the war. The key mobilization aspect of war films' lobbying for war usually drives toward a narrative telos that will happily balance the two in a new affective geography. The narrative achieves a scalar balance by covering the distance between the two, locating the private on the national map and thus scaling the individual to the national. The private map of desire can only be completed by scaling to the nationalized project of the war, and vice versa, while individual agency is maintained on both maps. The national effort to raise and motivate a fighting force can only succeed if there is some scale reached via the affective terrain of private desires and attachments. With their plots, war films consistently explore the way the one map interweaves behavior with the other map—it plays with the distance, scale, and affect across the two maps, as with *Dr. Hart* and *Inexpiable* above. In some films—for example, *Dr. Hart* or *Sword and Hearth*—the plotting covers the distance between the two maps by homogenizing landscape and integrating territory, but in other films, the spaces fragment and break, effectively descaling the individual from the national ensemble of the second map. With *Westfront*'s introduction of sound, of course, plot and story could grow much more complex, simply for reasons of representational exposition. But in terms of the scenes and information offered as plot, the film seems quite like a silent film, as one of its negative reviewers complained.[23] Instead, the dramatic power of the film resides in the distance and intercutting between these two maps, a scalar tension and intercutting for which Pabst deployed sound in creating some of its most memorable effects.

In his contemporaneous review of *Westfront*, Siegfried Kracauer focuses above all on the use of sound in the film. Kracauer dedicates two paragraphs to these effects in a review of merely six paragraphs underlining how he holds these mechanisms as central to the film's overall effect.[24] In many other reviews as well, the sound aspect was foregrounded, with, for example, the sound technicians receiving top billing in a *Filmkurier* advertisement shortly after its premiere (in May 1930)—their names prominent and centered and bigger than Pabst's name. In his review, Kracauer remarks on two specific deployments of the new sound technology that I think are useful to keep in mind, since they have become ubiquitous in the war genre, and their power and strangeness, clear to audiences whose habits were conditioned by silent films, would be very apparent to viewers at that transitional time. First, Kracauer underscores the way in which the film uses sound to "explode" the "borders of the picture" (sprengen . . . den Bildrahmen)—that is, he emphasizes, in dramatic rhetoric underscoring its novelty, the use of off-screen sound to expand the depicted space of the frame. This effect is central to war films, in which, to pick just a couple of relevant instances, the whiz of gunfire and the booming of artillery are regularly out of frame but, of course, have major dramatic impacts on character behavior without being directly depicted on screen. War films, one might say, depict the unsettling experience of ubiquitous off-screen sound effects and reacting to them: such sound destabilizes the space of the frame and suggests substantive, narratively significant distances and scales outside of it. In this way, Pabst choosing a war film for his first sound film seems particularly appropriate, as for maybe more than any other silent genre, sound would fundamentally transform both the spatial and scaling potentials of the film.

Second, Kracauer celebrates the way Pabst uses a variety of sound effects, especially matches on sound and sound bridges, to compress (at least initially) the distance between private and public spaces, a distance that serves in *Westfront* both to reference and to criticize the mobilization aspect of war films generally. Its opening seven-minute sequence includes a clever match on sound that reveals an important theme of the film. It opens with German soldiers relaxing away from the front in the French Ruhequartier (billet)—although notably they, resting in a pub in Bezincourt, are not at a full distance from the front back at home either. Most of the dramatic action in the sequence follows the soldiers' attempts to seduce, in their coarse fashion, the French woman Yvette/Jacqueline (she is called Jacqueline during the film and Yvonne in the shooting script[25]). In this largely failed undertaking, the soldiers literally fall over one another, with one soldier eventually spanking the other. Matched to the very moment of spanking, however, viewers hear the sound of incoming artillery, which puts the lights out and sends the soldiers scurrying for cover. Revealingly, the image track (sudden darkness) follows the cues of the off-screen sound. The sound of the soldiers' desire overlaps with and has been scaled to the larger, off-screen war: scale here negotiates the two maps mentioned above that are achievable, at least with this kind of economy of expression, only with off-screen sound. The thematic content of this effect is best illuminated by foregrounding the scaling of the two maps between which the film's off-screen sound navigates: that of the off-duty desires of the individual infantrymen and that of the on-duty agenda of the nation's war. The national scale invoked via sound is off-screen at first but still reminds the soldiers of its drawing ever closer and its covering the imagined, even fantasized distance to the actual fighting.

Such an interpretation of the film's distance, scaling, and double mapping also affords a reading of another noteworthy shot in *Westfront*'s opening sequence, one that even more effectively foregrounds the theme of distance via off-screen sound and returns my reading to the film's memory mechanisms. *Westfront*'s very first shot frames, in long shot, the windows and door of the pub in which the film spends its opening six minutes. It is a standard establishing shot of a dramatic location, and after registering this setting, viewers watch the student let himself in the door. Much later in the sequence, after the artillery and after the soldiers have been called to the town square to prepare to march back to the front—around eight minutes into the film and six and a half minutes after the film opens with the above-mentioned shot—Pabst returns to a reverse angle of the same door, windows, and cart. Now, however, there is no one pictured in the frame.

Over this empty image referencing the film's opening, the soundtrack offers, in another important deployment of off-screen sound, the voices of the infantrymen as they report to duty, barking officiously each soldier's name and "angetreten!" (present!). These parallel shots framing the important opening sequence demonstrate how the initial shot has been rescaled, via off-screen sound, to the intrusive war. It is a space that invokes personal memories for the soldiers that will become important later in the plot (and notably different from in the novel). Distance, scale, and (through them) loss are depicted as if the space of the Ruhequartier, that space of private desires that takes up the first six minutes of the film, could actually become a treasured, pleasant memory. It is exactly this Ruhequartier they remember personally, intimately, and on the map of private desires as they report to march off to the contrasting scale of the national.

Memories of the Human: Antiwar Affect at the Bodily Scale

Pabst's remarkable return to this opening shot highlights the war's memory function, a mnemonic mechanism at a time when the war had to be recalled some ten years after its conclusion. Within the film itself, the first sequence sketches a space to which the film will later return multiple times (notably more than the novel), that of the French Ruhequartier (billet) at the pub and the (literal) mise-en-scène of the student's romance with Yvette/Jacqueline. In this sequence, the film seems particularly invested in conjuring a space in which the soldiers' bodies can be specifically situated—a strategy of Pabst's that raises another dimension to space and scale and that I have not yet emphasized—namely, the space of the body and the way in which we inhabit our bodies even before places (and inhabit such places through our bodies). In her work on historical and remembrance modes within film and television, Landsberg has highlighted the importance of embodied, affective attractions in audiovisual media to engage viewers in a meaningful (and memorable) experience of the past.[26] *Westfront*'s opening sequence is particularly effective in evoking the past war—especially given what characters' bodies will undergo—because Pabst gives the bodies specific affective shadings throughout it, shadings contiguous with the space and this soon-relinquished scale of individual desire. The affect-intensified bodily scale will be a crucial means later for reestablishing distance and descaling from the national in the film's affective geography. The sequence opens with an exterior shot as the student enters with a pail of water: the door (and with it his point of view) sweeps open on a group of soldiers surrounding Yvette/Jacqueline—she is at the center of the group making coffee. Carrying a pail of water is, of course, a quotidian domestic undertaking, one that has a particular feel both in its manual sensations and in its effects on one's walk. The sequence extends these specific affective sensations when Yvette/Jacqueline comes to take the pail from the student, relieving his burden, and then finishes making the coffee. The film offers repeated close-ups of the wafting steam from the coffee, the deliberate pouring and sharing of it, and then a slow hugging of his cup by an old man, "a grandpa" (as he is called in the script), who will have no significant role in the film otherwise (figure 3.1).

Taken together, the images of this opening materialize the affective pleasures of coffee and domestic simplicity at the scale of the individual body. The coffee thus seems the focus here as much as any individual character, certainly an important relief for men mired in the grime of the front. To achieve these specific bodily effects that Landsberg foregrounds, the images conjure what Julian Hanich has called "somatic empathy"—a precognitive, affective form of empathy to which a cross-sense appeal contributes, often for a synesthetic effect in viewers.[27] The lingering shots of coffee achieve just such a cross-sense effect, invoking sight, smell, and touch even before the old man tastes it. The cross-sensory images of *Westfront* are so effective that they seem to have been copied by Steven Spielberg in his celebrated *Saving Private Ryan* (1998).[28] These specific effects are often temporary but then can contribute to a more general sense of a constrictive or expansive lived body in a sequence or series of sequences. Hanich observes that horror films (and, I would add, war films) work very deliberately with constriction in the affect-intensified body, a sense of generalized fear that

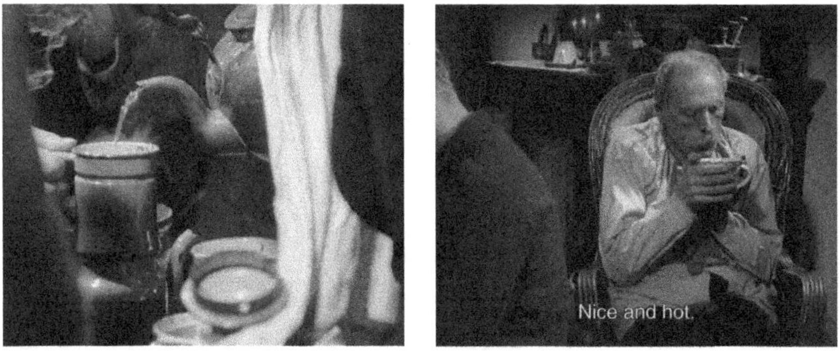

FIG. 3.1 Embodied affects of home: coffee more than character, *Westfront.* Digital frame enlargement.

compels the viewer to shrink or sink into her or his own body. Such a retreat can be materialized, for instance, in viewers' closing or covering their eyes, an effort at self-imposed and self-protecting constriction. Such direct, fear-driven constriction is to be contrasted to more expansive moments of the lived body, of joy, happiness, even ecstasy, which provide for a form of corporeal expansion in the viewer.[29] Even when limited to images and early sound, Pabst stages and shoots the sequence to foreground the soldiers' aromatic, gustatory, and then even tactile return to the domestic: he is deliberately using this opening to locate viewers at the happy scale of the individual's expansive body, not least by sketching this ephemeral space-place through the affect-intensified body. For a war film, of course, it is remarkable here how much the bodily scale is intensified away from the front, away from battle and its violence, underscoring how *Westfront* negotiates these different scales very deliberately.

Another haptic pleasure augmenting somatic empathy and an expansive lived body away from the front is that other handling highlighted in the film's opening minutes—namely, that of the soldiers' repeated, and sexist, groping of Yvette/Jacqueline's body. In the opening moment of the student's point-of-view shot on the group, viewers watch as a soldier takes her hand and rubs it over his beard stubble, emphasizing the tactility of both her hand and his face. When she goes to relieve the student of the pail, she runs her hand over his, the first, highly tactile hint of her infatuation with him. And when she brings the Bavarian and Karl their coffees, the former hugs her and suggests, "Let's give it a go! Let's give it a go!" (Machen wir einen Gang! Machen wir einen Gang!), until another soldier pulls her away and embraces her in feigned protection from the "no-good Bavarian," with one of his hands cupped conspicuously on her breast (the manual manhandling is carefully outlined in the shooting script as well;[30] figure 3.2).

Pabst shoots the Bavarian's lascivious face from her point of view, her upper body held by one soldier and her legs writhing in the grasp of the leering

FIG. 3.2 Tactile "pleasures" behind the front mapped onto the woman's body, *Westfront*. Digital frame enlargement.

Bavarian (figure 3.2). This segmentation of the female body via editing recalls Pabst's *Joyless Street* (1925), in which the male gaze similarly dissects the female body. When the group has to move to the cellar because of the initial shelling, Yvette/Jacqueline disappears into a shadowy stairwell with the student, where he holds her quivering hands ("zitternde Haende," says the script), and then they embrace, she running her hands over his face repeatedly. When the student has to leave to make roll call, Pabst offers a remarkable last look back from his point of view of her as he leaves, her body supine and clothes rumpled, registering the abandoned traces of his body on hers (figure 3.3). Like the return to the establishing shot of the (empty) doorway, this shot is a regretful look back that underscores the memories of the simple affective pleasures at the scale of the private individual. These carefully staged simple domestic pleasures—of hot coffee, sexist flirtation, and finally mutual love—create a sense of an expansive lived body in the carefully mapped and scaled place, of somatic joys to be all the more appreciated and remembered, given the war. But these are spaces, memories at the scale of the body, that will soon be rapidly fragmented by fading intimacies and newly produced scales.

These affect-intensified images of the quasi-private space of the Ruhequartier become, tellingly, the motivating memory, a personal memory at the scale of the body, for the student's negotiation of wartime scales later in the film. The scene of the student's leaving Yvette/Jacqueline for a marching column recalls precisely the scaling of the two maps in the war genre's standard affective geography: spaces of private desire succeeded by, often superseded by, the nationally scaled spaces of the army and war. This basic spatial trajectory, the scaling of private desire to the nationalized public of the army and war, is typical for war films, but this sequence of the student's very specific affective geography will tug at him, as memory, throughout the first hour as he suffers through the war. He feels the fragmenting of the two maps, the descaling of the individual from the nation, perhaps because Pabst, as noted above, so carefully produces the

FIG. 3.3 Fading affective pleasures become personal memory, *Westfront*. Digital frame enlargement.

specific place (the Ruhequartier) through the scale of the individual body. It is, indeed, the temptation of returning to this lost private memory from the war—negating collective memory and its scaling—that leads him to accept the lieutenant's request that someone deliver a message to command that they are being shelled by their own artillery. This attempt to preserve an affective geography of private desire leads the student on a journey through the memorable, and memorably desolate, landscape of the front—an echo and critique of the travel and landscape central to the genre, as I traced in *Dr. Hart* and *Inexpiable*.

The "Landscape of the Front": Reauraticizing Soldiers' Gaze

In his review of *Westfront*, Kracauer argues that the film distinguishes itself from previous war films not only by its use of sound but also by its focus on a Stacheldrahtlandschaft, a landscape of barbed wire. If chapter 2 suggests that landscape and its spatial transformations are central to the genre, Kracauer is suggesting that here, too, *Westfront* takes up and transforms this key element of the generic semantics and syntax. But as the first sequence, analyzed above, and Karl's trip home suggest, the film does not unfold entirely in that eerie terrain of barbed wire, collapsing trenches, and denuded trees—landscape is only part of its broader memoryscape. Rather, the film scales the two spaces—each part of a wider affective geography—by negotiating the distance between the characters' private lives behind the front and the pockmarked battlefield of the war. *Westfront* does leave, as it did with Kracauer, the impression that this latter landscape dominates because it is probably the key visual contribution of the film. In fact, the film foregrounds landscape in an important early sequence, also featuring the student, that invokes the cinematic tradition of travel—although, here in the antiwar war film, it is travel geared to fragment the usual wartime affective geographies, not least by descaling the individual from the nation. If homogenizing landscape and integrating territory are central mechanisms in the (pro-)war genre, a good portion of *Westfront*'s visual power lies in its descaling the landscape of the conventional war film, including on the journeys it uses to reinstall distances normally overcome in the genre.

One of cinema's most important early and conspicuous functions was its offering a traveling perspective and experience to viewers, a kind of cinematic tourism that foregrounds a "panoramic gaze," as both Wolfgang Schivelbusch and Giuliana Bruno have observed.[31] Panoramas reference, of course, the pre-cinematic attraction that featured faraway places and their landscapes, brought close in a realism, as well as on a scale, hitherto unknown. *Westfront* offers precisely this kind of traveling, panoramic gaze in the person of the student over the course of his journey. It is telling, however, that this descaling use of the panoramic gaze comes here with a soldier on foot as opposed to, say, *Dr. Hart*'s trains, horses, and cars. In this now pedestrian journey, unsurprisingly, landscape figures centrally in the film and its reception, because, in addition to its role in generic syntax mentioned above, the "landscape of the front" was an important aspect of the 1920s contestations around memories of wartime. But landscape also served at this 1920s historical moment for the kind of transformation in art and experience that a critic like Walter Benjamin was tracking. Benjamin's reflections on landscape in the 1920s demonstrate how these spaces and their transformations figured in culture more generally.[32] The unproblematic transformation and integration of landscape and territory that I tracked in *Dr. Hart* are now engaged problematically. Such engagement with landscape only underscores its importance for the genre and the modernizing cultural context in general. With landscape, Benjamin foregrounds both the conventional constitution of what he calls "the aura" and its transformation in modernity's evolving aesthetics. In its divergent depiction of landscapes (when compared to films like *Dr. Hart* and *Sword and Hearth*), *Westfront* revisits the aura and auratic experience in landscape to register the kinds of change in the experience of which Benjamin was writing in the wake of the wartime. Both the journey and these increasingly denaturalized landscapes radicalize the traversable distances established in the opening, effectively descaling the two affective-narrative maps that the film offers in its first hour. Here landscape is not so much transformatively scaled to the national as it was in *Dr. Hart* but rather invokes memory and loss of the personal in the war's relentless, merciless scaling processes.

The so-called landscape of the front had become an important locus for 1920s nationalist memories of the war, as Benjamin suggests in his 1930 "Theories of German Fascism." In this essay, a review of a collection edited by Ernst Jünger, Benjamin situates the soldier type sketched in the volume: "This soldier type is a reality, a surviving witness of the World War, and it was actually this 'landscape of the front,' his true home [Heimat], that was defended in the *Nachkrieg*."[33] Benjamin underscores how these "landscapes" became the Heimat for the soldiers in what Jünger insisted on calling the "*Nachkrieg*," a coinage signifying not the "postwar period" but the "postwar war," presumably of the

1920s.[34] The neologism emphasizes how belligerent nationalists and left-leaning critics were engaged in contesting the meanings of the war, its interpretations, and memories of it and how that very landscape of the front became the battlefield for these memories: "It should be said as bitterly as possible: in the face of this 'landscape of total mobilization,' the German feeling for nature has had an undreamed-of upsurge."[35]

Given the importance of landscape to the war film as well as the 1920s discourse of a memorializing "landscape of the front," it is not surprising that Pabst in his film and Kracauer in his review would foreground landscape as one of the film's most important visual innovations to the genre.[36] At almost exactly the moment he was writing critically of Jünger's landscapes of the front, Benjamin was giving the changing forms of landscape a central role in his history of perception via photography—in fact, in his skepticism about nature amid the wartime landscapes, he hints at how a transformation of landscape was at the core of the evolving modernist aesthetics with which he was engaged at the time. Indeed, around this time, the landscape for him became the paradigmatic model for the aura and auratic experience: "What is aura, actually? A strange weave of space and time: the unique appearance or semblance of distance, no matter how close that object may be. While resting on a summer's noon, to trace the range of mountains on the horizon, or a branch that throws its shadow on the observer, until the moment or the hour become part of their appearance—that is what it means to breathe the aura of those mountains, that branch."[37] The landscape, or rather the experience of looking at and being absorbed by it, serves as the model for Benjamin's elusive notion of the aura and auratic experience of the past. At the moment Benjamin was addressing its appropriation by the nationalists to set the mise-en-scène of the Erlebnis (experience) of the front—its consequential scaling to the nation—landscape also became the linchpin, in his eyes, of a fundamental transformation in art remade by technologies like the camera. This was a transformation figured above all through distance, the auratic distance to conventional landscape. Indeed, in "Little History of Photography," Benjamin traces how photography was moving away from this mode of the auratic; a modern photographer like Eugène Atget "disinfects" the photograph of the aura, which becomes "the most signal achievement of the latest school of photography."[38] In a revealing conceptual move for an essay on photography, Benjamin then turns to "Russian film" to emphasize how this newest of media in the newest of countries was dispensing with the aura and its consistent distances altogether. The medium itself traversed distances and homogenized spaces. Benjamin would return to a very similar definition of the aura some five years later in his much-cited "The Work of Art in the Age of Mechanical Reproduction" of 1935, in which he also cites auratic experience in "a mountain range on the horizon or a branch that casts its shadow on the beholder."[39] "Little History," in traversing from distant landscape photography to Atget to Russian film, serves to link the destruction of the aura to the tradition of landscape representation—the overcoming of distance I highlighted with *Dr. Hart* and its hillside but technologically augmented views of landscape.

Benjamin's destruction of auratic distance transpires in a way that elucidates how *Westfront*, as it does with other aspects of the war film genre, invokes but also sublates the so-called landscape of the front. In *Dr. Hart*, for example, the train speeding by the Hermannsdenkmal and its surrounding landscape (see chapter 2) deploys the aura of its rolling hills and distant monument to scale the private protagonist to the collective war. When Hart nods emotionally at the monument, the conventional (distant) aura of nature and of art conjures a new affective geography to scale the nation. *Westfront*, however, invokes such auratic distance only to memorialize it, effectively dismantling it and, with it, the genre. The film depicts the destruction of auratic experience amid the landscape that is nonetheless recognizable as a landscape, which should, as both perspective and experience within the journey form, be auratic. That is to suggest, on the one hand, *Westfront* invokes the auratic experience of landscape with the form of the soldierly journey and the wartime panoramic gaze that would conventionally accompany it; but then it works to deliberately subvert the conventional auratic experience of this wandering figure with a radically denaturalized, deauraticized experience, the now all too close landscape of the front. Much as it manipulates the mobilization's two maps to problematize their happy coexistence, the film thus works to undercut the auraticized, distant landscapes of the past with the battlefield of the present, evacuating the aura from nature as it drains humanity from the battlefield. This invocation followed by negation—thus sublation—forges the personal memory central to the film's mnemonic operations. *Westfront* invokes the panoramic gaze sketched by Schivelbusch and Bruno only to, as Benjamin puts it about Atget's photos, "suck the aura out of reality like water from a sinking ship."[40] Given the role of landscape in films like *Dr. Hart* or *Sword and Hearth* or, as we shall see, in the Nazis' Luftwaffe films, such a recasting of landscape and distance in the genre disrupts and destabilizes the genre's foundational scalar operations.

This memorializing dismantling of the panoramic gaze transpires above all in an eight-minute sequence about twenty minutes into the film, when the student volunteers to travel from the front to the regiment command post. The front lines at which the four infantrymen are serving are being shelled by Germans' own artillery, a discovery they make shortly after the opening sequence and one that underscores, as the first ten minutes at the front lines do, the ironic futility of the war. The lieutenant (he is the last of the eponymous four infantrymen) first dispatches a messenger dog to the regiment command to beg them to retarget their fire. When the shelling and therefore urgency intensify, he asks for a human volunteer to go. Only the student, to the consternation of his comrades, agrees, because he plans to use the mission to visit Yvette/Jacqueline back in Bezincourt—that is, to renegotiate, even revoke, the scale of the two affective maps that war always entails.

In line with the fragmented maps of war discussed above, the student's journey is to be from one map to another, from the spaces of the battle, with its constricted body, to that of his private memories of the expansive lovers' bodies. He takes the message and starts off on the sojourn to Yvette/Jacqueline, an ultimately eight-minute trip (in a ninety-minute film) that brings him through various, often surreal stations of the eponymous western front. The journey affirms the generic link of war and travel established in chapter 2, but here reestablishing the distance becomes decisive in the film's spatial logic. It dismantles the effective scaling via the traversing of distance from the opening Ruhequartier to the front, a distance that was quickly overcome with the film's space-eliding (space-destroying) cut to the front, unproblematically traversing the distance from the private map to the bodily deprivations of the trenches. In that sequence, the homogenization of space scaled the individual to the nation in the wartime's typical affective geography—distance was covered, and the national scale was quickly attained by the individual. But the student's later voyage allows the film to revoke this homogenization and its scaling, with its elision and destruction of auratic distance—the return journey, made on exhausted foot, makes viewers aware of the different notion of distances too often denied by war. These are distances both physical and emotional, of course. And the reestablishment of such distances, which the student's reverse journey slowly, deliberately depicts, destabilizes the scales at the cold heart of the genre's syntax.

As the student starts out, the camera cuts to a long shot that reveals more of the landscape than the low camera in the trenches has revealed up until that point. Viewers see, predictably, a desolate, denuded landscape but one that also deliberately establishes certain visual themes that recur later throughout the film. Here, in notable contrast to how *Dr. Hart, Sword and Hearth*, or *Inexpiable* work with landscape, there is no serpentine path guiding the viewer through the careful landscape composition, a path eventually diverted to the national scale. Instead, viewers see the overwhelming fragments of a conspicuously broken landscape. The film foregrounds the auratic in two important recurring fragments: (1) trees and their branches and (2) the cross, often naturally formed, sometimes deliberately deployed. Both elements of mise-en-scène invoke important examples of the auratic—the tree branch of which Benjamin speaks as paradigmatically auratic in "Little History" and the religious artifact foregrounded in "The Work of Art" essay—only to, as he says, suck the aura like water from the sinking ship of wartime reality. The trees and cross are present in this first journey image through the landscape and will recur as the student finally reaches the command post and then also when he encounters a workshop where they create crosses with which to bury the fallen soldiers (figure 3.4).

The student's encounter at the grave marker workshop is narratively the most unmotivated of the episodes on his journey and, indeed, emphasizes the episodic, almost sociological, cross section he witnesses while traveling between the film's two maps. This image of a stack of wooden crosses resonates with

FIG. 3.4 The student's dispersive journey, *Westfront*. Digital frame enlargement.

another aspect of the deauraticized landscape of death—namely, the radical seriality of human lives in war, one matching the seriality of modern mass society. The student's journey is, indeed, one marked not by recognizable sights and landmarks—as in *Dr. Hart*, where the journey integrated travel into the nation via the Hermann monument in a nationally scaled place of memory (*lieu de memoire*)—but by the quotidian seriality of death. Serial perception functions across the genre as a deliberate contrast to the militaristic/directed perception—it is a view of fragments that cannot be integrated, let alone scaled, effectively. Such meaningless seriality would also be the inverse of meaningful scaling to the multitude and eventually the nation: scale helps give meaning to multiplicity.

After this harrowing and exhausting trip through the landscape of death, the student does cover the distance, reaches the French pub, and is soon trying to get Yvette/Jacqueline's attention. The initial shot that relocates viewers in the Ruhequartier itself also hints at the awful seriality of war because it shows, a mere twenty-five minutes after the opening sequence here, a new group of soldiers strewn around the same floor. Viewers might well expect that Yvette/Jacqueline would have forgotten the student and would have a new soldier in her bed, just as the Ruhequartier has rotated out the student's company for a new one. But she answers the student's call, recognizes his uniqueness in a context in which viewers have seen uniqueness radically downgraded and nature deauraticized, one last reminder of the distance between the affective geography of private and individual memories and the serialized, denaturalized world of the battlefield. The shot of the student waiting for her to fetch him at the door revisits and rewrites the shot in the opening sequence (discussed and imaged above), creating a fondly remembered mise-en-scène with his person set to the scene of their love. It effectively restores him, against orders, to his personal memories at the scale of individual desire.

Despite the apparently successful journey—fulfilling his official mission and realizing, by navigating spatially, his private desire—the film spends its second half hour undercutting the established scale between the private maps of Karl and the student and the nationalized map of the battlefield. The film seems largely structured by these two journeys that re-etch the distance too easily covered in the film's opening and too easily traversed and homogenized in most war films. The film's opening went rapidly (via off-screen sound busting the frame of the image, pace Kracauer) from the private world to public military service, but the two journeys back highlight the sheer distance between the two, both physical and psychological. A scripted but missing scene reinforces this sense of newly emphasized distance between the front and home: the script, available in the Deutsche Kinemathek, offers a scene in which Karl stops in Belgium on his way home and buys various foodstuffs for his wife. Indeed, these copious foodstuffs are then visible upon his return to Germany in the extant copies of the film. Referred to in the memorable conversation with the student on the edge of a crater, the scene draws out Karl's journey, rendering it more parallel to the student's own lengthy sojourn back to Yvette/Jacqueline, as well as underscoring the distance between the starving home front and the rich foodstuffs near the western front.

The scripted but skipped scene also recalls the home as a locus of the bodily scale. When Karl finally arrives home, he learns he is the victim of another seriality (allegedly) common in wartime, that of infidelity. Revisiting a theme as well as iconography from Pabst's *Joyless Street*, Karl's wife has traded favors for meat from the butcher's apprentice. Karl loses faith in their marriage, fails to forgive his wife as he departs for the combat front, declaring that he only looks forward to seeing the comrades again, especially the student. His private map of personal memories has been ruined, fragmented by the infidelity, but the positively integrative, scaling aspects of the war (loyalty to fellow soldiers, feelings of camaraderie, etc.) are also already destroyed, as the viewer knows what Karl does not: the student has just been killed in combat back on the broken landscape of the front. This privileged viewer knowledge also underscores the obsolescence of the student's private affective geography when Yvette/Jacqueline is evacuated from her home, the setting of her love with the student, because of artillery. The cruel irony is that she is concerned with the student's knowing where she is when he is already dead. The crosscutting I flagged above that often traverses distance and integrates territory here yields fragments of their personal memories. The private scale is in utter fragments, its map in tatters, revoking the distance easily covered in the homogenization opening the film: both the scene of their love and one of the lovers are now gone, emphasized in a long-take of the ruined house and the off-screen sound of Yvette/Jacqueline's crying. The generic syntax's scales are fragmented amid the arresting ruins of the individual body, the loving couple, and the collective nation.

Countermemorialization as Countermapping

By the film's one-hour mark, the student has died unbeknownst to both Karl and Yvette/Jacqueline at the same moment that they, on their respective maps of private affects and memory, are anxiously contemplating reunion with him. The film's two lengthy journeys have reestablished the distance initially covered, with its fantasy of homogenized space from the opening sequences. Instead of compressing, integrating, and scaling space as wartime travel usually does, these journeys fragment what were assumed to be the connecting relationships and lasting scales of the war. Not surprisingly, the film's remaining half hour subsequently turns to the commemoration of death, the student's as well as others'—memory in a war mode, memory scaled to the national, is consistently entwined with death. In fact, Karl's own end comes in the attempt to appropriately commemorate—that is, integrate and create lasting meaning out of—the death of the student. Upon returning to the front and learning how the student was killed the week before, Karl is in despair. When he hears eerie off-screen screaming, he becomes convinced that it is the student, and when disabused of this notion by the Bavarian, he nonetheless decides to volunteer for an advance mission in order to recover the student's body. The first two parts of the film use off-screen sound to register the war by expanding the space of the frame: in the first part, the artillery and then sounds of being called up eclipse the map of private desires and attachments; in the second half, the wailing of loved ones, of Karl's wife and Yvette/Jacqueline, register the interminable suffering of war for the civilian inhabitants of that second map. The last half hour adds new off-screen sounds to the exploded frames of *Westfront*—namely, ghostly screaming and ghastly groaning from the maimed and wounded, additional sound effects emphasized by Kracauer in his review.[41] These off-screen sounds now signal personal loss, the spatial fragmentariness, and the memory-laden landscapes of war.

When Karl and the Bavarian move ahead to position themselves for what is expected to be a large French attack, they come upon the student's corpse in a puddle of water. His comrades quickly, silently bury him, and the film, having denied an image of the entire corpse, shows his upstretched and rigid hand slowly covered with dirt—an utter fragmenting of the expansive body that the film affectively conveyed as a corporeally empathetic space at the opening of the film. The silence with which the comrades bury the student is revealing: there are no words of commemoration for the student, no mythologizing of his death. The emphasis on the silence around the death of a beloved comrade is particularly telling because of the scalar importance of memorializing mythmaking around the death of "fallen" soldiers. Such memorials serve to scale the individual death to the survival of the collective nation such that the most singular, lonely moment becomes a living memorial for the entire country. In the context of World War I, such discourse was particularly pointed in the case of the deaths of young, naive student-soldiers. One of the most important legends to emerge during World War I, for the subsequent 1920s and then right up through the 1930s and 1940s, was the myth of the slaughtered student-soldiers at Langemarck on the western front.[42] The myth of Langemarck scaled individual deaths to the sacrifice of Germany's best and most innocent youths who allegedly (though implausibly) went into battle singing, at which they were mowed down by older, more experienced British troops. This myth was fostered in part to obscure the mistakes made by the German military command in sending inexperienced troops against thoroughly battle-tested ones: the deaths were commemorated throughout the 1920s and became an important flash point for the nationalist collective memory of the "Great War." Confirming the abiding meaning of this memory, the Nazis introduced a Langemarck penny, to be donated regularly to its own mushrooming war effort.

Pabst's film, however, with its silent burial of the innocent's stiffened corpse, is explicitly directed against such commemorative mythmaking and the collective scaling built on it. The film's mode of site-specific countermemory is confirmed in the last of its spaces, the field hospital colonizing a church. A Christian church is, of course, an institution built around the commemoration of death, one that foregrounds a memorialization of death-as-sacrifice in its most important artifact (and one of the visual motifs of the film), the cross. It organizes and scales the fragments of this myth in a strict hierarchy pointing, via a steeple, heavenward. To set the conclusion and climax of *Westfront*, during which at least two of the remaining three die and the third has a breakdown, in a Christian church underscores the kind of place-based countermemorialization toward which the film drives. The ubiquity of soldierly death in a church underscores the double aspect that historian Reinhart Koselleck ascribes to war commemoration: such commemoration recalls specific deaths while also charging those still living with a legacy and mission based on those deaths.[43] It is in this mode that war films deploy the deaths of beloved comrades, whose deaths are subsequently symbolized as legacies for the surviving comrades to uphold.

Westfront's concluding space of the hospital invokes the upscaling memorialization of individual soldiers but also shows, in a reference to the spatial fragments established in the workshop sequence mentioned above, how the protagonists die anonymously as only a pitiable few of an incalculable many. As with the (mis)balance of the two maps or the auratic landscapes sketched above, the film invokes traditions of war films only to sublate them. The invocation of memorialization comes first, in another memorable tracking shot, as medics carry the lieutenant into the field hospital/church, in a clear reference to the iconography of the *Pietá*. But the rest of the sequence undercuts the uniqueness and meaning of the deaths of those four (now three) infantrymen with whom viewers have spent the film. At various moments in the sequence, the camera focuses on fragments—episodically or station-like—including a number of characters whom viewers do not even know, emphasizing the mass of casualties and relative meaninglessness of the characters viewers do know. The Bavarian sings until he dies, with almost no one looking after him. Karl likewise expires without any attending medical personnel, on a cot next to a French soldier whom viewers have never encountered, a Frenchman whose words "pas ennemi" (not an enemy) accompany a medic pulling a tarp over Karl's corpse. As very few among very many, the four from the infantry will be forgotten: the film actually ends not with Karl's death but with another soldier, whom viewers do not know at all, about to be operated upon.

Instead of commemoration or offering his comrades a charge to keep—an integrating and scaling of the mnemonic fragments into some kind of collective future—Karl's death turns the film into a vehicle for a different kind of personal, not collective, memory. In his last seconds, the surviving characters around Karl do not get a moving deathbed exhortation, but instead, viewers see a flashback to his wife begging him, as she did when he departed home, for one kind word before he returns to the front. His last words to this apparition from the past are "We are all unhappy, we are all guilty." Maureen Turim has emphasized that in their flashbacks, films offer a model for memory and even history, and this is precisely what *Westfront* offers in this sudden, unexpected flashback, the first of the film:[44] a different mode of memory, at precisely the moment of death, that contravenes the nationalist discourse of memorialization, much as the film contests national discourse about the landscape of the front. If the film rejects mythologizing and upscaling the deaths of its characters but instead focuses on their utter futility, it is directed against the culture of memorialization that many would make of military deaths, as with the Langemarck legend. The flashback offers a different kind of memory, one that in Karl's last moments returns to the personal affective-narrative map and the insurmountable distance between that map and that of the nation. In his final moments, the film foregrounds not the scaling of the private map to the public war (as *Dr. Hart* did so effectively) but instead the unbridgeable distance between the fragments of the two maps, a descaled distance that haunts Karl in his memorable end. The wartime map of the nationalist war has come to irreparably rend the map of private desire and attachment.

Karl's personal memory has turned haunting and ghostly, underscoring the failed scaling of memories to the war in general. Nora's places of memory (*lieux de memoire*) normally scale individual memories to the nation, interweaving their personal and collective pasts together in a spatially realized tapestry (for instance, in the famous framing sequences of *Saving Private Ryan*, 1998). But Pabst's staging here offers a place of (personal) countermemory rending and descaling the individual from the nation. In *Westfront*, this kind of fragmenting location as countermemory does, however, point to the possibility of rescaling and remapping in general, and it is in this spatial sense that I would offer a tentative reading of the emphatically open-ended conclusion of the film (the last, declarative title card being "Ende?!"). The film has throughout deployed, manipulated, and refigured, as it does in Karl's expiring flashback, the two maps and their scaling of the war film, and these spatial manipulations point to the kind of remapping and rescaling it suddenly offers as its end. Its first sequences, I argued above, offer the student's private map of desire and attachment, but tellingly, this map is displaced to an occupied territory, to France, a fact that underscores how the film takes up both themes and iconography from the mobilization aspects of the genre but also works against them by remembering, rescaling, and remapping the war film's spaces.

Conclusion: *Camaraderie* and a Rescaled, Happier Homogenization of Space

Westfront's conclusion suggests that contingent geographies, rather than national origins, serve as destiny in the student's affair with Yvette/Jacqueline as well as for Karl's untimely end. Since the film has invoked but ultimately contravened the spatial figurations and scalar operations of the war film, it offers, with its final image of a French soldier next to Karl, another contingent space of solidarity—not between a German man and a French woman but between German and French soldiers. This refiguration of the war film with the contingent spaces of solidarity is taken up with the same precision by Pabst's other early 1930s film about recent history, one that seems a deliberate follow-up one year later to the fragmented memories and scales of *Westfront*, *Kameradschaft* (*Camaraderie*, 1931). The present study's spatial approach shows how in both antiwar films, *Westfront* and *Camaraderie*, Pabst employs the themes of sound, space, and distance to remember and rescale the postwar geography of the German war film.

Premiering in late 1931, *Camaraderie* had less than two years before it was (with Pabst's *Die Büchse der Pandora* [*Pandora's Box*], 1929, and *Die 3-Groschen-Oper* [*Three Penny Opera*], 1931) banned by the Nazis, but the praise for it was effusive. Writing in the *Welt am Montag*, for example, Hans Siemsen declares *Camaraderie* not only the most important film of the week or even the season but, indeed, the most important German sound film yet.[45] The film does seem an explicit reply to the wave of war films foregrounded above: this was a different processing of a different recent history and collective memory—namely, the Courrières mine disaster near the French border—reset to the interwar years. Courrières saw a major mine collapse in 1906 (Europe's worst ever, apparently, with over one thousand killed) that brought German miners and experts to help across the German-Franco border. Part of what Siemsen praises in his review is, to make a geographic point, the way in which "Germans speak German, and the French speak French—special thanks for that!"[46] This border-zone realism was (rather like *Westfront*) a crucial part of the film's approach: in fact, in discussing the film, Pabst deliberately emphasizes that the film should be seen not as political but, rather, simply as a border story.[47] For our purposes, this defense is telling: as I have been discussing throughout, spatial mechanisms in and around war films are revealingly political, and the entwinement of the border with politics is, of course, the core thematic point of *Camaraderie*. That Pabst could deflect political questions with spatial answers underscores the proximity of the two.

Even as he denies that his film is acting politically / making politics (that it "treibt Politik"), Pabst admits that when one brings peoples close to one another in this kind of camaraderie, the borders among them—be they between individuals or among whole peoples—will fall. Such a comment deliberately resonates with the contemporary wave of World War I films. For example, in one scene in *Camaraderie*, viewers assume the mental (internal diegetic) point of view of a delirious, hallucinatory miner who has a flashback to a World War I battlefield as he sees his rescuer in a protective (postwar) gas mask. Moreover, the publicity materials show the Aufhebung (sublation) of the border in the mine (as Pabst puts it) by rendering the miner uniforms ambiguous, such that they could be either war or postwar work-time garb. As Kracauer points out in his review, the spatial configuration of the border ("Frontiere [border] 1919," as the sign on it declares) serves as a marker and sign of both the border and the memory.[48] The specifically spatial figurations of the mine and the miners' experiences there—the narrative's spatialization, as Jameson put it[49]—function to reveal Pabst's fundamental politics, politics directed against the border practices of many of the recent war films.

Speaking in the *Neue Pariser Zeitung*, Pabst perhaps felt he could speak in more openly political terms: he says *Camaraderie* is a product of his sense of the brokenness of their "sacrificed generation" that had its Lebensrhythmus (rhythm of life) fundamentally altered, even broken, through the war.[50] It is no wonder, he says, that given this break, this abyss, the work of this generation has been marked by gasping uncertainty (Keuchen). His declaration makes clear that he sees the generation and its achievement in fragments, fragments he hopes to rescale in a nonwar but similarly mobilized mode to overcome borders, as at the end of *Westfront* and in the follow-up *Camaraderie*. Looking back at this troubled period and the revealing gyrations of genre and its spaces, it is telling that Fritz Kampers, as the star of both *Westfront* and *Camaraderie*, would be cast in two of the most promoted war films of the Nazi regime, *Pour le Mérite* (*Medal of Honor*, 1938) and *Über alles in der Welt* (*Above Everything in the World*, 1941), directed by "Professor" Karl Ritter. The casting of Kampers by Ritter in his Nazi war films would seem deliberate given the notoriety of Pabst and these two antiwar films. If Pabst, in his first sound films, aims to rescale the genre spatially, Ritter develops the genre emphatically skyward using the new military technologies and cultures of the air, the topic of chapter 4.

4

Combat Films and Their Aerial Spaces under the Nazi Regime

(*Medal of Honor*, 1938; *Squadron Lützow*, 1941; *Above Everything in the World*, 1941)

In a 1928 essay in *Zeitschrift für Geopolitik* (Journal for geopolitics), Erich Maschke poses the question of how one might best explore the relationship of politics to geography and to the earth generally. To do so—to depict, explore, and understand geography—Maschke suggests using cinema. There are two unique contributions cinema can make to these conundrums, according to Maschke: the first through the depiction of landscape and the second through the manipulation of artificial objects like models and maps and other "visual tricks" relating to space. If the present study has already, in examining key war films from the World War I and Weimar periods, foregrounded the centrality of landscape and territory in such cinema's politics, Maschke confirms this centrality—but with a telling deviation. He laments that most landscape in film is still shot at "eye level" and advocates instead shooting it from the ever-proliferating airplane. Footage from airplanes could be alternated with images of models in, for instance, a montage detailing how a city grows over time.[1] Maschke's proposals demonstrate how new transportation technologies transformed what Derek Gregory calls the "geographical imagination" at the time—an imagination at the nexus of mobility, technology, and cinema in the service of an increasingly geographical, even geopolitical, understanding.[2]

Perhaps more revealing is how Maschke concludes climactically by proposing a geopolitical film about Germany and its spaces—past and ominously future. In such a film, the sort of aerial footage he advocates could depict "all the spaces of the old Germany," especially its borders through 1914, and then use these images to trace the territorial impact of the Treaty of Versailles.[3] In a third part of the film following these aerial-visual contrasts, the footage taken from an airplane could then be deployed to underscore the "organic unity" of the country.[4] In this way, right around the same time that German cinema was producing a wave of films to (counter)memorialize World War I (see chapter 3), some geographers were exhorting a different cinematic angle on the impact of the war: one from the air that would offer a different perspective on the territorial and national fate of Germany, one that, Maschke thinks, would help refigure borders going forward. On the one hand, Maschke's proposals emphasize a wider discursive field in which the meaning of the war and the trajectory of the nation were being disputed throughout the 1920s, as described in chapter 3. On the other, this association of cinema, airpower, and the putatively unified spaces of the nation would be important throughout the 1930s and early 1940s, both in looking backward to World War I and in pushing forward to the next large-scale conflict. This chapter focuses on war films made under the Nazi regime in the 1930s and 1940s, which made this new technology of the air a central piece of the spatial assemblage of the ongoing genre.

Cinema made during the Nazi regime (roughly 1933–1945) has sustained a wave of rich and illuminating scholarship in the last thirty years, especially since the work of Karsten Witte and then Eric Rentschler in the latter's groundbreaking *The Ministry of Illusion* (1996).[5] In this burgeoning, and more sophisticated, interest in cinema under the Nazis, however, the war film has garnered little substantive analysis, rather mysteriously given war's profile in the regime. Part of the lack of interest may be that the initial wave of work on Nazi cinema, undertaken primarily by historians and highlighting these films' propagandistic content, did discuss war films. This early work, however, did largely lack more complex and nuanced film studies approaches, as has been recently manifest in work like Witte's and Rentschler's as well as in Sabine Hake, Mary-Elizabeth O'Brien, and Laura Heins.[6] Nonetheless, I think it is still somewhat surprising that war films have garnered little attention in the recent major studies by Linda Schulte-Sasse, Hake, and O'Brien.[7]

Another explanation for this relative omission is that there were, as several of these scholars observe, relatively few pure or straight "war films" made during the Nazi era (by Heins's count, the regime oversaw ten times as many dramas as war films).[8] But it is clear, I think, when one looks to films like *Wunschkonzert* (*Request Concert*, 1940) or *Die große Liebe* (*The Great Love*, 1942)—two of the highest-profile and most popular films of the Reich and two of the most analyzed ever since—that the war genre had become, by the time of World War II, a mode (like Linda Williams's melodramatic "mode") that could be deployed within films that otherwise did not "officially" appear to be war films.[9] I shall discuss this hybridization of the war film and a war mode within other genres in the next chapter, but for now, it is notable that in each of these two supremely popular films, the central male character is a Luftwaffe pilot. In attending to these war films, I follow Witte and Rentschler in investigating the pleasures of these films along with their politics. For me, these pleasures highlight the inviting affects associated with travel and mobility, particularly in the air, and how thrilling such affects could remake distance, place, and indeed, entire geographies. As Matthias Rogg has noted, when compared to films focusing on either the army or the navy, the Luftwaffe films constituted a markedly important component of the regime.[10] And in a conspicuous example of the thoroughgoing militarism the regime was cultivating, the core of many marquee productions is a fighter pilot, a figure carefully cultivated by German governments since World War I. This figure of the fighter pilot and his (invariably his) aerial contexts, as Maschke's contemporaneous speculations about geopolitical films in general suggest, underscore the sociospatial constellation that I locate at the heart of the war film. The Luftwaffe films were an important production trend within the genre and were intended to revolutionize it, much as the Nazis saw themselves revolutionizing society and culture.

Films foregrounding the aerial aspects of German war not only illuminate a core aspect of Nazi cinema but also, for my purposes, underscore the intersection of technology, mobility, and the remaking of space at the core of the war genre. As scholars like Paul Virilio, Caren Kaplan, Peter Adey, and others (Tim Cresswell, John Urry, Saulo Cwerner) have charted, airplanes, reconnaissance, and bombing have remade war and the societies around them.[11] Attending to the air-spatial assemblage—aircraft, their ground-based infrastructure, the subjectivities unfolded in and through both—underscores some of the basic spatial mechanisms of the genre while also driving it forward. This air-space nexus highlights how the semantics and syntax of the war genre transmogrify at different historical and technological moments. Finally, such a focus also helps rethink the theoretical and scholarly touchstone for twentieth-century war, air, and cinema—namely, Virilio's influential *War and Cinema* (1989). The force of his insights is such that many merely affirm his emphasis on visuality as it intersects wartime flying. But many scholars of air mobility, such as those mentioned above, are rethinking Virilio, something these air war and Luftwaffe films, I aim to show, further occasion.[12]

In exploring the explosion of air travel in the twentieth century, Henri Lefebvre notes that this new mode of mobility would mean, fundamentally, that "space is being recast."[13] More specifically and systematically studying this recasting, both Kaplan and Adey have emphasized how "aerial life" as it emerged in the 1910s and 1920s changed England's sense of space and its geographical sense of the world, particularly its colonial dominion in the Middle East. There emerged, echoing Maschke from *Zeitschrift für Geopolitik* above, an "aerial geography," not least as aerial views, photography, and survey evoked enthusiasm on the part of professional and scholarly geographers.[14] In chapter 6, on the 1950s, this intersection of colonial control and aerial geography returns, showing it to be one of the most important legacies of both war and its genre. It is notable for our purposes that a similar aerial refiguration of geography was foregrounded not only in the German 1920s, pace Maschke, but also into the 1930s as Germany prepared for war, not least in journals like *Zeitschrift für Geopolitik*.[15] For England, such aerial geography would mean an unprecedented level of detail in mapping colonial and contact zones in the Middle East in particular, where land-based survey and mapping proved difficult. The same was true of more tropical colonies both for England and for France, though these would pose different cartographic challenges. Aerial photography and survey would change cartography, and so geography and the spatial imaginary, forever, although, as both Kaplan and Adey describe, not least by abstracting considerably from those living on the ground. In the Luftwaffe films and their anticipatory contexts, I shall elaborate on this kind of aerial life and aerial geography that Kaplan and Adey foreground—and consider how it altered the existing, unfolding war genre. In Edward Soja's sense, Nazi airspace offered an attractive third space, a homogenized utopic place beyond (and sublating) conventional spatial contradictions.[16] Such contradictions in the aerial assemblage included its terrestrial moorings in airports and airfields and the politics surrounding them—all suggesting destabilizing scale jumping via the accelerated speeds of aircraft.

Karl Ritter's Airborne Bridge between World War I and World War II

In contemplating the confluence of aerial life, geography, and the war genre, I take up two well-known figures, Karl Ritter and Hans Bertram, both renowned in culture more generally under the Nazis. Ritter has garnered surprisingly little scholarly attention in the recent rich wave of work on film during the Third Reich, especially in light of what an omnipresent force he was in the German film industry in the late Weimar period—contributing to films like *Pandora's Box* (*Die Büchse der Pandora*), *Dreyfus*, and *Berlin Alexanderplatz*—and then throughout the Nazi period. Overall, Ritter worked on an estimated 120 films in some capacity, as screenwriter, director, and/or producer (on many as head of his own production unit for Nazi-era Ufa). His ubiquitous activities and seemingly boundless energy earned him the nickname "Vater Ritter" at Ufa, a reference perhaps as well to his two sons, Heinz and Gottfried, who often worked as his cameraman and editor, respectively. The lack of recent sustained scholarship on the elder Ritter is surprising given his films' popularity and his profile under the Nazi regime. He was credited with directing some of the most successful propaganda films of the time, including highly marketable ones like *Pour le Mérite* (*Medal of Honor*, 1938) and *Über alles in der Welt* (*Above Everything in the World*, 1941), which earned Ufa considerably more profits than the better-known *Jud Süss* (*Jew Süss*).[17] Moreover, his ensemble of regular performers included such high-profile figures as regime-designated "national actor" Paul Hartmann and especially Carl Raddatz, whose career Ritter boosted by casting the Berliner in *Urlaub auf Ehrenwort* (*Holiday on a Promise*, 1938), Raddatz's first feature-film appearance.

Although Ritter also made war films unrelated to the Luftwaffe (including those of his World War I "trilogy," like the much-praised *Holiday on a Promise*), Ritter was a dedicated aviator, having acquired his flying license even before World War I, becoming a major in the Luftwaffe, and even flying missions as late as World War II while in his fifties. For example, he claimed that he did firsthand airborne research for his popular *Stukas* of 1941. His late war service underscores his ideological loyalty to the regime and especially to Hitler, with whom he came into contact through the Richard Wagner family, into which Ritter had married.[18] Ritter met Hitler before the future führer's 1923 Beer Hall Putsch, and when Hitler was released from Landsberg, the Ritter household was among those he visited. Although Ritter ended up leaving the party in the later Weimar Republic to protect and foster his international film career—he worked in that period with Hitchcock, among others—he was restored to the special status afforded by a (very low) party membership number during the regime.

For Nazi-controlled Ufa, Ritter ran his own production group: he claimed he had been hired as Erich Pommer was leaving—implying, wishfully, a similar stature. He subsequently worked on a large number of important propaganda productions under the ubiquitous eye of Joseph Goebbels.[19] Despite the presumption that propaganda-minded directors were generally uniform in approach, there is clear evidence of directors' having specialties and even what one might term quasi-auteurist brands.[20] Ritter became particularly known for a so-called Zeitfilm style, an approach foregrounding contemporary events while cleverly cutting across genres, such as in *Above Everything in the World*. Ritter collaborated on films like *Hitlerjunge Quex* (*Hitler Youth Quex*, 1933) before being promoted to direct his own works, like the World War I trilogy of *Patrioten* (*Patriots*, 1937), *Unternehmen Michael* (*Operation Michael*, 1937), and *Holiday on a Promise*. Susan Tegel has understandably focused on Ritter's anti-Semitism, but such an analysis, important as it is, does little to help us comprehend why and how his films were so popular; the same is true of David Welch's investigation—it is remarkable that neither pays attention to those films' attractions or to Ritter's personal interest and investment in flight.[21]

Ritter's *Medal of Honor* was the follow-up to his World War I trilogy and deliberately stretched from World War I to the 1930s rebuilding of the Luftwaffe, part of the advanced preparations for the war that would start the following year. The film traces the fortunes of a Luftwaffe squadron as they fight in World War I, demobilize (sort of) after the shocking defeat, struggle with civilian life during the Weimar Republic, and then help Germany rearm in the 1930s. In mobility studies, as well as in cultural studies, of air travel, the discourse around the pilot tends to highlight his independence, self-reliance, and even brashness. Indeed, and parallel to the way the railway remakes Dr. Hart in *Dr. Hart* and Krafft in *Sword and Hearth* (see chapter 2), one could speak of this novel mode of transport fostering a new mode of subjectivity, clear, for example, in *Zeitschrift für Geopolitik*.[22] In many of Ritter's films, pilots play a central role, underscoring the intersection of the genre in which he was already well practiced with the new technologies that would transform both wars and the soldier-subjects fighting them.

The first sequence of Ritter's *Medal of Honor* would seem to confirm this new form of subjectivity from the outset with its introduction of brash, even brazen Lt. Fabian (Albert Hehn). After an initial few seconds with World War I biplanes among the clouds during the credit sequence, the camera finds the dandyish Fabian dancing with his fiancée at a Bavarian beer garden. Even though he is only nineteen ("18¾," as he proudly announces), he cheekily derides some older men when one takes his seat—soon they are mocking him for avoiding the trenches and generally shirking his wartime duty. But viewers learn the truth in the next scene, when his family receives a telegram that Fabian has been awarded the pour le mérite military honor—the highest for a soldier—at his proudly tender age. Fabian then has the audacity to deploy the newfound honor to pressure his fiancée, Gerda (Carsta Löck), to weekend with him at the Eibsee lake—a plan interrupted by his being called up to his western-front squadron.

One would think an order to abandon his home, family, and three-day getaway with his fiancée might hit Fabian hard, but not in a Ritter war film. As in the genre before it, the distance traversed from the home to the front is telling for the film's spatial operations. In one scene at his family's apartment, Fabian learns that his squadron leader, Einwald, has crashed in a test flight, and he, Fabian, will inherit his command; in the very next scene, convertible-driving Fabian pulls up to a French château, with beautiful stairs and an ornate fountain inside a walled courtyard, welcomed back by the a cappella skills of his comrades. As we shall see, many of these Fliegerfilme (air force films) stage an alternative sort of military drill—and the affective content of it of which William McNeill speaks[23]—in the form of a singing choir or chorus: this nonviolent but still body-based camaraderie fosters belonging to the troupe, not least to balance the much-touted, sometimes lamented individualism rampant among pilots. As McNeill notes, such "kinesthetic undergirding" is crucial to the lasting bonds of social groupings and is "inseparable from their gestural and muscular expression"[24]—such sequences thus shift from Virilio's gaze-focused analysis to, or at least supplement it with, embodied affect. It is the opposite of the fragmenting scalar mechanisms in Pabst's *Westfront* described in chapter 3, in which the intensified body is detached from the national scale by reestablishing the distances that homogenized spaces usually elide (*Westfront*'s two dispersive journeys, affect-intensive images on a microscale detaching from nation, etc.). Here, however, such drills are a good example of how the individual body can be scaled to the collective through pleasurable affects that help foster the "expansive body" that Hanich describes.[25] Fabian may have seemed a cheeky individualist in the first scenes at home—a common stereotype for a fighter pilot—but the choir collective and singing upon his arrival integrate him into his squadron and, ultimately, scale him to his national mission. In terms of the distance covered to the front, Fabian's trip to his squadron is so abrupt and fast that only the architecture indicates how rapidly Fabian has traversed the distance from his Bavarian summer frolic to the sunny western front, underscoring his association with speed and a different relation to distance. Likewise, he has no visible baggage for this surprise deployment, just goggles for driving his own car and, soon, for flying his own plane, highlighting the lightness and freedom of his movement. Such lightness of person and accouterments contrasts with the heavy kits that infantrymen usually lug on to lumbering, front-bound trains—the shooting script describes Fabian, first and foremost, as sporting "quecksilberner Unbekümmertheit" (quicksilver recklessness).[26]

The speed with which Fabian traverses the distance—the corporeal lightness coupled with his personal levity—underscores the remaking of distance described by Stephen Kern and famously characterized as space-time compression by David Harvey in modernity.[27] Of course, speed was central to the discourse about air travel and the way it would remake geography, as the assorted 1930s *Zeitschrift für Geopolitik* pieces on air travel also make clear.[28] *Medal of Honor*'s sequence also seems to emphasize—as Fabian zooms up in a car, is serenaded by his comrades, and is then hoisted skyward as they carry him into the château—the pleasing affect of specifically militaristic movement, here in the direction of the war. These very different affective pleasures of the pilots are confirmed in the next scene, when the squad sits down to a lovely meal in the château's baroque dining room, complete with painted reliefs, an ornate chandelier, and an elaborate candelabra. Such settings play a likewise crucial role in Ritter's 1941 *Stukas*, which registers the World War II advance into France with a series of increasingly elaborate (baroque and then rococo) dining rooms. *Medal of Honor*'s well-appointed tourist pleasures—seconds after Fabian was back at home with his family and fiancée—are a long way, literally and figuratively, from the infantryman's front, since the flight squadrons, comparatively fewer in number, could requisition comfortable quarters far from the fighting. These affective pleasures well behind the front echo those that open *Westfront* and that engage the viewer from the outset—likewise eating, drinking, joking—but such bodily pleasures are the pilots' regular purview, not rare leave, as in *Westfront*.

If distance and its traversal between the civilian life and fighting front are key aspects of the syntax of the genre, these Luftwaffe films remake them definitively for their own ends.

Of Enemies and the Airmen's Accelerated Scale Jumping

This first scene with Fabian's full squadron also marks another key difference between the pilot's spatial assemblage and the infantryman's front: the chivalric, even jocularly jousting relationship with enemy pilots. Per the war films mentioned above, the film spends relatively little time constructing the enemy as venal and/or evil—as I noted in the introduction, selling the war to civilians over the course of a film narrative was and is much more based on the positive aspects of love rather than on hate.[29] Since air travel was seen to be ushering in a whole new culture with a new mode of subjectivity, the bonds of this brave new world run deep, the film says, crossing even the literal and figurative borders in wartime.[30] Squadron commander Gerhart Prank (Paul Hartmann) has shot down and captured the celebrated British ace "Brown" (Theo Schall), whom the German pilots promptly fête with an elaborate meal in their château, toasting him and his skills. Such treatment is particularly noteworthy given that England had in many ways been the World War I enemy par excellence, bred in no small part from Kaiser Wilhelm's jilted feelings toward his own, though island-inhabiting relatives.[31] Moreover, in the context of these celebrations, such chivalry certainly seems overstated given, for example, the morbid fixation of "Red-Baron" Richthofen on the gruesome, even cruel midair inferno of the flyers who opposed him.[32] But in Ritter's film, in its imaginary celebration of air culture and flyer subjectivity, the relationship with the enemy pilot consists primarily of toasting him, mostly a friendly competition about air technologies. Positively coded interactions with foreigners seem an indispensable aspect of the film's tourist endeavors, as it was as early as the 1917/1918 *Dr. Hart*. With teasing pique, Prank asks Brown what he thinks of the Germans' improved Fokker fighter planes, while Brown brags about new "impregnated" observation balloons (said in English with German subtitles).

Brown's announcement of a new airborne challenge yields the film's first extended aerial combat scene, a scene singled out in both publicity materials and reviews for its excitement.[33] Tellingly for my argument about love of war rather than hatred of enemy, however, this excitement is achieved through targeting not some devious opposing fighter pilot but rather the large, lethargic, above all easily sighted balloons of which Brown brags. Upon Brown's announcement of the new balloons, the squadron's second-in-command, Senior Lt. (Oberleutnant) Gerdes, retreats from the dining room, pops up seconds later at the airfield, and is soon buzzing around in the air—an edge-of-the-seat dogfight, only against unnamed, largely inert balloons.

The sequence, just seconds after he was relaxing in the Louis XIV French dining room, alternates point-of-view shots of the English observational balloons and the expansive, beautiful French landscape around them. The aesthetic pleasures of his impromptu mission are as landscape based as those in *Dr. Hart* or *Sword and Hearth*, offering the viewer more tourist-like images of the French countryside. In contrast to *Dr. Hart* or *Sword and Hearth*, however, twenty years of technological advances have augmented and accelerated speed and the much more deliberate decoupage of point of view against the broad plane. But as far as viewers can tell, he never hurts or kills anybody, just sets the balloons alight. The film, even as it stages its first combat scene, avoids violence against enemies and provides instead another airborne spectacle, the balloon-fed flames gently raining down on the lovely landscape. The observers who were in the balloons all parachute successfully out, offering the film another lovely image of the early air war's airborne individual against the expanse of aerial space. Unlike Icarus, whose wings melt such that he perishes in descent, the parachutes work to preserve the enemy lives in a chivalric mastery of technology over nature (figure 4.1).

These images of the film's first combat sequence demonstrate one of Ritter's generic innovations: although they offer the viewer images of the landscape familiar from the genre, they refigure them with a new kind of speed-driven movement. The Fliegerfilm (flyer film), as it remakes the semantics of the Kriegsfilm, foregrounds the floating yet fast movement of the individual through this generic syntax of landscape.[34] As in the films from World War I, it is not the constitution of the enemy but the territorializing experience of this homogenized, longed-for space that matters most. Finally, perhaps most remarkable about this initial aerial sequence in Ritter's prestige production is that it is not particularly emphatic about airborne vision. Although Virilio emphasizes the visual aspects of air war (cf. his "*the function of the weapon is the function of the eye*"[35]), Gerdes's journey from the dinner table—a bodily emphatic setting—to the sky to shoot at balloons and then back to the dining table is about the spine-tingling affective experience of this kind of airborne travel, forms of multifaceted movement that only the fewest would have known at the time. The film foregrounds embodied effects beyond mere point-of-view shots: the roller-coaster arc from intimate dinner to boundless sky matters as much as the steely cold gaze. It is akin, I would argue, to the ghost rides that Gunning tracks in early cinema, the thrill of affectively rich motion itself.[36] As Brian Massumi has argued, any kind of movement can evoke these corporeal-affective reactions, which explains the contiguity that Gunning uncovers between amusement park rides and the movies.[37] Here, however, such affective geographies will be deployed increasingly to remake the geography of wartime, then postwar Germany.

After shooting the armored balloons down, Gerdes returns proudly to the dining table, where Prank and Brown to his right are still engaged in eating and

FIG. 4.1 Gerdes shoots balloons down, offering views of the French landscape, *Medal of Honor*. Digital frame enlargement.

drinking. Despite its being midday, the film seems focused on Prank's apparently many-coursed hospitality toward his Englishman enemy—the meal contrasting between the dining table indulgence and Gerdes's achievement. As noted above, part of the pleasure this first airborne scene offers is the jumping among what geographers have termed *scales* (cf. chapter 3), a breathtaking scalar negotiation that the newly forged speed and remade distance offer. It echoes and reinforces the rapid movement of Fabian in the opening sequence. Gerdes was able to leave his seat at the domestic table, test the new balloons in the air, and return to the domestic table in the course of one meal: the speed of the scale-jumping pilot's body knows few bounds. This upscaling of Gerdes's activity—from a formal dinner in a private château to aerial acrobatics on behalf of the nation—parallels the upscaling of the film's opening, which moved from Fabian on leave with his girlfriend to, rapidly, appearing with his comrades on the western front. This scaling of the individual to the national here hits a new pitch of speed and efficiency of the sort at which *Dr. Hart* (1917/1918), even in its transformative train ride past the Hermannsdenkmal, could only hint—it, indeed, becomes a kind of scale jumping for the individual pilots. In the wartime Kriegsspielfilmen, this kind of scale jumping is crucial to the refigured spatial syntax of the genre, but here they are exploited primarily for the pleasures, bodily and psychological, of such rapid airborne movement. Subsequently, over the plot, these foregrounded pleasures of mobility are deliberately mapped over the history of Germany through 1918, 1923, and 1935/1936. In nuce, this is my argument about the war film in general: the genre deploys the visual and affective pleasures of the travelogue or Kulturfilme (cultural, including travel, films) for the purposes of remaking the world spatially for its viewers—a remaking, then scaling of these affective pleasures of modern mobility up to the geographies of the national and transnational, to the spatial politics required for war.

For both the diegetic pilots and cinema-going viewers, the memory of the early plot pleasures of airborne travel—expansive landscape, the scalable individual imaged against it, the thrill of moving rapidly with views of both—comes to structure the plot as the film moves on, about forty-five minutes into its hour-forty duration, to depict the 1918 surrender. Intriguingly, the loss of these wartime affective pleasures is registered not so much in represented flashbacks or memories but rather in fragmented spaces descaling the wartime spaces mentioned above. The surrender and its aftermath offer not the spine-tingling affects of a body moving rapidly through the air, nor the aforementioned scale jumping, but instead riven spaces that will rule the film's Weimar period. It is as if the film had absorbed the late 1920s generic syntax of antiwar films like Pabst's *Westfront* in order to overcome them by suturing together fragmented spaces. When Prank returns late from a mission, he informs his men that revolution has broken out, their leaders have fled, and the war is effectively over. Prank's characterization asserts the stabbed-in-the-back myth, that German forces were "never defeated" in the field—Prank, for instance, had just emergency landed in enemy territory but had brought down his adversary nonetheless. Instead, according to this legend, unreliable elements and their revolution at home undercut the fighters' ultimate military triumph. Ritter emphasized this in some of the press on the film, saying that the fighter pilots returned to Germany without having been vanquished.[38] Such memories of the defeat help create a contrasting mnemonic mode to *Westfront*'s exploration of personal memory amid collective trauma. Defeat and memories of it are emphatically collective, a longed-for past to be found only in bygone comraderies and the affective spaces that bred them.

Airports and the Refigured Geographies of Air Travel

The trauma of the 1918 defeat is depicted by the intrusion of fragmented spaces, especially by a telling confusion of formerly well-networked airports and airfields. Recent postmobility turn analysis of air travel has postulated the peculiarity of the airport as a paradigmatic modern space, a heterotopia that materializes the dialectic of the simultaneously global and territorial, of the mobile and fixed. Airports offer the ground-based moorings for the most advanced mobility available to most of us; they also create, as noted in *Zeitschrift für Geopolitik* at the time, an alternate aerial geography with only tenuous relations to conventional borders.[39] This new aerial geography overcomes formerly insurmountable distances, compressing and integrating space in a paradigmatically modern mode. In this way, they are parallel to the secondary, wartime geography that John Keegan describes, as I foreground above in chapters 2 and 3.[40] For many critics, the contemporary architecture of the airport betrays the nonplace rootlessness of contemporary society: they are geared to move masses in as frictionless a fashion as possible while also distinguishing themselves from the global network in which they are merely one node.[41] Although these theorists tend to highlight the contemporary airport, many of these observations were true of airports already in the 1920s and 1930s, when Berlin's Tempelhof handled more civilian traffic than any airport in the world and geographers and other social scientists highlighted airports' role in the remaking of geography mentioned above.

In Ritter's *Medal of Honor*, airports and airfields serve as the central settings of the film, as the script's long list of Schauplätze (settings) makes clear: there are some twenty-three scenes set at airfields or airports, many more than the next important setting, a farmhouse that, tellingly, also hosts a secluded, surreptitious airfield.[42] But *Medal of Honor*'s airports materialize not the contradictions of globalized travel as much as the promise of a fantastical, so-called third space established in the film's first combat scene. In fact, as the barn-airfield indicates, the earthbound air infrastructure seems geared to ground (literally) the pilots in localities they can attach to as they embody frictionless mobility. After Prank announces to his men that the war is over—that they must relinquish the scale-jumping affects that afforded such pleasure to Gerdes (and viewers)—they decide to return their planes to the Heimat rather than to the conquerors. They abandon the field airports that have refigured the conventional (infantry) distances to the front for the film's first fifty minutes. Prank orders his pilots to bring their planes to Darmstadt, a famously science/engineering-oriented city for German aviation.[43]

In what one might term the *fog of the postwar war*, as Walter Benjamin puts it, Fritz Moebius becomes confused and lands his plane in Mannheim, where a sign informs viewers that the airport is now under the control of leftist workers' councils. Not reaching the correct node on the airport network was more common at that point in aviation history, but the film explicitly points to the fragmenting of Germany through the breakdown of its transportation and mobility infrastructure. What should be a seamless, frictionless, homogenized path from airport to airport has now become fragmented, confused, unpredictable for even the most modern means of transport. A Mannheim workers' council seizes Moebius and his plane; later, Prank will have to attack the Mannheim airport to liberate Moebius and his beloved "machine." Navigating the airports of home has become revealingly labyrinthine—Is one in Darmstadt or Mannheim?—even as the stakes of combat shift, via its airports, to the Heimat itself.

The postwar split of the squadron among different airports ushers in the fragmentary spaces of the Weimar period, spaces revoking the utopian aerial space established in the film's first half. The fragmentary spaces of Weimar highlight the chaos of a capitalist economy in free fall: a city garage where Prank refuses to lie to make a profit; a decadent music club where, due to his medal of honor, Prank is recruited to front a company that disappears as quickly as it was created; a decadent apartment where Gerhart Prank and his wife, Isabel, give themselves over to drinking and general indolence. With Gerhart and Isabel—as well as two comical underlings, Zuschlag and Krause, who refuse to demobilize and stay close to their former commander—the film offers a vision of urban modernity that is fundamentally fragmented, splintered spatially, socially, and psychologically. Rather than depicting the modern metropolis as foundationally mobile—as a node like the film's airports, full of frictionless and homogenous spaces that facilitate movement like urban sidewalks, streets, and rail tracks—Ritter's Weimar Berlin is replete with mobility obstacles and psychological stumbles. Even a back-to-basics garage playing on their wartime mechanical skills does not provide for any productive outlet, since the conniving and craven Weimar economy entails playing mendacious games of shifty supplies and seedy customers. Later, the office in which the "inflation profiteers" install Prank—in a gleaming architecture of art deco smoke and mirrors—has high-skirted "secretaries" (the film uses the English *secretaries* rather than the German equivalent) kicking up their heels one day and a caustic cleaning lady who announces all the furniture is gone the next.[44] The urban spaces are dark and smoke filled in contrast to the open landscape expanses of the opening flight sequences. With wartime spaces revoked and subjectivity transformed, Prank's behavior arcs from indignant disgust to benumbed torpor. Prank struggles with his own diminished motivation, suggesting a complex character defying the essential good-and-bad dichotomies to which Welch and some reviewers attribute the film's popularity.[45]

In a clear remedy to this lethargic Weimar metropolis, however, the film revealingly intercuts another type of airport altogether—namely, the capital of gliding in the 1920s, the Wasserkuppe in the Rhön.[46] By cutting from the dark, decadent spaces of the Weimar city to the wide-open Wasserkuppe, the film revives images of aircraft and their pilots against expansive landscapes from the opening half hour. As Peter Fritzsche outlines, the Wasserkuppe became a base for nationalist sentiment sublimated to reviving German aviation. Its nationalist place in Weimar culture was, tellingly, based on an exaggerated sense of victimization at the hands of the Allies and the Weimar government. For example, it was not the mythically maligned Treaty of Versailles that banned motorized military flights after the war. Moreover, private and commercial flights were long allowed in any case—after all, how else would Tempelhof have become the busiest civilian airport in the world in the 1920s? But the notion that the hated Treaty of Versailles had also ordered the destruction of beloved German fighter planes only fueled nationalist fires for flying (or, rather, provided the wind beneath their glider wings). In part due to these resentments, the Wasserkuppe became one of the most important centers for gliding in the world, along with a lesser-known locale in East Prussia, also with numerous records for flight duration and distance.[47] A victimization mythos unfolds aggressive German nationalism by way of a very modern, even cosmopolitan mode of transport and its novel geography.[48]

Medal of Honor marks the Wasserkuppe gliding as the heart of the nationalist movement that would best revive the collective Spirit of 1914 and its World War I fighter aces. This would include some of the "alte[n] Kämpfer[n]" (old fighters) like Prank who were falling prey to the temptations of the city. First, the film misleadingly makes World War I aces the heart of the gliding movement, as viewers' introduction to the Wasserkuppe comes with Gerdes's gliding to a new world record for duration (over seven hours in the air). He is cheered by a crowd of young enthusiasts, presumably pupils in a flight school that he references later. As Fritzsche outlines, these gliding schools did indeed later become "hotbeds of nationalism," but the gliding movement actually began as a pacifist means to celebrate German engineering and to reclaim aviation from the Luftwaffe.[49] Only later in the 1920s was the movement coopted by nationalists who self-servingly rewrote this early history and successfully reworked it as a contrarian political act. Second, and likewise misleading, is *Medal of Honor*'s depiction of the democratic government's opposition to the sport. In the film, the former Luftwaffe major Wissmann has joined the government's Ministry of Transportation, and the film depicts his furtively funding gliders through Fabian, suggesting a secret subculture subverting the Weimar government. But the democratic government, at various levels, openly supported the gliding movement throughout the 1920s.[50] Finally, Gerdes's flight and then interaction with a tax collector who tries to seize their glider—more government antagonism—are imaged with a well-known nationalist monument, an eagle with a plaque, atop the Wasserkuppe. In fact, the script clarifies that the year is 1923, the year the famous statue was dedicated with nationalist heroes (and perennial enthusiasts) like Prinz Heinrich and General Ludendorff, in addition to many thousands, in attendance.[51]

With the narrative arc of *Medal of Honor* and its refigured spatial assemblage for the war film, it is telling that these celebrated gliders are not really going anywhere, have no destination or target, are rather like aerial flaneurs. Mostly they circled geological formations where updraft winds were particularly suited to carrying them aloft and around (and around and around). Rather than mere combat, the aerial shots construct, as with Gerdes's first deployment against the balloons in 1918, the affective pleasures of this airborne mode of mobility. The editing further emphasizes the Wasserkuppe as an almost-imaginary, certainly fantastical space, as the initial cut to the location emphasizes. This unusual transition dissolves from a nighttime city street where Isabel speculates on how she and Gerhart should go there to escape urban venality to the Wasserkuppe itself—the film dissolves to the bright and wide-open spaces of the Wasserkuppe, even though it should be nighttime there too, obviously. Over the following ten minutes, the film heavy-handedly contrasts the city and the glider cultures by cutting from the increasingly depraved city to the wholesome gliding movement. This crosscutting construction of the Wasserkuppe—an invocation of the flying-floating affect from earlier in the film and a geographical contrast to the vilified spaces of the Weimar city—suggests it as a utopian third space. As with many moments in the genre, crosscutting helps assert the disparate spaces that war films regularly deliver. And per the above, the focus in such crosscutting is not so much on visualized targets, pace Virilio, but on the embodied affect and effects of the transition from the ground network to aircraft, here glider, levitation.

Weimar Geographies Remade by Air and by Land

This crosscutting to a fantasized third space (of the airport) is echoed in the film's second such escape from the urban spaces of the Weimar period. When he finds them suffering in their tiny and smoky city apartment, World War I comrade Fritz Moebius (the one who landed his previous plane in mistaken Mannheim rather than destination Darmstadt) invites the Prank couple to the fresh air and clean living of his farm. At first, Gerhart is skeptical but eventually relents when he realizes his urban work prospects have evaporated. The farm, like the Wasserkuppe, offers bright landscape contrasts to the dark city. There Moebius introduces Gerhart to his cows—all named after models of fighter planes—and reveals an ultimate surprise for his old commander: he saved and preserved Gerhart's old fighter Fokker from the war and has hidden it in one of his barns. Although Moebius had burned the other airplanes of their squadron rather than turn them over to the French amid the 1918 surrender, he has secretly and lovingly preserved Gerhart's plane in perfect working order. As with Ritter's particular staging of the Wasserkuppe, the modernity of the plane is apparently nourished by nature, landscape, and a Heimat-like setting. Such a contradictory aerial assemblage echoes the "reactionary modernism" that Jeffrey Herf has famously emphasized in Nazi culture.[52] These struggles, especially after the atomizing experience of the city, underscore the Nazis' trademark amalgam of modernity with (constructed) atavism. Isabel Prank declares Moebius's rural estate—a telling mixture of a dairy farm and an airport—"like a fairy tale" (Märchen), and when Gerhart first sees the barn doors sweep open to reveal his old plane, he cannot believe his eyes. In fact, he covers them with his hands and says, "I'll never forget this, Moebius." Such lines and gestures offer the film, in telling contrast and cure to the Weimar city spaces, another third space, a fantastical, fairy tale space for which one's eyes are hardly to be trusted—not a surprise, since the film, with its remade geographies, is cultivating corporeal affect as much as aerial views.

Celebrated by both publicity materials and reviews, *Medal of Honor*'s account of recent Weimar history thus unfolds between the maligned metropolis and two rural airfields: the well-known but secluded center of nationalist gliding on the Wasserkuppe and a secret airfield maintained by an old comrade in a Heimat setting. These fairy-tale, even mythical airfields contrast to the first act's compromised World War I airports, with the film drawing out these spatial contrasts in its plotting. But these fantastical third spaces of the rural airfield end up targeted, at least in the film, by the governmental powers that be during the Weimar period. A taxman (Zörbiegel) tries to seize Gerdes's glider on the Wasserkuppe, while a full, pitched battle ensues on Moebius's farm over Prank's plane when the Allies and the government come to seize it. In this way, in contrast to the sundry Weimar spaces, *Medal of Honor* continues the combat of World War I into the postwar period: it extends such combat, as does the war genre, from the aerial attack on the Mannheim airport to the machine-gunning defense of a farm. Combat, as noted above, has become a mode to be deployed even in peacetime, recasting the Weimar era as one long battle. These illegal battles in the postwar period eventually drive Prank into prison and then self-imposed exile so he can continue his military flying abroad. Although he could have flown as a civilian in Germany, he apparently prefers an exiled, militaristic airspace to a pacifist Heimat.

In a rather stunning elliptical edit, *Medal of Honor* jumps from these dark Weimar days to a deliberately bright 1935, with the film cutting to yet another space never seen before and never located specifically. It provides a paradigmatic fantasy any-space-whatever to sublate the contradictory spaces of Weimar Ritter's effects: a beautiful small town with conspicuously Germanic architecture (tellingly shot in Poland[53]) where the jubilant townspeople celebrate Moebius, Zuschlag, and Krause as they dedicate a memorial to soldiers at the center of the town square. The film's second example of a memorial-driven ekphrasis, it underscores how these *lieux de memoire* (places of memory) provided for right-wing identities during the Weimar years. The diegetic status of this memorializing celebration seems particularly unclear and fantastical, as it is abruptly accompanied by a voice-over that viewers have not heard in the first three-fourths of the hour-forty film: the sudden and unlocatable voice-over announces the 1935 Gesetz über Einführung der allgemeinen Wehrpflicht (Law on the Introduction of the General Draft) and the mandatory conscription it (re)introduces—so the cheering masses celebrate both Moebius's war memorial and the revived draft.[54] Such an unsourced, even unlocatable voice-over in a feature film is an example of what Michel Chion has termed the *acousmatic voice*, here used not to horror effect, as it had been in *Westfront* or, as Chion explores, in *Testament of Dr. Mabuse* (1933).[55] Rather, Ritter deploys it as the voice of history, or at least of the Nazi movement, that converts the film's second-act riven spaces into a gloriously unified third space that viewers have never even seen—apparently narrated by the voice of Goebbels himself.[56] It is a fascist acousmêtre played with deliberately by the syntax of the political war film that will return at the end of the 1950s.

Despite this rural grounding for *Medal of Honor*'s fantastical finale, the film concludes with a climactic reunion at, unsurprisingly, an airport. Parallel to Moebius's celebrating at the war memorial in Beeskow, Gerdes reads out a declaration from astride a plane: conscription, the Luftwaffe, and (with it) the Richthofen squadron have all been reinstated.[57] No acousmatic voice for the reconstitution of the Luftwaffe. This announcement is grounded in the film's real-life pilot—the actor who played Gerdes, as the publicity materials happily advertise, was an actual pilot licensed, unusually, for all three forms of air transport: balloon, glider, and motorized planes.[58] Basking in the light and levity of this reinstatement, Gerdes and Fabian convince the now uniformed "general" Wissmann to cable Prank abroad to invite him back to join them.

Soon they are underway to Hamburg to retrieve him and to return him to the base where the film concludes with the largest airfield and airplane display of its many such settings. Wissmann promotes Prank to colonel and appoints him head of the reconstituted Richthofen squadron.

The film's final shots dissolve from the many planes above the climactic airfield to the medal of honor, looping back to its 1918 opening, when the medal was awarded to "18¾ years-old" Fabian. Like the trajectory of Fabian's late adolescence, the film has spun a celebrated tale of recent history in Ritter's trademark Zeitfilm style, weaving together the fraying strands of the World War I surrender and Weimar's unraveling. It was, per the above, a tale told primarily through an affective geography of airports and airfields. Climactically sewn up by careful collective memorialization during the film's first part in 1918, the affective pleasures of war were moored to the field airports of the Luftwaffe squadron; during the difficult Weimar years, these affective pleasures were banished from mainstream Germany, exiled to rural airfields marginal to the marquee urban experiences of the time; and in the film's "happy" ending, the reinstatement of the conscription and the Luftwaffe unfolds in a renegotiated link between the small town and the now modern airport. If the contemporary reviews celebrated Ritter's handling of recent history, it was a history written through the affective pleasure of flying, then mapped over a series of airports, thus unfolding its memorialization in an outward direction, looking back to gaze forward and up.

Hans Bertram's *Squadron Lützow*: A "Miracle from the Heavens" Targeting New Spaces of East and West

Although he never enjoyed the influence in the film industry that Karl Ritter did, Hans Bertram did have a considerable profile in German culture and, if one brackets the World War I aces mentioned above, counts as one of the best-known aviators of Germany at the time. He became most famous through the experiences recounted in his best-selling *Flight into Hell: My Australian Adventures*, which describes his 1932 effort to fly around the world. These efforts took a famous detour when he had to emergency land in Australia, with him and his mechanic left to survive fifty-three days in the outback, crocodiles and all, before being discovered by accident. Bertram resumed his around-the-world objective but then crashed and destroyed his plane in Java, concluding prematurely that particular effort but not his general enthusiasm for flying, as the publicity for *Kampfgeschwader Lützow* (*Squadron Lützow*) trumpeted. For example, he became a consultant on the aerial footage for *D III 88* and then was entrusted with directing his own film that extended many of the themes, and even plotlines, of *D III 88*, which recounts the education and training of Luftwaffe pilots. Made in the run-up to the beginning of World War II, *D III 88* offers vivid aerial footage of novice pilots confronting the challenges of schooltime rivalries and unreliable machinery as they attack dummy targets. After the war, Bertram would continue to make films into the 1950s, including the similarly travel-minded 1952 *Towers of Silence* (set in Syria), and he even became an important aviation entrepreneur, helping found a regional Bavarian airline as well as a leading aerial photography firm.[59] Bertram, in his biography, his writing, and his film work, was indeed one of the individuals who helped conjure a new, affectively rich aerial geography for the German public.

Despite Bertram's aerial notoriety and this film's air-oriented name, Bertram's 1941 *Squadron Lützow* offers viewers a familiar scene of soldiers mobilizing to battle by train—a clichéd war film setting of the sort I have tracked since World War I. Such scenes belong to the generic syntax of the war film, demonstrating how integral the literal and figurative distance of the home to the front, and its negotiation, is to the war genre. *Squadron Lützow*, however, varies the established syntax of the genre considerably because this mobilization scene transpires not near the film's opening, as it had in *Dr. Hart* or *Inexpiable*, but over an hour into the ninety-five-minute film. This tardiness for the mobilization setup occurs because, by that point in the film, the conventional train mobilization has been well framed within an imaginary geography created by the Luftwaffe, one geared to turn traditional train-riding soldiers into pilots. Here too, in Bertram's feature film directorial debut, the war film is foregrounding a geography of its own making and, as Adey observes, introduces a specifically aerial geography according to the broader aerial life it sketches.[60] While the scene similarly affirms the narrative negotiation of the distance from the home to the front as central in war films (cf. *Dr. Hart*, *Westfront*, and *Medal of Honor*, discussed above), *Squadron Lützow*'s pilots are traveling neither from a real home nor to a real front—thus a purely imaginary geography of the home, front, and distance between them reveals the film's peculiar spatial logic.

As narrative strategy, this reconfigured mobilization over an imaginary geography proved effective, because *Squadron Lützow* became one of the most popular war films of the Third Reich. It was a prestige production, declared both "Staatspolitisch/künstlerisch" (state-political/artistic) and "volkstümlich" (ethnonationally) valuable, with Joseph Goebbels, Walther Darré, and Heinrich Himmler at its Berlin premiere at the Ufa-Palast am Zoo on February 28, 1941. These Nazi leaders would have watched how the film's young pilots board the mobilization train not from their own homes but from a Heimat-like community they helped create during the course of the film—namely, an artificial Heimat of the relocated refugees, who had to rely on these young pilots to find a place for them to settle after they had been driven from their homes. As the Luftwaffe moved into the war itself in *Squadron Lützow*, it was charged not with looking back to recent history, as in *Medal of Honor*, but with negotiating and even creating a new geography for Germany at war, one, as I shall argue below, achieved by the speed of its attack and precision of its airborne targeting.

The film is useful to track the emergence of wartime spatial assemblages because it deliberately extends Hans Bertram's earlier *D III 88*: *Squadron Lützow* offers the same characters, many of the same relationships and rivalries, but effectively resets *D III 88*'s plot, as befits the actual war. *Squadron Lützow* relocates the bombing training from *D III 88* to wartime targets, underscoring how such airborne targeting—a crucial theme in recent critical military studies—needs to be thought of within the wider spatial operations of war films.

A Familiar, and Close, Commander at the Wartime Airport

The film opens with that space central to the Nazis' wartime spatial assemblage, an airport. In all these Fliegerfilme of the Third Reich, the airport is deliberately remade as a place where personal relationships colonize the modern space as warm, personal, and comfortable—this is to be a fast and precise modernity made congenial and homey. For its wartime purposes, *Squadron Lützow* renders the airport the setting not so much of warm collective memories (*Medal of Honor*) or budding squadron camaraderie (*D III 88*) but of the surprisingly affective relationship between a commanding officer and his young, underling pilots. The opening shots offer the viewer precisely what one would expect from a film entitled *Squadron Lützow*—namely, a slow crane and then tracking shot over the squadron's coat of arms and then its looming hardware in a long row of HE II bombers—the expanding perspective of a mobile camera renders the coat of arms the old-time signifier of the latest air technology. This opening camera movement was, in fact, singled out in the film's lengthy Presseheft, or "press packet," which declared *Squadron Lützow*'s opening as memorable as the ending because this kind of camera movement reminds how the medium of film is absolutely "no painting gallery."[61] The young Luftwaffe pilots are lined up in front of the long row of aircraft, in an orderly line mimicking that of the planes, emphasizing military discipline and technologies of both body and machine.

On the tarmac of the airport, the squadron is about to be formally handed over to a new commanding officer, for whom the pilots are standing at attention. One older soldier, Guggi (Hannes Keppler), even warns a younger comrade (Hellweg) that he better pay attention—the new commander is supposed to be a tough one.[62] The suspense surrounding the new commander builds as the film cuts away to his ceremonial arrival and then formal speech to the assembled pilots. The commander is Colonel (Oberst) Mithoff (Christian Kayßler) from *D III 88*, so he is already familiar to a number of his pilots from, as he puts it in sudden jocularity, the "old school of Fliegerhorst Westerförder," as depicted in *D III 88* (the script even has him clapping them on the back, something that does not transpire in the film). These relationships rapidly establish the film as a sort of sequel to the Bertram-advised *D III 88*, with a trajectory from the first film's flight school with feigned maneuvers to full deployment amid a real war.

The links between Colonel Mithoff and the pilots—especially pilots Eckhard (Hermann Braun) and Paulsen and gunner Zeistler (Adolf Fischer), who all feature centrally in *D III 88*—are made explicitly paternal when, in the very next scene, Zeistler asks Mithoff's permission to marry Lina (Carsta Löck), his girlfriend from *D III 88*. Not only does the commanding officer grant his permission—he ends up presiding over the wedding, offering the marquee toast and being a somewhat weird focus for the attentions of the bride. The office and then marriage scenes are likewise emphasized in the Presseheft, both for the warmth that Mithoff surprisingly shows and, one suspects, for the assumed sexist appeal of an early wedding scene.[63] As I have argued throughout, the (literal as well as emotional) distance with which the commanding officers are depicted is crucial to the narratives of the film as well as the spatial ensembles they offer. Here the commanding officer, who remained a bit of an aloof presence to the pilots in *D III 88*, is now personally affectionate to his men in the film's opening three scenes, a fact highlighted as well in some of the reviews of the film.[64] These three scenes construct the commander as both physically and emotionally proximate to his men, not least to fortify the pilots for the war that then takes off immediately after the long wedding sequence. A major arrives at the matrimonial festivities to hand over orders to Colonel Mithoff for the bombing of Poland—and he does so quietly, all without interrupting the conjugal ceremony. War has become a mode within "normal," even matrimonial, domestic life.

Precision Targeting to Produce Refugee Spaces

It is telling that the publicity materials promoting *Squadron Lützow* emphatically foreground, notably for a Fliegerfilm, "Volksdeutsche" refugees from Poland. This narrative attention is afforded the refugees even though they are not introduced until some thirty minutes into the ninety-five-minute film and do not figure at all in its climactic last half hour, with its attack on "Engelland." Despite this subdued narrative role, the publicity pamphlet foregrounds the refugees as it sets the stage for *Squadron Lützow*. Its second sentence reads, "Augusttage des Jahres 1939. Der polnische Staat wütet mit Mord, Brand und Verfolgung gegen die Volksdeutschen, seine Herausforderungen gegenüber Deutschland werden immer unerträglicher" (The August days of the year 1939. The Polish state rampages with murder, arson, and persecution against ethnic Germans, and its challenge to Germany is becoming more and more unbearable).[65] As recent years have underscored, the displacement of noncombatants, whether long or short term and whatever their ethnicity, seems a lamentable, repeated consequence of modern war. Beyond the suffering that such displacement invariably causes, this kind of wartime movement underscores, for our purposes, the centrality of mobility for the remade geography of war: mobility not only of the modern, militarized machines of war but also of civilians inhabiting the contested territory where those machines are terrifyingly active.

For the Nazis' aggressive policies in the late 1930s and 1940s, highlighting ethnic Germans to the east justified foreign interventions and invasions—such accounts, as Omer Bartov, Bill Niven, and Paul Cooke have all underscored, made the Nazis and other ethnic Germans the alleged victims of the nations they then aggressively attacked.[66] This would be especially relevant in war films, in which the preparation for war often focuses on the emotional vicissitudes of individuals rather than on abstract political causes, even if the films scale conflict up to the nation. Certainly, there were issues with and/or concerns about ethnic Germans in countries ruled by people of other ethnicities, but as Richard Evans recounts, the Nazis exaggerated their persecution to secure concessions in the Sudetenland and then to launch their war on Poland: Goebbels deliberately multiplied the number of victims by at least a factor of ten and likely even of twenty.[67] For our (generic) purposes, it is revealing that a multipage essay in the Presseheft on the "Necessity of the War Feature Film" (Kriegsspielfilm) cites this sequence, in detail, as the starkest evidence for this eponymous necessity, since it emphasizes the "human-personal" element standing behind it all.[68]

Squadron Lützow's staging of ethnic Germans in Poland emphasizes their victimization as well as the Luftwaffe's unique ability to help them. After the initial bombardment of Warsaw and its nearby Okęcie airfield, the squadron continues to prowl the Polish skies and soon happens upon a column of fleeing civilians whom pilot Paulsen identifies immediately as ethnic Germans. Any question about the aircrews' becoming involved is quickly resolved when they witness what the film carefully constructs as a brutal war crime: as Polish gendarmes corral a column of ethnic Germans along a dusty road, one older man collapses. To dramatic music, one of the gendarmes stops his bike, dismounts, draws his pistol to shoot the pitiable straggler. The long-take tracking shot that has been following the column does not show viewers the actual shooting, but viewers hear the shot off-screen as the camera lingers on the gendarme's now parked bike, a seemingly harmless metonymy for the menacing murder.

This death-march sequence is shot on-level, which locates viewers' perspective among the other refugee ethnic Germans, making them close witnesses to the staged atrocity. Despite this on-level, tracking-shot focalization on the refugees, the film cuts abruptly back to pilot Paulsen looking down from his cockpit window, down from a godlike perspective a few hundred feet above these events. Such aerial views offer the much sought-after coup d'oeil, or assessment of the entire situation at a glance, as Carl von Clausewitz first described it and as technology increasingly facilitated.[69] Declaring the Poles a "Schweineband" (gang of pigs), Paulsen launches himself and his crew into action: he leads his and two other planes in a quick attack on the column. The improvised supplement to their mission emphasizes a suspiciously recurring aspect of air war that Samuel Weber has discussed—namely, the "target of opportunity," in which an unexpected "opportunity" presents itself to a pilot's privileged perspective—and emphasizes, I would highlight, the exalted subjectivity of the pilot as well as aerial views in this context.[70] A montage sequence rapidly crosscuts among the three planes, their raging machine guns, and the collapsing Polish forces. A revealing shot at the end of this sequence revisits the abandoned parked bicycle of the Polish gendarme, now presumably gunned down—a higher power intervened, a quasi-religious act confirmed by the *Illustrierter Film-Kurier* in its summary of the film, in which it writes, "Das Wunder, das große Wunder ist geschehen. Es ist wahrhaftig vom Himmel gekommen" (The miracle, the great miracle, has occurred. It has truly come from the heavens).[71] The fleeting target of opportunity has become a lasting miracle in the suddenly healing hands of the pilot-heroes and the Luftwaffe in general.

The characterization of the bombers' interceding as a "miracle" is telling, since, as Donna J. Haraway has observed, the view from high above performs what she calls the "god trick," the dream of an omniscient and omnipotent perspective from the sky.[72] This dramatic montage of bomber machine guns and refugee rescue demonstrates one of the key fantasies of this god trick that recurs regularly in these Fliegerfilme and, indeed, of all war films: the selective targeting of the enemy while miraculously avoiding the civilians who are in close physical proximity. Adding to this miracle, insists the *Illustrierter Film-Kurier*, is the way the pilots render the Poles, who are trying to make the refugees into Zielscheibe (targets), themselves the targets of their bombs, without hitting any of the ethnic German civilians.[73] The need for effective targeting became immediately clear to military thinkers and aeronautical engineers when they realized how inaccurate assault from the air was, given the many variables (speed of aircraft, mechanical failure of bombs, poor visibility, especially the challenges of the weather and wind, etc.): it was estimated that fewer than 50 percent of bombs reached their intended targets during World War II. Besides Samuel Weber's work, there has been much written about the importance of targeting in critical military studies, but this sequence underscores again how targeting, as with most military activities, needs to be seen and analyzed within larger spatial mechanisms (and ideology).[74]

Caren Kaplan describes how the shockingly low level of effective targeting led to a "cult" of precision among military thinkers and their engineering minions: an obsession with precise strikes from the air.[75] I would emphasize how this cult of precision aerial targeting reduces the complexity of space ideologically: it emphatically denies the many vectors of space—What is nearby? What is hit and lost next to / beside the target?—that Massey underscores are always in play, not least in the cities that were often targets of the bombing.[76] In calculating the vectors of the variables that could affect the trajectory of a bomb—like wind—military planners, by design, denied other such vectors, like the social density of space in a city. It is notable that the press materials about *Squadron Lützow* emphasize this ideological spatial assemblage of precision in the film: "In the age of the autobahn and ever-increasing motorization, the sharpest and fastest weapons spread throughout National-Socialist German with astonishing speed and precision," which the materials declare contribute to "a revolutionary way of waging war."[77]

This expertly selective targeting transforms the wider spaces of the eastern front and Poland, as I have traced since *Dr. Hart*'s exploding of a sight line obstructing windmill. As with *Dr. Hart*, such targeting and transformation of space also conjure surprising new social relations.[78] After targeting the Polish gendarmes—and miraculously avoiding the civilians—Paulsen lands his plane near the relieved refugees and approaches them to provide comfort. In this action—the large bomber reaches them in a remarkably small field—the film advertises how airplanes are able to access spaces formerly difficult or impossible to reach, further homogenizing and integrating distant, here disparate spaces into Germany. Paulsen picks out an older gentleman "who seems very reasonable" to take leadership ("die Führung") of the group. He encourages them to hold on (*durchhalten*) a couple of more days, since the German forces are only two or three days away, news that astonishes the refugees because they have been subjected only to Polish propaganda. After the bombers unload some provisions for the refugees and return to the battle, Wehrmacht ground forces march into the neighboring town and take control of the territory. In a clear parallel to the Luftwaffe's refugee assistance, the conquest of the territory results in the transformation of the town battlefield into a sanctuary for the refugees, who, unlike the chaotically fleeing Polish forces, line up in an orderly fashion for military-delivered food. In this way, the film follows the quickly edited and dramatic combat scenes with longer-take, slow tracking shots that establish the calm coherence of the conquered space, transforming it for the refugees the film holds at its center.

This transformation of town-as-battlefield into town-as-soup-kitchen foreshadows the film's main plot turn: the pilots create a new home for the refugees in a nonspecified village, one tellingly in the direction of Germany but clearly still in Polish territory. As Kaplan also reminds us, aerial views of this sort in which *Squadron Lützow* traffics prove crucial to statecraft—that is, to the conjuring of the state and the affirming of its legitimacy.[79] In terms of cinematic style, this transformation of Polish into German territory counteracts the twenty-minute combat scenes discussed above by remaking the frenzied montages of battle. There is, at first, another correspondingly quick montage of the pilots' rapid running, but this time, their speed and efficiency are displayed to provide the refugees with more food and clothing, especially with a delivery of hay for a local school to transform into beds. The script deliberately emphasizes the satisfaction of the soldiers at helping establish a Heim (home) for the refugees as well as the refugees' emerging sense of a Heimat (home as in homeland).[80] The music accompanying these images returns to those themes played out during the wedding, mentioned above, that third sequence of the film that establishes

Kampfgeshwader (attack squadron) as a personal, even familial affair. The script describes how the pilots' Don Kosaken choir performs for the refugees and is accompanied by the Okarina, all last seen and heard at the wedding.[81]

Ritter's *Über alles in der Welt*: Revoking Cosmopolitanism, Rescaling Europe

Somewhat unusual for the kind of Ufa prestige production that Ritter usually directed and/or produced, his *Über alles in der Welt* (*Above Everything in the World*) had its March 19, 1941, premiere not in the festive Ufa-Palast am Zoo but in Posen/Poznań, in what had been Poland.[82] Poznań, located in East Prussia, comprised ethnically mixed Germans and Poles but was located in newly minted Poland in the contentious redrawing of borders after World War I—it had been captured early, ending what Germans had declared twenty years of Fremdherrschaft (foreign domination). This territorialization and colonization builds on the eastward spatial transformation emerging in *Squadron Lützow*. A piece in the *Illustrierter Film-Kurier* hints that a premiere for such a film outside the Reich capital was unusual,[83] but Ritter's film opened in Poznań's largest cinema (holding 1,500 people) as part of the Cultural Days of the Warthegau, at which Goebbels spoke about the centrality of culture to the German "colonization-will" in the East.[84] In that eastward direction, Goebbels's speech declares that such cultural efforts should make dedicating "a couple of years of their lives in the East" nothing but an honor for young Germans.[85] For such cultural inroads, Ritter's film hit a couple of key notes, especially with its eponymous reference to the *Deutschlandlied*, and indeed, the music of the film was celebrated in the press, perhaps not least because its composer was Herbert Windt, who had worked on *Triumph des Willens* (*Triumph of the Will*). Culture and, with it, film thus followed the troops eastward in their own wartime theaters, a territorial and territorializing strategy that geared to colonize the east for future generations.

It seems especially fitting that Ritter's film should travel for its premiere, since the film has as its basic plot premise, like most of the war films in this study, both travel and its role in deterritorializing and territorializing processes. The prepremiere press highlights numerous exotic locations (from Danzig to Spain to the Großglockner mountain in Austria) and promises "constantly shifting settings."[86] In terms of the film's traveling eastward for its premiere, one piece points out that in bolstering the cultural bulwark of the "reconquered" Poznań, it could expect to find a special resonance, since it foregrounds German sacrifices made to launch the 1939 war as well as the attack itself.[87] Somewhat unusual for a film with combat at its core, however, it starts not at home to trace trips abroad, which provide the general trajectory of many war films, thematizing, exploring, and crosscutting the distance from the home to the front. Rather, *Über alles* begins abroad with a series of ethnic Germans who are working in foreign countries when the war starts in September 1939. Fritz Kampers was part of the war film star system, familiar to audiences from *Westfront*, *Medal of Honor*, and *Squadron Lützow*, and here he plays Fritz Moebius, a Siemens mechanic working abroad in Paris; Carl Raddatz (recently of *Request Concert*, 1940, soon of *Stukas*, 1941) is Karl Wiegand, a well-known German journalist likewise posted in the French capital; and the final of the "foreign workers" is a singing group of Tyrolians who perform folk songs for adoring audiences in London. The film then traces these three expat stories—all arrested abroad, all moved (figuratively and literally) by Germany's fight against its enemies, all seeking to get back to the Heimat—as their loved ones back home struggle with their absence.

Given these myriad plot strands, the telltale collective protagonist in *Über alles* moves not from the home to the front but rather in the deliberate direction of Germany. The many border crossings in that direction underscore the film's peculiar spatial mechanisms, especially its generic innovation of very modern cosmopolitanism. *Über alles*'s peculiar collective protagonist provides for, in fact, the possibilities of cosmopolitanism—a term usually deployed to mean something like a "citizen of the world," whereby one belongs to some kind of global civil society.[88] This sense of belonging and membership means that cosmopolitans can belong as citizens of "their immediate political communities, and of the wider regional and global networks which impacted upon their lives."[89] I would highlight how modern cosmopolitanism in the twentieth century relied upon an increase in mass mobility. By differentiating these modern mobilities, Zygmunt Bauman explores how the sorts of citizenship regimes already discussed could be taken "as the metaphor for the new, emergent, stratification," laying bare the fact "that it is now the access to global mobility which has been raised to the topmost rank among the stratifying factors."[90] *Über alles* foregrounds both the mobility and the stratification in cosmopolitanism that it conjures. Indeed, at least Karl Wiegand (the very mobile character played by Ritter-regular Carl Raddatz) embodies precisely the elite worldliness of which Bauman writes and that the film is at pains to dismantle.

With such a plot approach, *Über alles* seems unusual for a combat film because it places in the foreground preexisting sorts of German cosmopolitans: ethnic Germans living and working abroad, speaking foreign languages, with friends and defenders from these countries that quickly turn into Germany's enemies. These ethnic Germans abroad are different from the refugees from *Squadron Lützow* because they have willfully traveled away from Germany. Particularly Wiegand, per the above, has strayed far from Germany both literally and figuratively: with French-language skills good enough to fool native speakers, he has a French girlfriend, Brigitte, who tries to keep him near—she even has him arrested by French authorities to hold him on her side of the increasingly contested border. If the distance to the front and how it is covered often reveal a film's narrative logic, in *Über alles*, the characters have to return home to sojourn farther, to the front and in military garb, later. This would seem to raise questions about *Über alles*'s status as a war film in general, although the film tracks the early days of the war, and in its final half hour, combat dominates the diegesis and concludes its multiple narrative strands. Some reviews dissociate it from a war film in the mode of *Squadron Lützow*, although others are equally clear Ritter was a director predominantly associated with war films, like *Holiday on a Promise*, *Medal of Honor*, and soon, *Stukas*. This suggests how combat was increasingly deployed within other genres, as a mode within a larger context, not least to normalize it for viewers. But the war film becomes a telling mode at this fateful historical moment, nonetheless manifesting many of the genre's recurring traits (a phenomenon I also explore at length in the next chapter). For example, linking these hybridized elements in *Über alles*—the arrest(ation) of German cosmopolitanism and its subsequent militarization—are the travel and exotic locations deployed throughout, confirming the distant shores of the war film that I am tracing throughout this study.

As with *Medal of Honor* and *Squadron Lützow*, the press and interviews about the film did ruminate explicitly on its genre. In distinction to those two films, *Über alles* was designated a Querschnitt (diagonal cutting) film in the mode of Ritter's *Holiday on a Promise*. Ritter was explicit that such films should arc away from individual-focused stories or big-named star turns—code words for the Hollywood cinema with which these films felt themselves to be in competition.[91] His statements in interviews, in fact, indicate that he was interested in the fundamental aesthetic approach of cinema, which he suggested had not reached anything like artistic maturity.[92] In these generic ruminations, Querschnitt refers to the core stylistic element of *Über alles*, both to the space-homogenizing and space-synthesizing crosscutting that I have been emphasizing throughout in the war film and to the fate of the ostensible protagonist in the plot. Ritter's Querschnitt crosscuts among individual stories to aim at a collective depiction realized in a spatially expansive Germany. In this approach, too, one can sense an effort to converse with the excitement of the *Die Deutsche Wochenschau*, which was taken explicitly as a model for Kulturfilme. As with *Westfront* and *Camaraderie*, foregoing stories in favor of more expansive collectives and their spaces suggests how *Über alles* aims to transcend the scale of conventional film plotting.

The above analysis of *Westfront* and *Camaraderie* foregrounds the importance of scale in war films and their remaking of the films' geographical and geopolitical aspects. *Westfront* radically interrupts the usual scalar mechanisms—the rescaling upward—of combat films to focus on the body and its suffering under wartime conditions. It does so in part by fragmenting the sorts of homogenized spaces that a pro-war film like *Dr. Hart* or *Squadron Lützow* deliberately produces. Like *Westfront* and *Camaraderie*, though in the opposite direction, *Über alles* invokes the scalar syntax of the combat genre to manipulate it. While Ritter's *Über alles* focuses on travel in a different direction than most war films (from abroad homeward, not vice versa), it also affords the opportunity to consider wartime scales within a new framework—namely, the specifically European plans in the Nazis' larger project. Benjamin Martin has explored the extensive cultural work the Nazis undertook toward realizing a Europe-wide and Europeanizing vision.[93] In *Über alles*, the transnational rescaling of cosmopolitanism and, with it, the very subjectivity of the cosmopolitan are problematized. Scaling up by cosmopolitanism is arrested, while Heimat-based upscaling is endorsed, all with the vision of a new Europe (literally and figuratively) looming.

As in *Camaraderie*, the stakes of *Über alles*'s intensified geographical scales emerge in an early sequence at a border. But Ritter, contrary to *Camaraderie*'s political optimism, will emphasize not the homogenizing potential—rather, he highlights the fragmenting mechanisms of border control. The opening minutes of the film track the immediate impact of the war's 1939 start on the spaces and bodies involved but not with the familiar spectacle of mobilization. Its opening minutes recall instead a contradiction that Kaplan has noted in war: that even while war galvanizes mass mobilization, it simultaneously "polices borders and limits freedom of movement" so that, as I have argued throughout, the marquee mobilization and mass mobility function within larger, contradictory spatial mechanisms linked to territory and sovereignty.[94] After opening with famous landmarks of Paris and London—and putting travel and foreign destinations in viewers' minds from the outset—Ritter stages the Paris arrest of Fritz Moebius as the war begins and then cuts to the film's second expat cosmopolitan, Karl Wiegand. The latter's luxury convertible advances rapidly toward the camera, emphasizing both the velocity of Wiegand's attempted flight from France and the speed at the core of the film's crosscutting style. Wiegand is attempting to cross the French border into Belgium, presumably to avoid the same arrested fate as Moebius. After initially believing both Maria and Wiegand to be French, the border guards follow up with their papers, at which they realize Wiegand's origins: they summarily arrest him and confiscate the car. Being ordered to cease and desist highlights how the vehicular homogenization of space is fragmented by the border and its policing. This kind of checking of papers and questioning of subjects also affords the plot a convenient moment of exposition—the border incident reveals Wiegand's profession and his suspect inclination for things French, especially his girlfriend. But it does so by foregrounding a confessional moment of the border that international relations theorist Mark Salter has emphasized, with the border a contested space in which the territorial abstractions meet Foucauldian biopolitics.[95] That duality highlights the rescaling of the border, demoting the border-crossing cosmopolitan to the nationality of the individual bodies. An intensified biopolitics is especially relevant given his attempted flight with his nationally other lover. Weltbürger Wiegand (cosmopolitan Wiegand) is forced to confess his nationality and submit his body to the wartime border regime.

The confessional and classificatory mechanisms of the border undercut Wiegand's cosmopolitan upscaling beyond his nation: the border halts the sort of facile mobility that Bauman, for example, locates at the core of modern cosmopolitanism.[96] In a similar mode, the border and his arrest there also put an end to his cosmopolitan career in journalism. As with *Westfront* and *Camaraderie*, a central means of producing (and understanding) scale is economic activity, especially decisions about the levels (aka scales) of cooperation and competition in work and industry. Journalism is a profession that self-consciously navigates multiple scales, mediating between the individual's voice and concentric journalism-consuming audiences, be they (much like scales) local, regional, national, or supernational/international. As is often cited, journalism and the consumption of news mass media were integral to the imagined community of the nation, something duly noted in the more recent literature on the scale of the national.

Arrested at the Belgian border and ushered from his journalist job, however, Wiegand is sent to a concentration camp at the Stade Colombes, near Paris, where he encounters the similarly apprehended Moebius. The film invokes the kinds of concentration camps that had been used since the earliest days of the Nazi regime, in a classic case of projection, only here the French camp remains sunny and seemingly harmless.[97] To escape the camp—to reactivate both the mobility and the journalism at the core of cosmopolitanism—Wiegand agrees to his girlfriend's plan of cooperating with anti-German agents. These agents, one Austrian named Samek and an Englishman named Brown, are likewise linked to journalism and the manipulation of sentiment at the national and supernational scales, with Samek's work for German-language radio broadcasts and Brown's for national newspapers. This murky world of Paris-based anti-German agents allows the film to dip into the decadent demimonde of Paris, including a scantily clad song-and-dance routine at a revue (the script refers to "Negertanzerinnen zu Hot-Musik frech tanzend"[98]), before turning the journalistic screws on the now ambivalently cosmopolitan Wiegand. Samek and Brown are publishing anti-Germany articles in his name and expect him to speak at an anti-Germany rally, emphasizing the negotiation of scale inherent to modern mass media. The agents are committed to exploiting Wiegand's scale-jumping profession for their own ends.

While *Über alles* gives interwar cosmopolitanism an increasingly negatively cast—not least through the France-based, Jewish-coded Austrian radio broadcaster—erstwhile expat Wiegand is rescued by the distant but distinct signals emanating from the Heimat. They reach him in part through Germany's own supernational radio broadcast, as he secretly listens to the Wunschkonzert (request concert) program in a Paris apartment. Wiegand's listening to the Wunschkonzert program is one of the film's many examples of intertextuality in its marquee propaganda productions, which together created a legible national unity out of the diversity of cultural products. Such a transmedia diversity of cultural products underscores the notion of a war assemblage within this milieu, one intersecting and dovetailing with its spatial ensembles. It is also through the radio that Wiegand is emotionally moved by the retooled cosmopolitanism that *Über alles* is at pains to produce—namely, when he learns, at a telling distance from home, of the cross-border attack and foreign invasion. With this radio-driven refiguring of Wiegand's identity—the recasting of his Francophilism as more "innately" national—the film is remaking its opening cosmopolitanism in the war mode that I am exploring throughout this chapter. The film replaces an economically driven cosmopolitanism manifest early in its plot with a new kind of rescaling and scale jumping—namely, the militaristic extension of the individual. This reminted mobility manages to revisit the far-off, exotic Europe that it vividly offers viewers in its first twenty minutes.

When sitting at a scenic Paris café, as one imagines he formerly did to compose his foreign-correspondent articles, the air-raid siren screams a German bombing raid: as the Austrian handler and Wiegand's French girlfriend, Brigitte, flee, Wiegand looks up—with a weird wistfulness given that he is at repose in the middle of a big target—at the German planes and sighs "A German attack" in the direction of the Heimat (figure 4.2).

This cross-border rescaling of the expat to the national, this refiguring of the film's individualist cosmopolitanism, is tellingly shared by Wiegand's fellow expat Moebius. Moebius has likewise been released from the camp but, unlike Wiegand, immediately flees Paris for the French-German border. When on the run in Alsace, Moebius also looks up, similarly wistfully, at the German attack planes as they fly toward central French targets, both admiring and expectant (figure 4.3). Ritter dissolves from the refigured cosmopolitanism to the German plane itself: the film's assiduous border crossers are being written as more German, rewritten in the geography-defining air.

In this way, the supernational reach of radio (Wiegand's listening to Wunschkonzert) is fulfilled by the border-crossing scale of the air war: both are beacons to the lonely traveler increasingly longing for the Heimat, both offer the means for rescaling the itinerant individual, thereby binding his—notably his—body via the air war to the national scale of wartime.

The looming import of Germany's air war, however, is admired not only by the film's two main characters, from below and at a distance. Rather, those piloting the planes also become key characters in *Über alles*'s myriad narrative strains. As noted above, although the plot begins with and predominantly features Wiegand and Moebius as reformed cosmopolitans, *Über alles*, per Ritter's Querschnitt revision of the war genre, offers multiple narrative lines from its onset. Despite these many plot strands, however, the film ultimately favors the Luftwaffe contribution to the war and its reclamation of the recovering cosmopolitans. Among the many narrative lines, there are some scenes at sea (a

FIG. 4.2 Wiegand admires a German attack in/on France, *Above Everything in the World.* Digital frame enlargement.

German tanker is scuttled, its crew captured by the English fleet to be rescued by a U-boat); a few on the ground with infantry (Moebius's son is mobilized by train to the earthbound front); and, literally above all, scenes of the Luftwaffe's aerial prowess first in Poland and then, increasingly, in the west. Aside from those with Wiegand and Moebius, the Luftwaffe scenes are the most frequent, longest, and most spectacular, favoring its contributions over the other armed forces'. If Ritter's Querschnitt style is premised on the breathlessly fast and breathtaking excitement of rapid crosscutting among the many narrative lines and collective protagonist, the aerial plot, in fact, ends up unifying them all, including Wiegand's and Moebius's divergent trajectories. Wiegand's brother Hans, it turns out, is a Luftwaffe pilot who ends up crashing quite close to Moebius as the latter crosses from France to Italy. This only-in-the-movies serendipity—one moment in a concentration camp with a fellow German, the next moment that German's brother crashes nearby to likewise assist—highlights the big and welcoming family of the Heimat to which the two expats are now returning and rescaling. This serendipity of supernational scales, across at least three countries and over multiple borders, comes largely through Germany's aerial reach.

The aerial portion of *Über alles*'s multifaceted plot is favored not only narratively—the story, in fact, seems to fade in favor of the film's visual and geographical spectacles, as the Querschnitt montage of its plot climactically accelerates. As with *Medal of Honor* and *Squadron Lützow*, airborne mobility offers a cinematic means to produce new scales visually and then to jump among them geographically—emphasizing anew how Virilio's association of the visual with (air) war cinema should be analyzed within broader spatial mechanisms. On the visual side, the airborne point of view allows the pilots and viewers to marvel from above at Warsaw and then, eventually, the western front, producing and integrating new scales into Germany's ever-broadening military campaigns (figure 4.4).[99]

FIG. 4.3 Moebius similarly admires a German aerial attack, *Above Everything in the World.* Digital frame enlargement.

These perspectives on foreign cities, through pilots' points of view on faraway geographical features, prove crucial to the film's imaginary work of travel, affect, and territorialization. The film opens with exotic capitals that hinder and arrest the expat protagonists at the ground level but then offers such foreign cities anew from the perspective of bombers and fighter planes. If cosmopolitanism indulged foreign pleasures early on, the film's later war modes deliberately detach characters from these foreign charms to offer them at a marked (bombing) distance. It is the fort/da of travel destinations to be territorialized anew, not in the initial economic cosmopolitanism (a European scalar model the film is at pains to reject), but rather in military conquest. These cockpit-based visual perspectives, pace Maschke at this chapter's opening, operationalize the affective-geographical expansion of the film's reach. After the fragmented cosmopolitanism of expats scattered in European capitals, the film's staging of German airpower signals the increasingly homogenizing and integrating reach of its air access to distant territories.

In terms of how such perspectives produce scales—and do the work required to navigate between and among those scales—such a visual/geographical impact of airborne travel was contradictory, as Kaplan notes: it flattened out landscape and geographical distance while also allowing an observer at altitude to observe topographical distinctions, differences, boundaries. This paradigmatically modern form of travel allows the contradictory, dialectically entwined process of homogenizing space (flattening it out) while also fragmenting it (rendering differences clearer from an airborne perspective).[100] This contradictory production of new scales from the cockpit of the Luftwaffe attack planes establishes a geographical and national hierarchy decidedly lacking in *Über alles*'s early cosmopolitanism. The national scale now beckons to the individual expats—Germany recalls them from France and London as it integrates that supernational scale from the air. For example, when Wiegand's brother coincidentally crash-lands near Moebius, they help each other over the mountainous

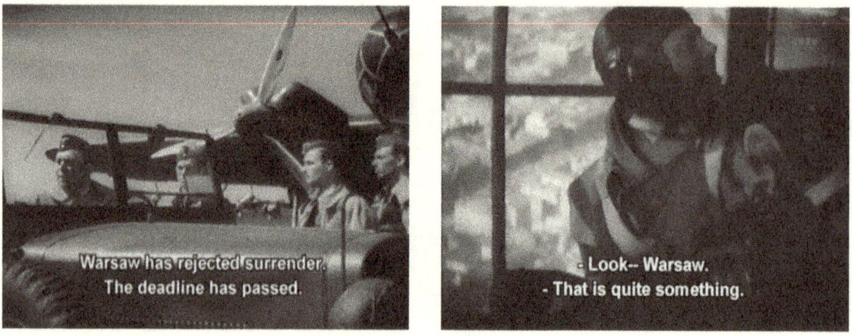

FIG. 4.4 Aerial tourism of Warsaw, about to be bombed, *Above Everything in the World*. Digital frame enlargement.

and scenic French-Italian border and end up with the German-friendly Italians at a festive dinner in Genoa—under a picture of the duce, as the script makes clear.[101] They thus head home while producing a refigured supernational scale, simultaneously serving up more (and more integrated) exotic travel images of wartime leisure and fun.

The narrative, visual, and geographical unity, achieved by *Über alles*'s rescaling through airpower, reaches its greatest heights, so to say, in the film's climactic scenes. Despite the film's Querschnitt and its fast crosscutting among its many narrative strands—scenes are rarely longer than two to three minutes before the last half hour—the longest sequence occurs in the final ten minutes and lasts over six minutes, as it stages aerial combat reminiscent of that in *Squadron Lützow*. The approach to this unusually long sequence emphasizes how both Wiegand and Moebius are integrated back into the Heimat after their stuttering returns from the cosmopolitan life in France. After crossing the front and being embraced by his German brethren, Wiegand convalesces first in a hospital train, whose well-cushioned comfort is reminiscent of *Dr. Hart*'s and *Sword and Hearth*'s medical trains, and then in a scenic mountain hospital, where his pilot brother Hans visits him before the latter flies off in the film's final sequence. Moebius's fate confirms the plot's favoring the Luftwaffe narrative strand even more starkly. After tracking him in civilian clothes throughout his flight from Paris—through Alsace, over the French and Italian border, to Genoa, and back to Germany—viewers suddenly see the very middle-aged Moebius burst out of an airport door in full Luftwaffe uniform. As we saw in *Medal of Honor*, the airport functions as a key transitional and transformational space throughout these films. It serves as a signpost for the film's skyward aerial plot that underscores the centrality of mobility and its affective remaking of the world.

With both Wiegand and Moebius rescaled to the national, the film unifies its sundry strands and sends them out centrifugally from Germany over its national borders. Afforded more and more narrative time, in by far its longest sequence, the film's Luftwaffe pilots now repel an attack of (reportedly) fifty-two English Vickers Wellington bombers—(allegedly) thirty-six of which are shot down by German fighter planes, presumably saving the port city of Wilhelmshaven. In *Über alles*, however, this uniquely long, seven-minute sequence—the film's opening economic cosmopolitanism culminating in concluding combat—gives way to a final battle-geographical montage of a little over three minutes. After the English bombers are downed or repelled, viewers see stock footage of Germany's invasion of Denmark and Norway (purportedly to prevent British attacks, hailed in the voice-over by Hitler) and then, starting in May 1940 and accompanied by march music, the attacks on Belgium and France on the western front. The montage starts with names of places and dates: Liège/Luettich (May 13, 1940), Antwerp (May 18, 1940), Boulogne (May 24, 1940), and Calais (May 26, 1940). These place names and dates are superimposed on the dissolving tourist images of foreign cities, recalling the film's sunny opening in Paris and London, a roll call of engagements very akin to a tourist trip westward—a pleasure trip laid over the newly minted affective geography of war.

These images and voice-over largely mimic newsreels but with a telling difference: the superimposed text of "Boulogne May 24, 1940" is accompanied by an image of a German tank with Karl Wiegand atop it. The battle montage homogenizes and integrates new space as territory as it has since the 1910s, but it also deploys characters very specifically in the ongoing constellation and ensemble of the genre. Wiegand now recrosses the border in an armored vehicle, recalling but recasting the film's first ten minutes. *Über alles* has remade his failed border crossing as it has refigured his movement and the space around it: approaching the camera not in a luxury convertible but in a top-heavy tank, accompanied not by his French girlfriend but by his fellow tank crew members, and so on. The film offers a parallel revision of the border sequence mentioned above when the collage of the conquering is interrupted by the Jewish-coded Austrian announcer approaching the border to Spain (in a convertible) but then being asked for a visa. His travel is interrupted, and he will be, presumably, caught and deported eastward. After a happy image of the Luftwaffe pilots, marching cheerfully in their gear on an air base, the film zooms in on the corner of the newspaper *12-Uhr* where a text box announces, "Now it is about England," to which the sequence dissolves to a crescendoing montage of German fighter planes and bombers. If the film traces various modes of mobility, from Wiegand's opening convertible to merchant ships to tanks and planes, *Über alles* favors, in the end, the Luftwaffe. The closing shots display the iron cross superimposed on the bombers as they move toward—like Wiegand's opening car and closing tank—the camera and viewer. It is a trajectory, an affective geography, navigated by the reform of modes of transportation, with homogenization and integration of space still at the heart of the refigured genre.

5

Out of the War Mode: Demobilizing the War Genre in the Postwar Rubble Film

(*Request Concert*, 1940; *The Great Love*, 1942; *Ways into Twilight*, 1949; *The Sons of Mr. Gaspary*, 1948; *Birds of Migration*, 1946/1947)

The first three German feature films made after World War II—*Die Mörder sind unter uns* (*The Murderers Are among Us*, 1946), *Irgendwo in Berlin* (*Somewhere in Berlin*, 1946), and *Und über uns der Himmel* (*The Heavens Above*, 1947), the first two licensed by the Soviet Union and the last by the U.S. forces—all open with their male protagonists in a deliberate and deliberative walk.[1] These opening figures invoke a recurring postwar apparition, that of the Heimkehrer (someone returning home, here a soldier) walking home to rebuild the country in whose name the most nefarious crimes in world history had been committed. The Heimkehrer is almost always imagined as walking, walking out of the prisoner of war (POW) camp, walking back to the disgraced Vaterland (fatherland), and even walking back into the lives of family and friends from thousands of kilometers away. Through this figure of the Heimkehrer, these so-called rubble films memorialized a particular mode of mobility amid a very different postwar affective geography, one that hints at what I explore as a revised generic subtext relating to space, mobility, and transportation technologies.

In analyzing these films, critics have tended to underscore the ways in which rubble films of the late 1940s broke from the films directly preceding them. During the yearlong, Allied-imposed Filmpause of 1945/1946, there were many calls to abandon the Traumfabrik (dream factory) style of the Nazi-coordinated film industry and instigate a socially critical, historically engaged, cinematically realist approach.[2] But the spatial subtext of mobility and its ancillary technologies that I have been tracing throughout this study was one of the subtle ways in which films of the 1940s engaged with their immediate cinematic predecessors, despite many claims of a radical break from the cinema of 1933–1945. In this chapter, I will investigate the deliberate negotiation of postwar affective geographies—or more specifically, spatial transformations of the period, to invoke the phrasing used by Fredric Jameson and others.[3] I would suggest that images and metaphors of mobility abound in the rubble film in large part because Nazi cinema of the early 1940s, in some of its most popular films, established very particular spatial transformations via mobility and the affective geographies it conjures. Thus, consciously or not, a bridge is forged between the two periods on either side of the 1945/1946 rupture.

In the previous chapter, I foregrounded several leitmotifs of the diverse and uneven Nazi project, including Lebensraum (living space), Drang nach Osten (push to the east), and Blut und Boden (blood and soil). All such motifs suggest a spatial and subsequently geographical project interwoven with militaristic, racist, and genocidal goals. Films made under the Nazis—like the immensely popular *Wunschkonzert* (*Request Concert*, 1940) and *Die große Liebe* (*The Great Love*, 1942), two of the era's most successful films[4]—deploy the military and its transportation technologies to arrange geographies both spatial and affective-emotional. The military is deployed representationally not only to negotiate the dynamic national notion of Germany in specific ways but also to map, in a deliberately sketched geography, the private emotional lives of the main characters. Both of those films highlight the mobilization aspects of war films, including the mobilization of protagonists for war in ways that reflect a society girding itself for combat. Revisions to the generic syntax of war films demonstrate their refiguring of space both for the genre and for Germany. Such films juxtapose and intertwine the usual subjects of feature films—that is, the intimate affective-emotional lives of their protagonists—with a militarized project of national mobilization for war. Cinematically, they achieve this scaling, as I have termed it, by building on film's long-standing relationship to travel and transportation as well as conjuring what I would call a new affective geography.[5]

Scholars have often mentioned the theme of the Heimkehrer in postwar rubble films and frequently focus on questions of reintegration into private households and traditional gender roles.[6] But I want to suggest that at least some of these films revisit and even indulge the kind of scaling mobility and mobilization so emphatically achieved, as in chapter 4, in popular cinema under the Nazis—they take elements of both generic syntax and semantics important during the Nazi era. While the Heimkehrer is a recurring theme of rubble films, few have questioned how the Heimkehrer figured not only as an absent male returning to the heterosexual family but also as a former soldier—militarily conditioned and experienced—returning from a war that had required a specifically mobilized and mobile mindset. There has been a consistent focus on their reintegration into postwar society but little on the militaristic baggage and imaginary former soldiers and recently released POWs would have carried. For many of these soldiers, mobilization for war would have exposed them to some of modernity's most distinguishing aspects, including industrial organization, modern technology, and I suggest, travel to distant lands and contact with foreign cultures. The absorption and manipulation of the affective thrills associated with these experiences had been central to the genre since World War I and, I would suggest, would have to be addressed in these very different films of the postwar period.

In more general cultural histories of this period, there is a similar and parallel neglect of probably the most consistently executed of the famous "four Ds" of Allied occupational policy (denazification, demilitarization, decartelization, and democratization). Much work has focused on the denazification and the negotiation of the Nazi past, yet demilitarization was the goal on which the Allies most agreed and at which they were probably the most successful.[7] By suggesting that some of the most popular films of 1933–1945, especially 1939–1945, were of the war genre (or at least deploy the "war mode," as I argued earlier) with a heavy emphasis on mobilization, one can appreciate the ways in which rubble films were meant explicitly as demobilization films, films directed against the military-spatial habits, mores, and psychologies that the Nazis had inculcated during the war years.[8] A central aspect of these both wartime mobilization and postwar demobilization films, I have been arguing, was an affective geography built via military (literal and metaphorical) technologies. These demobilizing rubble films indulge in but also attempt to dismantle this kind of wartime affective geography and its sundry spatial aspects.

If a new spatial assemblage and geography around it had taken hold during the Nazis' "total mobilization"—that is, its particular instrumentalization of industrial modernity—then the postwar period would have, at least as one of its sundry aspects, to invoke and dismantle this kind of geography. This is precisely what a cycle of three films associated with Rolf Meyer, a director as well as the head of the production firm Junge Film-Union, achieves in each one's curious, often-haunted negotiation of postwar affective geography. With these references to a prewar and then postwar spatial ensemble, I will attempt a reading that focuses not so much on character or cast but rather on images of space, transportation, and general mobility within them.[9] On the one hand, there was a clear invocation, and even suspect indulgence, of the militarized, affective geographies of cinema under the Nazis that I sketched earlier; on the other hand, there was an effort, with varying degrees of conviction and success, to dismantle it for the literally millions of returning soldiers who had not only learned but lived the Nazis' spatial assemblage of affectively charged travel unto territorial aggression.

The War Genre as a Deployable Mode in Popular Cinema under the Nazis

Three aspects seem especially relevant to the spatial depictions and practices of mobilization in two key Nazi-era films, *Request Concert* (1940; Eduard von Borsody) and *The Great Love* (1942; Rolf Hansen), against which postwar rubble films were, at least in part, made. These films confirm some of the mechanisms charted above with the Luftwaffe films but also vary them in the direction of generic hybridity. Mobilization from private life to military service was relatively subdued in the Luftwaffe films because they often started in medias res, whereas these two—tellingly among the most popular of the regime—foreground the tensions between civilian life and war service. In fact, *Request Concert* and *The Great Love* were not usually discussed by the regime or the press as Kriegsfilme or Kriegsspielfilme, but they both offer pivotal scenes, narratively speaking, premised on the linchpin of wartime combat.[10] In this way, they confirm a sense of war and combat as a mode within other genres during the Nazi era that anticipates the increasing hybridity of genre in the postwar period, blurring how life is war and war is life. I have in mind not only the genre's hybridity (as I shall discuss in chapter 6) but also the "melodramatic mode" that Linda Williams has influentially described in her rethinking of the melodrama genre.[11] Developing this war film mode within other films fit the regime's ideological agenda, since they deliberately normalized combat as part of civilian life. Normalizing combat in other sociocultural realms is, in nuce, the very definition of militarism—that is, of military principles and practices colonizing other spheres (as they do territories) of usually civilian life.[12]

These mobilization and demobilization films of the Nazi and postwar periods, respectively, deploy novel affective geographies to navigate their both narrative and contextual challenges. In their particular spatial transformations, the films highlight the impact of technology on (cinematic) perception and derive their visual and affective pleasures from that nexus; they also sketch, to narrativize a film's disparate spaces, a secret second map of the narrative trajectory, as I explored in chapter 3; and finally, they depict the slippery plotting of power and desire according to an entire secondary affective geography that varies the assumed coordinates of a plot's primary map.

* * *

1. The mobilization that these two films foreground builds on the affective pleasures and attractions of new technologies and their impact on perception, much like the Luftwaffe films. For many scholars whose work foregrounds the intersection of technology and space, the history of that technology, especially of modern transportation technologies, has influenced changing perceptions of space. Paul Virilio, Wolfgang Schivelbusch, and Giuliana Bruno in particular focus on the impact that mobility and its ancillary transportation technologies have had on perception.[13] For example, Schivelbusch's *Railway Journey* proposes that the train introduced an entirely new mode of "panoramic perception" that replaced the more "organic" spatial perception of the horse-drawn coach, a transition in mobile perception manifest in both *Dr. Hart* and *Sword and Hearth*.[14] In *War and Cinema*, Virilio highlights how technologies of aviation "become one [different] way, perhaps even the ultimate way, of seeing."[15] Both Virilio and Schivelbusch highlight how these technologies of mobility served to transform the nature of the perception of space, most often creating a new detachment and distance from the perceived objects, an abstraction and "geometrification" (as Virilio calls it) from spaces that were perceived and experienced at greater proximity before the technologies were introduced.[16] These modern transportation technologies form an important and often-neglected foundation for filmic imaging, for the kinesthetic aspect of cinema, as Jameson calls it when he analyzes the modes of movement among spaces in film.[17] Both Virilio and Jameson, however, underplay the affective pleasures of this intersection of film and mobility—that is, that this intersection constitutes a key aspect of cinema as an attraction and as an affective thrill, which explains both its popularity and its capacity to be manipulated for other ends.

For example, in both *Request Concert* and *The Great Love*, it is not only that space and mobility matter to their narrative trajectories but that modern mobility, transportation technologies, and the military mobilization bred of such technologies structure the films' affective geographies—geographies central to their narrative unfolding. As Jameson observes about a series of different films, spatial representations can even overpower the narrativization of character and desire rather than vice versa.[18] In the case of Luftwaffe films, they foreground a male protagonist who is a military pilot repeatedly called up and away from his prospective love interest to war (to the Spanish Civil War and then World War II in *Request Concert* and to World War II in *The Great Love*).

In contrast to the Luftwaffe films, however, both *Request Concert* and *The Great Love* are delivered more in a melodramatic mode and actually constitute clear generic hybrids between war and melodrama.[19] The films contrast the land-bound love stories and airborne military duties of their protagonists, which normatively collide at the most inconvenient moments, duties invariably undercutting but thereby becoming intertwined with desire. As war films become a mode to be deployed within other genres, both films offer crosscut sequences that combine the affective thrill of aerial battle and the challenges of melodramatically deferred courtship; and both have sequences that cut from the body of the female love object to the sublime beauty of the skies shot from the cockpit. In parallel sequences, the male gaze is juxtaposed to the point of view of the fighter pilot looking through the skies at the enemy, such that what Ernst Jünger calls the "cold gaze" of technology is entwined with the conventional male gaze as well as the affective pleasures of airborne travel.[20] Their narrative schemes thus hinge on the thrill of militaristic transportation technologies and the visual-affective pleasures they afford.

2. In *The Geopolitical Aesthetic*, Jameson argues that the operations of narrative mapping become intensified—at least representationally—when it is revealed that there is a secret second map behind the presumed spatial order of things: a second, initially unknown layer permits a shift to a different landscape (literally) of agency.[21] This remapping within the narrative then undergoes a triangulation effect among the two different layers and the observer, who comes to see the surface as well as the deeper map over which the surface is stretched. These mechanisms underscore how, insightful though they certainly are, Schivelbusch and Virilio do not go far enough in examining broader spatial mechanisms when foregrounding visual perception. With such broader, and deeper, mechanisms, *Request Concert* and *The Great Love* assert more complex spatial systems derived from these two conspicuous maps, as Jameson argues in his essay on *North by Northwest*.[22] They subsequently settle on a third space amid new affective geographies that resolve the conflicts of the first and second. In this way, the tensions between these two spaces drive at a transformed affective geography by the films' ends. I would suggest that any number of films that are, as Jameson puts it, more spatial than others include this kind of remapping over the course of the narrative: there is a remapping of older geographies, unfolding a double layering of space that can permit an effective refiguration of character, plot, and desire via a spatial shift.

Both mobilization films begin with the early stages of a courtship and accordingly visit the familiar venues of the romantic picture: the couples meet in a public place (the Berlin Olympic Stadium in *Request Concert*, a theater in *The Great Love*), proceed to semipublic places to develop their acquaintanceships (restaurants and/or nightclubs and/or parties), and eventually head toward the bedroom. Courtship and the challenges around it are much bigger parts of the plot than in any of the Luftwaffe films mentioned above. But then, in both cases, this privatizing topography of romance is undercut and ultimately displaced by a second affective geography, that of the military and, in particular, the Wehrmacht's wartime mapping of Europe. The fundamental tension in both pictures is precisely that between these two geographies—spatially at odds—and the films cut between them as two different contemporary spaces. In both cases, the second military geography is initially kept secret but then erupts into the narrative to interrupt the expected trajectory of courtship. In *Request*

Concert, the male protagonist, Herbert, is suddenly called up to serve in the Spanish Civil War, and he has little time to inform his love interest, Inge, to whom he has already proposed marriage. He is forbidden to explain why he is leaving so abruptly, although viewers know the military secret, which then unfolds the film's second geography of the Spanish Civil War. In *The Great Love,* Paul is called up from leave repeatedly when he thinks he might enjoy a few romantic days with Hanna, the singer played by the beloved Ufa star Zarah Leander. Cinematically speaking, the private spaces of German romance are thrown over for the aerial geography familiar from the Luftwaffe films, the topography of Berlin in each case replaced by scaled and scaling maps of European conquest—exactly the geography of distorted cosmopolitanism at which the Reich was aiming, as I argued with Ritter's *Above Everything in the World.* This narrative navigation and tension between the amorous (civilian, private, intimate) and the military (official, public, coldly impersonal), supported by the spatial tension between the romantic metropolis and war-torn continent, is paradigmatic for what I am terming the *mobilization drama.*

Although the two films are parallel in this tension between the standard romance and the surprise air war careers of the protagonists, there are differences in the way in which the pictures negotiate these primary versus second geographies, differences that register the intervening (war) years between the two works. In *Request Concert,* after Herbert Koch's secret mobilization undercuts the trajectory of his courtship of Inge Wagner, the eponymous radio program (Request Concert) emerges to mediate between the two of them: the national radio program navigates wartime nationalized scales to the private and intimate as well. Given the spatial shift from Berlin nightspots to the wartime front—between which abrupt intercutting then emphasizes the distance between Inge and Herbert—the radio program is able to unite the two lovers when Herbert requests, for all to hear, the march that was playing at the Olympics, where they met. The implication is that the war would require a remapping and production of a new affective geography: first, that of the mobilization that threatens to undercut private life, but then that of the publicly mediated community that the Reich's technology can create with the radio. This latter one is a utopian third space, in Edward Soja's sense, where the scale of the private to the national is perfectly realized and balanced.[23] Despite some further travails—about which more below—the radio program brings them together, bridges the gap between the primary and second geographies of the film. In *The Great Love,* Paul is called up repeatedly, but Hanna attempts to schedule her musical shows in the major European metropolises where an actively deployed military man might be able to meet her: first Paris and then Rome, both cities that had, in the intervening years, been incorporated into the sphere of the Reich, so the film is deliberately sketching a new pan-European geography. The tension between love story and mobilization is resolved at the intersection of entertainment—Hanna's singing—and the military's new affective geography of Europe. Her audience in various cities comprises the Wehrmacht troops on a trip that Alon Confino emphasizes.[24]

3. If these narratives oscillate between the primary and second geographies of the spatially intensified plots, they offer parallel shifts in the locations of the narratives' (agentized) power and desire, as if these two key facets of any narrative are run through a refracting prism between the two geographies. This also diverges from the Luftwaffe films, in which the films' agentized core stays consistent from beginning to end, despite airborne challenges along the way. In *Request Concert* and *The Great Love*, this phenomenon is a variation of Jameson's reading of Algirdas Gremias on the actantial aspect of narrative—that is, the idea that stories locate agency in particular narrative figures that change over the course of the narrative. Jameson emphasizes this actantial aspect rather than mere agency because such actantial aspects can be located either in an individual character or in groups or types of characters as well as in space itself.[25] Similarly, toward the end of Ritter's *Above Everything in the World*, there is an actantial shift from any individual character to the Luftwaffe. These films featuring mobilization refract actantial power in surprisingly emphatic ways via the two geographies discussed above. Where agency seemed to reside is abruptly transformed based on the second geography, such that suddenly the actantial center of the film shifts to military time and space.

Although it is safe to say that in most narratives there is some transformation and even relocation of the narrative's actantial aspects, *Request Concert* and *The Great Love* do so in a spatially emphatic way: with the goal of producing new affective geographies, there is an intensified remapping of agency and authority whence it initially resides or was assumed to reside. For example, in *Request Concert*, the suave suitor Herbert Koch—the film's libidinal engine for its first twenty minutes—is suddenly subordinated to his military superiors and deployed, such that the nation abruptly exerts narrative sovereignty. But what the nation takes away, it gives back, at least representationally: the Request Concert radio program is able to repair the private damage it has caused in a newly mass-mediated Volksgemeinschaft (national community, emphatically ethnonational community). The mapping of the narrative relocates actantial efficacy from Herbert as private citizen and suitor to the Wehrmacht to the radio program, the last two both emanations of the nation in which trust is thereby fostered. The narrative's driving desire is similarly interrupted—Herbert, on repeated planned rendezvous, gives up Inge because "Dienst ist Dienst" (Service/duty is service/duty)—but is ultimately reinstated through a new geography: the radio program and the air force hospital that delivers Inge to Herbert at the end.[26] In *The Great Love*, the trajectory is similar. The private courtship is interrupted repeatedly by Paul's mobilization but ultimately reinstated with the kind of affective geography mentioned above. Both films restore the couple initially interrupted, but now their desire has mobilization built into it, a refiguring accomplished spatially as well as emotionally.

Rethinking the Heimkehrer as a Veteran: Continuities and Ruptures from Cinema under the Nazis

> Man sollte endlich auch auf der Leinwand Schluß machen mit den Landknechtsmanieren, mit der in den Kasernenstuben und in den braunen Jugendheimen gedrillten und dozierten Ideologie, mit der dazu gehörige Terminologie und mit der zur Schau getragenen deutschen Innerlichkeit . . . Auf dieses Tonart aber ist dieser neueste deutsche Film [*Wege im Zwielicht*] gestimmt. Sie ist uns nur wohl bekannt, und wenn sich nicht hin und wieder auch ein koketter Nihilismus in platten Allerweltsformulierungen einmischte, könnte Herr Goebbels das Ganze . . . in seiner Produktion aufnehmen. So gut paßt es da hinein.
>
> One should finally quit it with the soldierly manners, those that observe the drilled and memorized ideology from the barracks and the brown youth homes—quit as well its terminology and the German inwardness that belongs to the whole spectacle. But this new German film (*Ways into Twilight*) is tuned to such a key. It's well known to us now, and if, here and there, a bit of coquettish nihilism is mixed into the flat everyday formulations, Herr Goebbels could have integrated the whole thing into his productions. That's how well this kind of thing fits right in.

This unusually harsh review of Gustav Fröhlich's *Wege im Zwielicht* (*Ways into Twilight*, 1949) suggests something frequently neglected in the scholarship on the rubble film: the uncomfortable continuities from cinema made during the Nazi regime. It is generally presumed that rubble films intended and achieved a break from the Nazi-coordinated film industry and style, that they dispensed with the Traumfabrik (dream factory), or at least held it at bay provisionally. But this critical review underscores the unavoidable, if often-unmentioned, connection between (extremely) popular cinema under the Nazis and early postwar films. I aim to argue that one of the important but neglected continuities of the postwar film industry was the way in which rubble films invoked and played upon the travel and mobilization aspects of the war genre—that is, a certain kind of war film that was produced especially to initiate viewers into the increasingly militarized society, its affectively invested geography, and the growing personal sacrifices that would be demanded by the "total war." In tracing these continuities, I shall concentrate on a market that one important director-producer, Rolf Meyer, targeted, that of disoriented and often-angry returning veterans, for whom certain psychologies and predispositions would persist from the wartime imaginary. Meyer and his Junge Film-Union assumed that there would be a large audience for these kinds of veterans' entertainment: by the end of the war, some eleven million veterans landed in POW camps, the majority of whom returned to Germany. In three films it produced in this period, Meyer and the Junge Film-Union offered films with veterans as protagonists and invoked the complex geographies of mobilization I sketched above. *Ways into Twilight*, *Zugvögel* (*Birds of Migration*, 1946/1947; Rolf Meyer), and *Die Söhne des Herrn Gaspary* (*The Sons of Mr. Gaspary*, 1948; Meyer) all offer narratives that invoke, indulge, and at least attempt to refigure the mobilization kernel of the war genre mentioned above. All the films emphasize, with veterans as their main characters, a changing spatial sense via metaphors of mobility, the means of transportation technology, and a renegotiated affective geography for the postwar period.

Veterans were certainly one of the biggest and most conspicuous of the various social groups drifting around the chaotic, even anarchic, German landscape at the time. Studies like James Diehl's *The Thanks of the Fatherland* and Frank Biess's *Homecomings* have emphasized how these veterans—usually freed former POWs—became increasingly important to German self-understanding in both the post–World War I and post–World War II periods. It is often forgotten or overlooked how much veterans and, in particular, veteran organizations impacted society, politics, and culture in the Weimar Republic and the Nazi era; for a nefarious example, the Stahlhelm group started as a veterans' organization before becoming an important political player by 1926. These organizations were particularly effective at portraying veterans as victims rather than as any kind of perpetrator. Although the Dolchstoßlegende (stabbed-in-the-back myth) eventually (and revealingly) acquired a general resonance, its origins were clearly in casting and understanding the average veteran as victim par excellence. Veterans' celebration of the Fronterlebnis as a form of transcendence amid a putatively experience-famished civilization helped create a culture that could then be instrumentalized by the Nazis. The Nazis deliberately built on these powerful social, cultural, and political currents, officially satisfying veterans' demands as well as building them into the political culture of the Reich by introducing national holidays, staging ceremonies, and dedicating monuments.[27] For instance, Nazi officials gave veterans long-sought-after medals in recognition of their service, organized visits by World War I veterans to families of current soldiers, and mobilized them for home-front, particularly air, defenses.

Veterans thus played an important role in German political culture, as well as in the discourse about German victimization, from the late 1910s through the mid-1940s, such that their status would, in the early postwar period, undergo a fundamental transition when the Allies raised demilitarization to the level of core occupational policy. Demilitarization was the goal on which the Allies could agree the most, not least because it was, at the time, a basic interpretive frame for understanding the rise of Nazism, even if it has received shorter shrift in historical and cultural studies ever since.[28] After World War I—but in a very different direction—the veterans became an important flash point for debates about how to "cure" Germany: besides the official end of the Wehrmacht, there was an attempt to demilitarize the general culture, for instance, by tearing down war monuments that had gone up after World War I. Debates about the "deutsche[n] Soldat" (German soldier), the Heimkehrer, and the Kriegsgefangenen (POWs) were ubiquitous in the postwar public sphere.[29] In their resolve to transform the centrality of militarism in German culture, the Allies even considered exiling the Wehrmacht officer corps from Germany, an astonishing consideration if one recalls that no one who played a role in the Third Reich was (officially) exiled. This exiling was, of course, eventually ruled out, but the benefits for veterans were kept deliberately low (or canceled altogether, as they were in the Soviet Occupation Zone, or the SBZ) to try to root out remnant militarism: the goal was to discredit the previously privileged military class in Germany. On the other hand, the persistence of militarism as an ideology and even modus vivendi is confirmed by some German veterans' applications to join the British military as well as the conspicuous growth in the French Foreign Legion.[30]

Like the numerous newspaper and journals articles and debates, these postwar films about former Wehrmacht troops reflect ways in which political and cultural undercurrents could and did return in a culture that liked to claim it had broken cleanly from those of the 1930s and early 1940s. The review above that ties Nazi propaganda to *Ways into Twilight* could refer to any of these three films, as all focus on sympathetically depicted experiences of those from the Kasernenstuben (barracks). Although other rubble films offer veterans as protagonists—films like *The Murderers Are among Us*, *Somewhere in Berlin*, and *The Heavens Above*—these films focus on the challenges of the veterans' reintegrating into civilian life, a conflict that, in fact, comes to displace other struggles with demobilization. In the films I am discussing, however, the plots extend the mobilization aspect of war because the young veterans—often multiple veterans who remain together in the wake of their wartime camaraderie—have no home to which to return and spend the entire plots on the move.

An article at the time, in fact, divides the returning veterans into different groups of exactly this sort, and these films follow those veterans committed to resisting reassimilation into lawful civilian life.[31] *Ways into Twilight* follows a group of three young veterans who are on the run from the police because they are believed to be responsible for an accidental death, a metaphor for the fate of the veterans who could not deny the prevalence of death but who had not held themselves as responsible. *Sons of Mr. Gaspary* follows two brothers who were separated by the Nazi regime: one fled to Switzerland with his father and has grown up in the lap of Swiss luxury, while the other was left to fight for the Wehrmacht. In the postwar period, they are reunited in Switzerland but struggle with their divergent wartime experiences. *Birds of Migration* follows the travails of a group of young veterans as they try to find themselves in the postwar context; one of the protagonists, Georg, a veteran who left the hospital too early, learns that he will die from his untreated illness. Georg is played by Carl Raddatz, the star of the popular *Request Concert* (1940) and *Stukas* (1941) and analyzed above in *Above Everything in the World* (1941). His casting emphasizes the links of these rubble films back to the Nazi war films. I shall focus on the spatial aspects of *Ways into Twilight* but also connect its narrative trajectory to the other two films to argue that all the films rely on the spatial mechanisms that I have above located in the mobilization aspect of the war film: they all foreground transportation technologies and the affective pleasures therein, all eventually divulge a secondary map that displaces the narrative geographically, and all trace the consequences of that displacement for agency and desire to settle on a refigured, compromise third space between the two geographies.

Ways into Twilight opens in the Hannover train station, although its very first shot is unusual for this period because it refuses the conventional establishing shot of the setting. Instead, viewers first see a close-up long-take of Lukas, played by the film's best-known cast member, Gustav Fröhlich, who had become a star at age twenty-three as Freder in Fritz Lang's *Metropolis* and who continued as a matinee idol through much of the 1930s and early 1940s. Playing upon his fame and reputation as a suave gallant, the shot deliberately invokes the markings of the Heimkehrer familiar from films like *The Murderers Are among Us*, *Somewhere in Berlin*, or *Liebe 47!* (*Dear 47!*), including a craggy face, an eye patch, and a conspicuous limp yielding a noticeably slow gait. When the camera pulls back, viewers see that this seeming Heimkehrer is wandering through a train station whose floor is thickly settled with homeless people, refugees, and as viewers see in a remarkable panning point of view, veterans (figure 5.1).

This pan eventually settles on a group of three veterans, on whom the film will focus: Stefan, Peter, and Josef, all conspicuously dressed in uniform and playing cards on a Persil (laundry detergent) box (figure 5.2). The box is a clever metonymy for their indifference to denazification, as the certificates clearing one of denazification were known colloquially as Persilscheine (detergent certificates). It turns out that the film will not be, as the first shot implies, the story of Heimkehrer Lukas and his struggles to reintegrate into postwar society: Lukas is no typical Heimkehrer, as he is not returning home to a ruined household, to an alienated family, or with the symptoms of post-traumatic stress syndrome, all tropes familiar from other rubble films. Rather, he is already the gentlemanly mayor of a small town. The film will focus instead on the travails of these three young veterans, who, like Lukas but in a different way (expanded upon below), also invoke but dispense with the standard Heimkehrer film, in which a single returning protagonist typically finds his way back into an estranged family (*The Murderers*, *Somewhere in Berlin*, *The Heavens Above*, and *Before Us Life*). *Ways into Twilight* will focus on the fates of these young veterans, who have no home

FIG. 5.1 The Heimkehrer in the train station, visual clichés of the postwar period, *Ways into Twilight*. Digital frame enlargement.

to which to return and who are extending their wartime camaraderie into the postwar "black market."

The film introduces this social group (of veterans) in a space associated with soldiers and troop movement since the first mobilization films—namely, the train station. The first twenty minutes of the film—those in which the plot tension is usually set up, that particularly plotted problem that the rest of the film will attempt to resolve—is established in this transit space that implies a certain lifestyle in it, something made note of in various reviews of the film at the time.[32] It is no mistake, of course, that the primary mapping of the film is in the urban train station, which has long been associated with both mobilization and war films more generally. As we have seen since at least the mid-1910s *Dr. Hart*, trains had long been indispensable to German war planning and fighting, thoroughly interwoven with German troop movement to and from the front. Tellingly, they had entered the cultural imaginary, right down to the card playing, as they relate to mobilization—for instance, in the very different literary depictions of mobilization via train in Jünger's *Storms of Steel* (1920) or Thomas Mann's *Doktor Faustus* (1947). *Request Concert*, although it focuses on the fate and visual pleasures of the pilot Herbert Koch, nonetheless offers an important train-mobilization sequence in which Koch's love interest, Inge, accompanies her childhood friend, the young recruit Helmuth, to the train station to see him off. The long and visually striking sequence is remarkable not only because it foregrounds the train departure of soldiers going to war but also because of its deliberate construction of the departure not so much as a sad parting but as a festive celebration. Although families are breaking apart—husbands leaving wives, fathers leaving children—a cheerful mood pervades the entire sequence. To read *Request Concert*'s train station spatially, one can see how even as private lives are being uprooted and deterritorialized, new cheerful lives of mobilization are being reterritorialized via and in the train itself.

Even before their redeployment at wartime, train stations had always served as a particular kind of spatial intermediary, a contact zone: Schivelbusch

FIG. 5.2 Veterans and a visual gag about denazification "Persil" certificates, *Ways into Twilight*. Digital frame enlargement.

describes how the train station had served as the interface between two different modes of traffic, between the industrialized transportation technology that made modern society possible and the narrow medieval alleyways of the inner city.[33] Trains and train stations materialize what Henri Lefebvre calls "abstract space"—that is, formerly organic and preindustrial space changed irrevocably by modern industry.[34] In fact, their hybrid character highlights, in Lefebvre's memorable emphasis, the production of (abstract) space out of older urban forms. This Janus-faced character of the train station is reflected in the familiar architecture of European train stations, with their grand facades backing to the systematized lines of the industrial anterior. In the war genre, the military train and train station signified a number of transformative encounters that seem to elaborate the kind of interface that Schivelbusch suggests: they were where the locality met the faraway, where the home front met the war front, where the private family met the national project. This kind of transformative space housed the contradictions of those consenting to war, contradictions played upon effectively in Rainer Werner Fassbinder's invocation of the rubble genre in *The Marriage of Maria Braun* (1979), Lars von Trier's in *Zentropa* (1991), and Christian Petzold's in *Phoenix* (2014). They were also, as *Ways into Twilight* suggests and Jünger's *In Storms of Steel* describes, where the social relations of the private home were dissolved and welded anew into the camaraderie of the military.

In its 1948 postwar train station, however, *Ways into Twilight* deploys this modern transportation technology and its links to the war to underscore how this production of homogenized, abstract space has gone awry. If the train allowed for mass movement in a new way—for mass mobility and migration—by organizing and transporting a large number of people in an industrial fashion, *Ways into Twilight*'s train station represents a postwar return of the repressed masses: people are strewn about the floor, the industry has broken down into illegal contraband, and open violence is poised to erupt. The kind of industrialized society symbolized in the train and train station, the film suggests, has failed, something asserted even more sharply by the other setting in this primary map of the first twenty minutes: the ruins of the cathedral into which Stefan, Peter, and Josef pursue a commercial adversary, Fleck. As we saw, both *Dr. Hart* and *Westfront* transform their churches into wartime spaces—the former optimizing, the latter admonishing. Lukas watches from the cathedral shadows as the band of veterans chases and confronts Fleck, who throws some church cobblestones at them before tumbling down backward in the rubble. In following these black marketeers, the film cuts among high-contrast, low-key shots of the various religious icons and artifacts to highlight how society—the modern balance between the railroad station and the cathedral—has broken down, an invocation of the postwar hand-wringing about the prevalence of nihilism.[35] The film's poster also highlights the tension between the traditional, religious architecture and the young, misbehaving veterans. When the police appear to investigate, the band flees to the church and jumps on a train, where they happen to encounter Lukas again. Convinced he will report them, they also flee from him by jumping off the train in the countryside, a symbolic flight from industrial society that ultimately saves them.

With its train station full of homeless veterans, cathedral ruins used by black marketeers, and crowded train ride overflowing with the postwar period's wayward masses, the film's first twenty minutes sketch a destroyed industrialized space, mapping the failed war on to the broken society, militarization, and mobilization. This mapping that invokes the modern city, mobility, and war becomes all the clearer once the film suddenly shifts to its second affective geography in the countryside. As with *Request Concert* and *The Great Love*, the film offers an initially covert secondary space onto which it will map the protagonists and initial scenario sketched in the first segment of the film. In those mobilization films, however, the second geography was the militarized geography of Europe at war, a second affective geography that undercut, in each case, a private courtship—revisiting John Keegan's point about war's second geography (cf. chapter 1). In *Ways into Twilight*, the trajectory is the opposite: the first twenty minutes show the venality of veterans in the postwar period, veterans who inhabit the lingering, demolished, and discredited industrial spaces of the postwar period. There will be a stark transition from this life to the second geography in the countryside, reinforced in a transitional sequence that occurs right around twenty minutes as the three veterans hop off the train, when a montage of short episodes ensues that shows them roaming with no particular destination or goal. These kinds of social collages were common to other rubble films, and they seem directed at offering a kind of sociological cross section, as Gilles Deleuze puts it, into the peculiarities of the postwar landscape.[36]

This montage sequence of *Ways into Twilight*, however, opens with a scene that underscores the struggles with demobilization as well as that central aspect of the Nazi imaginary—namely, airpower. Having departed the train and on their own in the unfamiliar countryside—thus indulging the military imaginary of travel in distant and lovely lands—the three veterans approach abandoned bombers on an airfield in a memorable shot that invokes the visual pleasures of the Luftwaffe films (figure 5.3).

As they get close to one bomber, however, a sudden, off-screen voice, in American English, warns them off the plane, and they quickly run out of the frame. With the attraction of these visually striking bombers—so crucial to the pro-war Nazi films—*Ways into Twilight* is reinforcing the veterans' military habits and their persistence in the postwar period. When left uncertain, the veterans would revert to the military, military technology, and the association of airpower with World War II. Once displaced from the train station and train, they seem, in this context, to seek what Virilio, following Henri Bergson, terms the unique "perceptual luxuries" of films during wartime.[37] The rest of the montage sequence then reenacts the process of demilitarization and the uncertainty of demobilization after it. Since they have been admonished by a faceless Allied authority, they hurry off, wander around, searching unsuccessfully for work in the unfamiliar postwar landscape. It is at this point that they arrive, not coincidentally, in the small town of which Lukas is mayor, something viewers learn as Lukas returns and is greeted with a complaint about a destroyed bridge that a farmer in a horse-drawn cart needs to move his wares. This sequence arranges the scenario that will help the veterans find their way back to honest work and happiness: Lukas offers them work on the bridge as an opportunity to prove themselves.[38] It also begins to assert the film's covert second geography, since Lukas, who seemed to be just another Heimkehrer wandering in the postwar urban landscape, is actually the mayor of a small town where the rest of the film will unfold.

In a manner even more explicit than the plane scene, the sequence in which the three veterans stumble on the second affective geography of Lukas's small town cites *Request Concert* and, I would argue, the mobilization aspects of the war genre directly. When the veterans first find their way into Lukas's town, they are seeking shelter from a rainy night and let themselves into the steeple of the town's church. Two of the veterans sleep until the third, Josef, wakes them up abruptly by playing the church organ, an act, undertaken in the middle of the night, that gives away their whereabouts immediately. A veteran in a church who suddenly plays the organ references a scene in *Request Concert* in which a group of three soldiers hides in a church in France waiting for their comrades to return from an attack. There is, however, thick fog and the battle smoke, such that one of the soldiers in the church decides to play the organ and guide his lost comrades back to safety.[39] The organ-playing soldier, who is promptly killed by Allied artillery targeting the source of the music, connects the primary and second geographies of *Request Concert*'s mobilization spaces: in the film's second twenty minutes, during which viewers become acquainted with the localized Volksgemeinschaft (national community) around Inge on the home front, this same pianist entertains his neighbors with Beethoven piano pieces. In this manner, *Request Concert* apotheosizes the high culture of home

FIG. 5.3 Renouncing the pleasures of aerial warfare in the postwar period, *Ways into Twilight*. Digital frame enlargement.

but also deliberately refunctionalizes it for war and, ultimately, consecrates it with a soldier's death in a church. *Ways into Twilight* references this scene too but also refigures it in a way revealing for the demobilization aspect of the postwar genre. Here the organ playing is a cultural luxury after the war, giving vent to a musical urge that had to be repressed—adamantly not, as in *Request Concert*, fulfilled—during the fighting. This cultural indulgence, in fact, negotiates the way of the veterans back to the small town, negotiates between the initial spaces of bad German modernity in the Hannover train station and the second geography of the church, small town, and humble bridge rebuilding under the paternalistic but kindly mayor.

This reading of the primary and second geographies—as well as their association with metaphors of mobility and transportation technologies—is confirmed in an extended sequence about Peter, the clown of the three veterans. This sudden subplot, occurring at about fifty minutes into the film, lasts some five minutes in an eighty-minute film but seems abruptly introduced as well as subsequently out of place. The most plausible interpretation, it seems to me, is one that emphasizes its deliberate repetitive symbols—namely, the railroad and the bomber. Once the three veterans are enjoying their country idyll—happily working on the bridge and Stefan falling in love with Edith, Lukas's secretary—an abrupt sequence intercedes that threatens their relocated and redirected camaraderie. The film cuts suddenly back to the train, this time to a finely clothed, carefully coiffed, and heavily made-up young woman, Liselotte, portrayed by Sonja Ziemann in one of her first roles. It turns out that she is bound for the same small town in search of her boyfriend, the veteran Peter. Upon her arrival, he happily hosts her in his rustic room and primitive bed, at which she, in her urbane tastes, cringes. She convinces Peter to leave his provincial work and friends and return to Hannover and within the day has him sitting back on the city-bound train, which the viewers have not seen since the first twenty minutes (after which the veterans had been increasingly integrated into the small town). From this sudden development, however, the sequence rehearses an almost-direct repetition of the earlier plot and spatial points: regretting his decision to abandon his small-town friends and return to Hannover, Peter jumps from the train; leaves behind the urban modernity and the homogenized, abstract space it implies; and returns to the country to help finish the work on the bridge. The repetition even includes, as it did in the montage sequence mentioned above, his passing an abandoned bomber on an airfield, but this time, he walks right by without even hesitating and without having to be warned off it by the Allied authorities. Repetition and variance, as Raymond Bellour has observed, are a central part of the filmic narrative's generation of meaning and registering change, and the sequence rehearses the transition from the film's primary mapping in industrialized society to the secondary mapping in the country.[40] The variation within the repetition comes in Peter's willfully choosing it this time: he is not fleeing the train in desperation as they were in the original sequence, and he does not need to be convinced to stay away from remnant military technologies.

The sequence reiterates their conscious relocation on the second affective geography of the countryside by demonstrating how desire has been remapped. Urban sophisticate Liselotte embodies the desire for that kind of urbane modernity he has renounced, so his desire is likewise rerouted through the second geography of the film's cheerful country setting. He cedes his desire to remain loyal to his friends and to finish the project they have undertaken for Lukas. Power is thereby likewise rerouted in the country: at the train station, Lukas seems weak and ineffective, just another Heimkehrer limping across the postwar landscape, while in the small town, he is the mayor and benevolent patriarch to the young veterans. Although there is some unconvincing dramatic tension around Edith, his secretary in whom both the old mayor and the young veteran Stefan have a romantic interest, the main trajectory of the plot is clear: moving the three veterans from the Bahnhofsleben (train station life) in Hannover to the country allows them to reconcile to postwar society—and to return to life back in the German city. The film's excursion to the countryside, the narrative trajectory from a primary geography of bad German modernity to a second geography in the countryside that negates trains and planes in favor of horse-drawn wagons, ultimately allows a successful reentrance into society—namely, studying in Essen. It is a successful reentrance that is figured as a second, improved demobilization of the three comrades who finally left their uniforms behind.[41] The film's memorable closing image revisits and refigures, as the entire film has, the opening sequence in the train station: viewers see a long shot of the repaired bridge from downriver, such that the degenerate, black-market-ridden train station is replaced with the wholesome infrastructure of the country. This little bridge and its stuttering small-town traffic deliver a deliberately more modest form of mobility than that offered in films like *Dr. Hart* and the Luftwaffe films. In this very last shot of a film named with "Ways" in the title, viewers do not see even any characters they recognize, just anonymous carriages and trucks crossing the bridge slowly, as if to enforce that the entire filmic journey has indeed been about reforming the train station for the rural bridge, about the vagaries of postwar traffic.

This kind of narrative remapping and production of space via traveling veterans—one that engages the military's wartime imaginary to reform it—structures two of the other films made by Rolf Meyer and the Junge Film-Union in this period. The two other films operate similarly in terms of their protagonists (veterans), narrative trajectory (also involving travel amid multiple geographies), and even parallel scenes of indulging but then swearing off the perceptual luxuries of transportation technologies made popular in the cinema of the Third Reich (as with the airplane and train in *Ways into Twilight*). *Sons of Mr. Gaspary* focuses on two brothers who were separated before the war when their father, author of a book critical of the Nazis, fled with one of the boys to Switzerland. From there, they had very different fates: Hans grew up wealthy, happy, and (as the film and its posters are careful to depict) skiing in Switzerland, emphasizing again the intersection of the war and travel genres. On the other hand, Günther remained in heavily bombed Hamburg, fighting in the war and then landing in a POW camp. The secondary affective geography here is that of Germany itself, which, over the course of the narrative, wins out over cosmopolitan, affluent, but ultimately soulless Switzerland, where the film begins and which offers the many visual and affective pleasures of driving and skiing among the soaring Alps.

After an opening sequence with the father, Robert (Hans Stüwe), and his son Hans (Hans Holberg) enjoying themselves on a drive after skiing—they even come across Christina (Inge Landgut), a Danish skier whom both brothers will pursue—Robert brings his other son, Günther (Michael Tellering), and his estranged wife (the sons' mother) to the Swiss slopes for a reunion of the eponymous progeny. But it becomes clear by the end of the film that this is a fantasy life in which there is no future for either of them. The contrast between the brothers corresponds to the constructed geographies of the film, to the contrast between Switzerland and Germany, a contrast drawn with repeated references to mobility and the war: Hans, the son from Switzerland, brags to Christina how much he has been able to travel with his father, an altogether different kind of cosmopolitanism than Günther, who viewers learn, in another repetition-and-variance sequence, also saw the world, although only with the Wehrmacht.[42] Günther embodies the militarized cosmopolitanism that Ritter's *Über alles* explores and normativizes, and *Sons of Mr. Gaspary* even parallels Ritter's critical contrast with the image of Hans's superficial travel around the world.

The centrality of the air war to the German wartime experience is confirmed by one of the film's most interesting scenes that references both this kind of deviate cosmopolitanism and the nexus of airpower and perception that underpinned the Luftwaffe films. When the newly reunited family is relaxing on a ski lodge deck, they see some planes high above, and they hear an American debating a Frenchman about what kind of aircraft they are. Günther tries to intercede and correct them, but the American says, "I should know what it is; I flew one," to which Günther retorts, "Well, I shot many down." The American replies, "Apparently not enough, and anyway, the Germans started all the trouble." A tense exchange between an Allied soldier and former war adversary is rare for a rubble film, as is Günther's subsequent defense of the war: "We were only trying to live, we had the whole world against us, and now we have to listen while others shoot their mouths off." He rushes out and considers leaving Switzerland altogether. The scene is highly unusual on a couple of counts, not least because it gives depoliticizing and dehistoricizing vent to the complaints of many veterans; it is also no accident that the disagreement focuses on airpower, underscoring the centrality of airpower to the German military's self-understanding as well as the discourse of German suffering during the war.

In the end, in the tension between the two maps, that of Switzerland versus of Germany, the refigured complexities of Germany win on all fronts. The power would seem to reside with Robert, the father, who has brought his estranged wife and son to Switzerland and who has paid for their mountain travel that offers the film the bulk of its visual pleasures. Robert has specific plans for the future: he has invited Günther to study in Switzerland—even applied for him and offered to finance his fees—so that he may study with his brother, Hans. Completely inverting what viewers might expect from the adoring scenes of Swiss snow, however, Hans instead decides to join Günther back in Hamburg to study there and to found a typical postwar business: they sell their father's expensive car that Hans has driven from Switzerland and buy a truck that will allow them to do commercial hauling. Even the woman torn between them, the Danish skier Christina, chooses the brooding German complexity of Günther over the cheerful Swiss levity of Hans. Both authority and desire are thereby filtered through the contrasting geographies of the narrative, with narrative preference, as with Stefan in *Ways into Twilight*, for the suffering but recovering veteran.

The suffering, angry veteran of Meyer's *Birds of Migration* is, not coincidentally, Carl Raddatz, the actor who played the protagonist fighter pilot Herbert Koch of *Request Concert* and who was in the Ritter war films *Stukas* and *Above Everything in the World*. Given the success of both *Stukas* and *Request Concert* and the relatively advanced age of Raddatz for the role of a young veteran, the casting of him for the film's protagonist, Georg, must have been, at the least, conspicuous.[43] Like the films discussed above, *Birds of Migration* offers viewers a group of veterans wandering around the countryside, here hitching rides on passing trucks, flirting with likewise wayward young women. In a new twist on Meyer's now familiar traveling trope, however, the foregrounded mode of transportation in *Birds of Migration* (despite the aeronautical implication of its title) is water—namely, kayaks. Wolfgang, a young veteran, leads two comrades and two women they have met to a hidden cache of kayaks intended for him and his friends' comrade Georg, for whom he is still waiting. Whereas *Ways into Twilight* replaces the panoramic view of the train with adoring, pedestrian shots of the rural landscape, and whereas *Sons of Mr. Gaspary* afforded, in contrast to ruined Hamburg, the pleasures of mountaintop travel and skiing, *Birds of Migration*'s entire middle section offers viewers the nautical exploration of postwar Germany. It is a novel way to avoid the ubiquitous ruins and stands in stark contrast to the industrial visual pleasures of the 1930s and 1940s. In this way, it seems to echo the parallel alternative geography of the canals of war-torn Berlin that Helmut Käutner's *Unter den Brücken* (*Under the Bridges*, 1945) offers—a film also starring Raddatz. Given that the kayaks were hidden before the war from the bombing—abiding reminders of school-age adventure and antimodernity—they, too, offer an alternative mode of transportation to the modernity that concluded so unpleasantly in the war.

Paddling with his comrades in his kayak, Wolfgang pulls up alongside a ship at one point and finds Georg hidden in the shadows of its hold, as if Raddatz had been held in POW abeyance since *Request Concert*.[44] Georg has just returned from a POW camp, depressed, brooding, and sickly. Although Georg is clearly delighted to see Wolfgang and joins their revived kayaking group, he continues to brood, including during his first night with the group, when, next to the obligatory bonfire, he sits off by himself and then returns to the group to tell a harrowing (and presumably autobiographical) story about two prisoners who suffered endlessly in POW captivity. Slowly, though, both the beauty of the landscape seen from the kayaks and the attentions of a woman, René (Lotte Koch), in the group soften Georg: as in *Ways into Twilight*, the second affective geography closer to nature helps veterans heal such that they are ready to return to land and the postwar landscape of toil. The transformed second geography is neither the German countryside, as in *Ways into Twilight*, nor the Swiss Alps, as in *Sons of Mr. Gaspary*, but instead Germany's system of rivers and canals, a forgotten network close at hand that allows them to evade the difficulties of landlocked lives for a final indulgence of prewar/leisurely travel. But as with the countryside in *Ways into Twilight* and Switzerland in *Sons of Mr. Gaspary*, there is the need to overcome it: on the affectively resonant aquatic adventure, the group slowly pairs off two by two such that they are ready to relinquish their kayaks to return to the shore.

The only casualty of this return from the film's second geography is Georg himself: unlike *Ways into Twilight* and *Sons of Mr. Gaspary*, *Birds of Migration* rejects a happy ending for the angry veteran at its narrative core. Georg, viewers learn, had some unnamed illness, but frustration and despair led him to flee the hospital early. His newfound joy and love on the kayak trip lead him to seek out a doctor, who informs him he left the hospital fatally early. If the advanced medical culture of Germany has played a central role in the war genre from its earliest days during World War I, here it resurfaces not to save but to seal the dismal fate of a veteran. This is even more remarkable given that this veteran is played by Raddatz, a central member of the war genre star system under the Nazis. Eventually, Georg decides to give himself over to nature and paddles out to a watery death. Wolfgang aims to save him, but he cannot paddle out after him due to a dramatic (and dramatically shot) storm. Wolfgang ends up with Renee, the woman who had fallen in love with Georg. Renee gives up her love for Georg for the humdrum but healthy Wolfgang, whereas power seems to rest with the doctor, who became, for the context in general, as Jennifer Kapczynski has argued, an important figure of seemingly unreproachable social authority.[45]

The Long Journey to a Rediscovered Heimat

In two long journal articles about veterans' returning to Germany from POW camps (one entitled "Heimkehr: Der Kriegsgefangenen aus England" [Returning Home: POWs from England], the other "Heimkehr aus russischer Gefangenschaft" [Returning Home from Russian Incarceration]), both authors emphasize the parallels between the suffering of captivity and the challenges of returning home. Both articles, revealingly, foreground a key difficulty of this returning from the war—namely, the finding of a "second" or "third" Heimat back in Germany upon arrival in what will be, in many ways, an unfamiliar environment.[46] One article admits that even POW camps might have become familiar, even in some sense comfortable, so returning to find a new Heimat would challenge those soldiers yet again. The articles are both concerned with the kind of production of new spaces—the changes in space and psychologies as well as the intertwinements of those two—that would be required in the postwar period. In this chapter, I have focused on a key reason, and subsequent subtext, for this rediscovery and remapping of a postwar Heimat: that Nazism, both in its cultural imaginary and in its military execution, relied on organized mobility—that is, military mobilization and the refiguring of geography it brought with it. The impact of this mobilization would have to be worked through in a demobilization that not only sent the soldiers home but also required a deliberate recasting of the spatial relations that the Nazi culture industry had been careful to assert in some of its most popular products.

All three of these films follow a group of veterans on their travels that provide the films with many of their visual and affective pleasures. This travel negotiates multiple maps and produces multiple geographies—that is, an initial space is undercut by a second geography that relocates both desire and power from their primary mapping. The films, at their conclusions, settle on a third space, a compromise space that negotiates between the films' primary and second geographies. None of the films goes very far in representing such third spaces: the films are about the (literal) journeys to those spaces, journeys that afford the films the opportunity to indulge but also refigure the kind of narratives offered in the mobilization genre. The actual character of these third spaces—the ultimate rediscovery of the Heimat, as these two articles suggest—is something left for later. As the very harsh reviews suggest, these three films extend important aspects of the Nazi imaginary, even if ambivalently. They focus on wartime travels and tourism to which viewers would be accustomed while leaving open the precise character of the new Heimat for the 1950s, when the genre could be remade yet again, as I explore in the next chapters.

6

War in the Reconstructive 1950s: Genre, Espionage, and Cold War Subjectivities in the War Film

(*Canaris*, 1955; *The Fox of Paris*, 1957; *Rommel Calls Cairo*, 1959)

By the 1950s—after the beginning of the Cold War and the lifting of Allied cultural controls on the young Federal Republic—the war genre returned to West German screens full force. In fact, the war genre became the second most popular film genre in a decade ruled by them.[1] Although there were specific institutional and economic reasons for the prevalence and power of genre production in the 1950s, it is nonetheless remarkable that the war genre in particular would become so widespread soon after the disastrous war.[2] Although war films had been among the most popular of the Nazi regime (cf. chapters 4 and 5), that they could attain this kind of currency so soon after "the catastrophe" underscores the abiding attachment to these generic products. I would suggest, however, that reading the transformations of the genre—its institutional as well as commercial ups and downs—reveals not only the unfolding history of feature cinema but also the tectonic shifts in the culture of the early Federal Republic and the sorts of subjectivities that culture unfolded in the wake of the latest world war.

Although the Heimat genre has come to serve as a synecdoche for 1950s repressive memory culture, the war film was deliberately interwoven with an engagement with the wartime past. As Robert Moeller and others have argued, the early postwar years were marked not so much by silence about the past but rather by deliberately distracting modes of working through Nazi and German aggression and crimes. In this reconsideration of the putative repression about the past, various scholars have emphasized sundry aspects of this diversionary working through. For example, as both Moeller and Omer Bartov have detailed, such modes of working through the past often self-servingly highlighted Germans' own (highly constructed) victimhood at the hands of the Nazis.[3] Moeller has further highlighted the attention given to wartime expellees and postwar refugees; Elizabeth Heineman has emphasized the images of women in this period; Frank Biess has focused on the discussions around returning veterans; my own work has addressed the way in which debates about "Germany's young" and reeducation served wider memory contestations.[4] In all these studies, it becomes clear that the early postwar public sphere was marked not so much by silence via repression but rather by deliberate displacement and consolidation.

A central aspect of this complex, often-diversionary discourse of coming to terms with the past was, indeed, the prevalence and popularity of the war film genre in the 1950s. In fact, the genre itself helped work through the past, a generic mechanism I underscore with history and collective memory in chapter 3. For example, many films in the early postwar period refer to and (occasionally) critically engage the popular war films from the 1940s. The 1950s combat films suggest such continuities not only in their popularity but also in the many films made by directors and actors and so on who had worked during the Nazi time.[5] In this genre, then, it would certainly be misguided to speak of a Stunde Null (zero hour of slate clearing). Most of the films, however, tend to foreground the average German soldier as a victim of the Nazis and Allies alike while obscuring any sense of complicity or guilt in the Nazi-led war, war crimes, and other atrocities. As Jennifer Kapczynski writes, films like *Canaris* (1955) and *Der 20. Juli* (*The 20th of July*, 1955) negotiate the recent past in largely self-serving ways that offer the audience opportunities to follow characters whose behavior suggests that not all Germans were the same kind of perpetrators and, indeed, some were victims of, and even resisted, Nazi crimes.[6] Other scholars, like Erica Carter, Mark Gagnon, and Moeller,[7] highlight the way in which the films tend to divert attention and responsibility away from their protagonists at a historical moment in the 1950s, when West Germany was remilitarizing, joining NATO, and reinstating the draft.[8]

The longer-term history of the fictional genre I am attempting, however, reveals a slightly different aspect of these 1950s war films—namely, their transitional character. A certain sort of cultural hybridity, I want to suggest, fit these evolving German 1950s, a hybridity that grows clear in the arc of war films over the reconstructive decade. Although many scholars seem to write as if the 1950s war films constituted a homogeneous ensemble of films—that is, in film-industrial parlance, a fairly unified production trend—I would argue that there was a trajectory or arc over the course of the decade in terms of these highly popular films. While some have observed a trajectory of these war films over the course of the 1950s, they do not consider the reasons and terms of what John G. Cawelti has called the "mechanisms of generic transformation" late in the cycle.[9] For example, in reviewing the later *Fuchs von Paris* (*The Fox of Paris*, 1957), critics from the time linked the film to the then still unfolding war genre. But a number of the reviews also remarked on *Fox*'s novelty of a self-conscious fusion of the war with the spy genre, calling it "eine Mischung aus Landserdrama and Spionagereißer" (a mixture of war drama and espionage thriller; in German, the genre is usually called the Agentenfilm).[10] Some reviews considered this generic alloy effective, some not, but what is particularly noteworthy, I argue, is not only the hybrid generic product that *Fox* provides but also the way that the espionage genre emerges from within the war genre over the course of the narrative and from the arc of its key soldierly subjectivity. Both Janet Staiger, in a widely cited essay, and Rick Altman have analyzed how the film industry consistently works with hybrid genres, but they have not linked this phenomenon with the later stages of a generic cycle in particular, as occurs in *Fox* and the 1959 *Rommel ruft Kairo* (*Rommel Calls Cairo*).[11]

In both *Fox* and *Cairo*, the hybridization occurs late in the cycle to rejuvenate, literally, the genre as well as to take it in a different direction. This rejuvenating transformation is different from the generic mechanism of mythification that I traced in chapter 3. Rather, in this series of 1950s films, the genre is revived through a hybridization that manifests broader cultural trends of the Cold War. Unusually and revealingly, the spy aspects in these films are, I would suggest, self-consciously nested within their (by that point familiar) war aspects. Rather than building on the films' own moment of the early Cold War—which was, after all, rife with espionage—the emergent espionage genre in these films unfolds within the older war genre. This hybridity underscores the challenges of the transition to the postwar period: psychologies were still mired in a militaristic milieu to a surprising degree and in unexpected ways. Espionage is "nested" both in the sense of initially at home within, and then subsequently departing from, the semantics and syntax of the conventional war genre. Both films begin with generic semantics like soldiers with conventional uniforms, military missions, and battle maps, but then the films' syntax departs the standard generic mechanisms, in effect sublating such mechanisms in the later genre.

This genre hybridity fit the broader-based rethinking of the military and defensiveness that found itself in a peculiar postwar crucible: acknowledging the disaster of its military history while manifesting an increasing ambition to remilitarize. Despite the devastating destruction wrought by the war, West

German leaders were formalizing plans for rearmament as early as 1950.[12] By the mid-1950s, to parallel the controversial West German remilitarization, there was to be a "revolution in [our] thinking about national defense," as one lengthy piece in *Zeitschrift für Geopolitik* declared.[13] It was a piece indicative of a widespread rethinking of Germany's defense policies within the new geopolitical order.[14] After reviewing the previous "revolutions" in this kind of defense thinking—from the industrial, colonial, and then World War periods—the article calls for an end to the old practices of violence. Notably, there has to be a shift away from weapons and toward new methods, which include both economic pressure and espionage. Instead of soldiers submerged in massive armed forces, the new kind of defense action will be individuals working alone and in small teams. This is precisely what one finds in the reformed war films of this period: espionage becomes a key pivot point in this period, for both national and increasingly individual agency, and helps remake and recast the war film in the direction of postwar subjectivity. And this transformation in soldierly, increasingly spy subjectivity is negotiated in these films via the changing affective geographies of the conventional genre.

A Late-Cycle Trend: *Canaris* as a Humble War Film

Alfred Weidenmann's 1955 *Canaris* offers an earlier example of this generic hybridity, one that establishes an important industry context for the war-espionage films later in the decade. Despite its similarities, it also provides a telling contrast to the later films I shall be investigating, highlighting the arc of the hybrid genre as the genre cycle progressed over the 1950s. The very popular and award-winning *Canaris* deliberately negotiates the wartime past with a new type of citizen-soldier—or, rather ironically, quite an old citizen-soldier, refigured and recast for the postwar situation. The film would seem to be deliberately revisiting and revising, as Erica Carter notes, the "genius" films of the Third Reich that emphasize the depth of "personality" of figures like Otto von Bismarck, Carl Peters, or Paracelsus.[15] But in the postwar context, *Canaris* offers, in lieu of this putative genius, a humble servant of the nation whose reflective manner and modest cardigan signal a different type of military leader–protagonist for postconflict West Germany. Such a refigured mode of military subjectivity was especially important for the particular historical moment into which *Canaris* was released.[16] By the mid-1950s, West Germany was in the midst of its controversial remilitarizing, and the film was released just a few months (January 1955) before West Germany's joining NATO (May 1955). In these various regards, the film belies the "repressive hypothesis"[17] that the 1950s was not engaged with Germany's recent past and demonstrates how war films, as one of the most popular genres of the 1950s, helped negotiate both past wars and future politics, especially as West Germany looked longingly toward "normalization" via the Western Alliance.[18]

Canaris is, however, a rather peculiar war film, if one has in mind the longer-term syntax and semantics of the combat genre. Its protagonist never fights in a battle nor even physically participates in one because he is the head of military intelligence and thus operates primarily through his ring of clandestine operations, disguise-adopting agents, and distant contacts. Deeper into her analysis, Carter briefly admits that the film is an "alloy" of war and spy film, but I wish to highlight and elaborate upon this curious generic development for one of the decade's most celebrated "war" films. By being sensitive to the film's generic operations, one can observe how it anticipates the further hybridization of the war genre later in the 1950s.[19] If one takes, as I am suggesting, this set of three war-espionage films (Weidenmann's *Canaris* from 1955, May's *Fox* from 1957, and Werner Schleif's *Cairo* in 1959), one can observe how this hybridity continues to unfold—and continues to negotiate the novel sort of soldierly subjectivity, and the spaces that house it, at the core of the postwar genre.

Canaris follows the late career and ultimate arrest of one of the most important commanders in the Nazi intelligence community. Wilhelm Franz Canaris was appointed head of military intelligence in 1935, thus an elevated position fully supported by Hitler, whose agenda Canaris served happily through the Spanish Civil War, through the Austrian Anschluss, and into the Sudetenland crisis.[20] The film, not surprisingly, downplays this highly Hitler-complicit background and foregrounds instead an old-fashioned military man, not least by contrasting him to the aggressively Nazi Reinhard Heydrich (Martin Held). Above all, Canaris remains "loyal to Germany" and therefore to protecting his men even from Hitler, against whom he eventually conspires, first with the group around Ludwig Beck in 1938 and then with Claus von Stauffenberg in 1944 (although his role in both plots is disputed by historians). The film manages to recast Canaris the commander as a privately reflective individual deeply disturbed by the Nazis' wars of aggression and their version of public history with which they justify this aggression.[21] At various moments in *Canaris*'s plot, the film stages these wars largely through newsreels that would have been familiar to many viewers from the 1940s. But even as he reproduces the images and voice-over from the Nazi era, director Weidenmann carefully stages Canaris's reactions to, and interpretations of, them. Viewers watch this replay of history but now with Canaris's skeptical reactions amounting to a counterhistory to the Nazis' triumphant trumpeting of one victory after another.

The film offers in the person of Canaris an important update to the genre's recurring military commander: here the commander is someone who, against the grain, contemplates the meaning of his own military actions and recent history generally, with the commander's "contemplation" (*nachdenken*) a repeated theme. If the physical distance of commanders from the front was often marked as a problem in the genre (cf. *Westfront*, discussed above), *Canaris*'s distance allows him to reflect more honestly and accurately on the nature of this dubious war. These newly contemplative commanders are even willing, as Canaris is, to plot against their own leaders in the service of higher values. This is, indeed, a renegotiated aspect of the commander from earlier in the genre, where most contemplation was on the meaning of camaraderie and loss (e.g., the commander's private moments in *Medal of Honor* and *Squadron Lützow*), highlighting the love and sacrifice at the core of the war genre's positive messaging.

Tellingly, however, this celebration of the older, wiser, and even staid Canaris is balanced throughout the film with an ensemble of younger players who offer the film many of the conventional "pleasures" of a war film, especially those pleasures of the genre that I have been tracking throughout this study—namely, those of faraway spaces, of foreign travel to arrive there, of the affective thrills of modern mobility. Carter highlights the clear contrast between Canaris and Heydrich as one between Wilhelmine tradition and Nazi modernity, and certainly there is substance to that dramatic conflict (not least on how they differently regard the Nazis' blitz victories in 1939 Poland and then in 1940 France).[22] But even as the film revisits many of these events, it, as film, affords the genre's familiar affective pleasures through its youthful operatives. The film also manages to connect cardigan-wearing Canaris to the heady heights of modern espionage and the alternative geographies it creates: with his own spy network, complex phone systems, and clandestine communications to manipulate them.

With Canaris and his team of young agents, the film would seem to be suggesting an alternative, better modernity and future for Germany's military. This alternative thinking looks forward to a postwar order for smaller-scale military activity and secret missions that was propagated above in the reform-minded 1950s military thinking. With his paternalistic relations to agents like Fernandez (Peter Mosbacher), Captain Althoff (Adrian Hoven), and Irene von Harbeck (Barbara Rütting), Canaris gathers intelligence throughout Europe, with the film offering subplots in, and pulse-quickening visits to, France, England, and Spain. Here the intelligence-gathering forays may, plotwise, be very brief, but their excitement is explicitly exploited in lieu of the war film's standard territorial conquest—both territory and conquest would have been problematic in the 1950s. Rather than large-scale attacks and territorial capture and conversion, Canaris's stable of agents uses multiple disguises, minicameras, and even postage-stamp codes to communicate their furtive findings, underscoring the genre's, and war's, transformation for the later 1950s.

This curious alloy of the war genre in the film underscores the metamorphosing character of culture in the 1950s, and *Canaris* offers, in a well-known cultural icon, an older and older-style officer renegotiating the subjectivity at the core of the West German military as it looked toward normalization. The model of "citizen-soldier" became increasingly important later in the decade. Further, I argue how the film innovates the visual and affective pleasures of the genre by extending the war film's travel and foreign offerings to the very modern geography of espionage. This refigured spatial assemblage for the genre pushes the newly minted citizen-soldier one finds in the protagonists of *Canaris* or *08/15* (see Mark Gagnon) into literally new territory—indeed, a new kind of affective territory, to be infiltrated and engaged rather than conquered. The trend will further emerge in May's 1957 *Fox*, which also unfolds Germany's better military commanders' willingness (allegedly) to act against Hitler. But it shifts more of its plot from older commanders like Canaris to the young spies only hinted at in the earlier film. And the 1959 *Cairo* takes an actor from among *Canaris*'s highly mobile and disguise-adopting agents, Adrian Hoven, and builds a plot around him even further afield, and farther in the field, in the colonial/postcolonial struggles of British-controlled Egypt.

A Fox in Paris? A Young Tank Commander amid Urban Topographical Spaces

Canaris was a phenomenal success and foreshadowed an important industry context for the later direction of the West German war film.[23] In this reconstructive decade—for instance, in both *Fox* and *Cairo*—at the core of the narrative is a young soldier of the sort one would expect from the conventional genre. But because this soldier serves increasingly as a spy, he operates differently politically as well as spatially. In unfolding the subjectivity of a spy versus soldier, the films negate many of the genre's traditional scalar operations (cf. chapter 3). On the one hand, in these late-cycle hybrid war films of the 1950s, there abides the affective thrill of mobilizing travel, especially across borders and into foreign lands, what I term the genre's *affective geographies*. The genre's shift to espionage allows the films to continue indulging in the unabashed pleasures of wartime tourism. On the other hand, espionage films unfold very different subjectivities and scalar processes with their mobilizations. If a core aspect of the war genre is an effectively collectivizing scaling of the individual to the unit and then nation, espionage films increasingly negate the relevance of this unit, leaving the link to the nation more attenuated. Undercutting the careful scaling at the core of the war narrative, such films conjure an ambiguous relationship to the unit and then subsequently to the armed forces and the entire nation. What was a mass mobilization unto collective psychology in the conventional genre becomes increasingly individualistic foreign travel in these generic hybrids.

These newer subjectivities and scales are spatialized in specific ways, underscoring how both genres are among the "more spatial" of films and genres, as Fredric Jameson describes.[24] For example, rather than conventional accumulation in collective, industrial spaces one sees in conventional war films (like *Sword and Hearth* from 1916, *Inexpiable* from 1917, *Camaraderie* from 1931, or *Junge Adler* [*Young Eagles*] from 1944), the culture around these late 1950s war films has shifted to the bodies of individuals as the locus of a strategy of accumulation. The individual body, as David Harvey has put it, becomes a crucial tactic for accumulation in late capitalism.[25] Instead of transforming social spaces, per the earlier genre, these films change individuals and how they fit into their sociospatial contexts. The revealing location, the perfect nonplace, for such a fundamental shift in the spaces and scales of accumulation is a foreign city. Such an extraterritorial locus serves as the key (neo)militaristic setting in the affective geographies of these hybrid war-spy films. As we saw above, faraway cities or towns were featured ambivalently in films of the Nazi regime like *Request Concert*, *The Great Love*, and *Above Everything in the World*. But this late-cycle recurrence of foreign cities in an increasing espionage milieu realizes the revealing transformations of the genre's key spaces, especially from what geographers track as a hierarchical topographic to a networked topological space, with its accompanying shifts of subjectivity.

In the opening scene of *Fox*, for instance, viewers find themselves on street-level Paris by way of a typically French street café—I write "typically" advisedly, since *Fox* is deliberately inviting the tourist-viewer to read this setting as the heart of a place and its culture, much as one would be invited to read attractions like the Eiffel Tower. Such an ontological reading of the café by a tourist-viewer is confirmed in the film's publicity packet, which includes a postable page of text (and a small insert photo) about the relationship of the French to their cafés. It identifies the café as the place to gain insight into the "essence" of the city and the French generally. In this way, as *Fox*'s marketing suggests, the film's slow dissolve from the orienting urban signpost to the café affords viewers, within its overriding cinematic tourism, an exhortation to ethnographic engagement: it deliberately offers up a chance to read the typical French experience in addition to the Parisian destinations suggested in the signpost. Eventually, the film will arrive at the familiar attractions of/around Paris—Versailles, Sacré-Cœur, and Notre Dame—but it initiates its viewers to the film's novel affective geography via this typically quotidian place. For a war film, it is a telling location and locus indeed.

What transpires in this scenic, vibrant forum, however, underscores the late genre's complication of urban territories. This is not, as it was in *Westfront*, a pleasant touristic detour to civilian life then contrasted to combat later. Instead, *Fox* offers the same complication for space as contested territory that the war genre has afforded since its beginning, only now within the inscrutable maze of the city. The voice-over informs us that as Germany awaited the continental invasion, and France its liberation, the "underground war of the intelligence services" was in full swing. The camera finds two men in trench coats intensely observing a young woman sitting at one of the outermost tables. Although the two men seem engaged in a flirtatious jousting of gazes for the woman, one of them (in a fedora) abruptly observes that "he" is not coming anymore, that he must have been warned. The exchange shifts from the apparently amorous overtones of a typical café interaction into something more considered, slips into something more sinister. Within seconds, a gentleman appears and stands without looking next to the woman, who whispers emphatically, "André, Gestapo!" He tries to flee, but the two men who had been observing the young woman jump up and apprehend him.

With its opening-scene street café, *Fox* explores the Janus-faced character of the familiar visual pleasures of the city, reminding viewers how the visually engaging city also became the groundbreaking laboratory for modern surveillance. The rise of urban surveillance was interwoven with cities' status as modern spaces, especially as venues for the key technologies of modernity (like electricity), as Wolfgang Schivelbusch has explored in *Disenchanted Night*. Long before Foucault singled out the panopticon or Gilles Deleuze thematized technologized tracking in "societies of control," Robert Louis Stevenson noted how the illumination of the urban spaces would heighten the horror of the city by casting a surveilling light on its street.[26] Slightly later, Walter Benjamin regarded surveillance as entwined with the modern experience of Paris itself: the modern city not only hosted and grounded the famous flaneur but also yielded the detective surveillance of the flaneur and the streets he (always "he" in Benjamin's description) roamed, not least through the new technology of photography.[27] As with various aspects of modernity—like the airplane in chapter 4, above—the Nazis radicalized the inchoate, incipient tendencies of the late nineteenth and early twentieth centuries: in their careful monitoring and managing of dissent, the democratizing public sphere of the café (pace Jürgen Habermas) became, as in *Fox*, a sinister venue for surveillance and control.

What appeared to be the typically pleasing place in the affective geography of France—where, the marketing materials for the film highlight, the tourist can best get to know the Gallic culture—has been shown to be contested territory between the occupying and native forces. It is a secretly vectored, surveilled space that, in this war-espionage hybrid, rises to replace the shellable landscape or bombable cities of the earlier genre. But from this novel place, the hybrid film follows the arrested resistance operative André and the arresting agents to a more conventional setting for the war genre, to the local commander's headquarters. The genre's recurring distance to the commander is mapped over the city and here, tellingly, to a requisitioned luxury hotel. *Fox* locates the commanders in the famous but now occupied Hotel Lutetia, where viewers meet the film's uniformed contingent, including Generals von der Heinitz (Paul Hartmann) and Quade (Martin Held) as well as Colonel Toller (Viktor Staal) from the führer's headquarters back in Berlin. As in the wartime *Medal of Honor* and *Stukas*, requisitioned luxury quarters were long part of the genre's depiction of Germans in France. It is notable that Hartmann (here Heinitz) and Staal (Toller) are both actors well known from the longer-term war genre of the Nazi period, with the former (Nazi-era) "national actor" Hartmann in both *Medal of Honor* and *Above Everything in the World* and a noticeably younger Staal as the male-lead Luftwaffe pilot of the extremely popular *The Great Love*. Along with Held (Quade) and Peter Mosbacher (Major Wedekind)—both appearing in the Reinecker-written and national-film-prize-winning *Canaris*—*Fox* is invoking the star system of war films, built in part on generic continuities from the 1930s and 1940s as well as their postwar innovation. Another such generic linkage to the wartime war film is the decidedly younger but likewise uniformed protagonist: playing the eponymous "Fox" Captain Hans Fürstenwerth is Hardy Krüger, one of the young people discovered for the 1944 *Young Eagles*, the curious Luftwaffe film that offers little by way of actual aerial combat. The late-war *Young Eagles* focuses instead on the economic aspects of the genre, especially young people's collectivized contributions to the factory manufacture of fighter planes—in many ways, it is more of an Erziehungsfilm (educational film). From this somewhat dubious debut, Krüger went on to become one of the most beloved actors of German genre films in the 1960s and 1970s, and in *Fox*, he comes to embody the transition from a wartime eastern-front soldier to a Paris cosmopolitan, a longed-for itinerary of many postwar German citizens.

First, however, as with most young protagonists, a certain education needs to be initiated by the film's narrative. After the opening café arrest, the camera finds the young Fürstenwerth entering the commander headquarters in the Lutetia, where he asks to see General Quade (Held), who viewers soon learn is Fürstenwerth's uncle. The lavish Lutetia lobby likewise attracts a tourist gaze—in addition to guests like Picasso and Josephine Baker, Joyce was said to have written part of *Ulysses* in the famed hotel—but the spectacular interior is dominated by uniformed Wehrmacht. While waiting for his uncle-general to appear, Fürstenwerth happens to watch as a handcuffed André, accompanied by the SD agents (the Nazi security services operatives) from the café, enters for questioning: the Lutetia was, in fact, the infamous headquarters of Nazi counterintelligence. When André is approached approvingly by Colonel Toller (Staal)—"Ah, we've finally got him!"—the Frenchman abruptly flees, sprinting through the lobby and out a window and into a waiting car under gunfire from the guards. A frustrated Toller turns to Fürstenwerth, who has watched these events with detachment and asks why he did not also fire his pistol at the long-sought-after underground operative. A completely unflustered, even impudent Fürstenwerth answers that he did not know that one is supposed to fire at civilians in Paris. The Wehrmacht's shooting of civilians was a key issue throughout the war and then postwar West Germany, where many continued to defend the army's putatively pristine "honor." This telling interaction in the lobby—a key urban space since at least the 1920s, as Siegfried Kracauer has noted in his famous short piece[28]—underscores the entirely different nature of combat in occupied Paris. Although some of the semantics of the war film are there, including uniforms, guns, and numerous actors from the star system of the longer-term genre, the hotel-inhabiting Toller is educating Hans that the city will be a different affective geography, a different kind of battlefield indeed.

These different kinds of battle and battlefield spaces are confirmed in the next major sequence, when the assembled generals discuss the military challenge in front of them with Toller and his staff.[29] Here, too, the genre's manipulations of space reveal the kind of transformation that I am highlighting in the 1950s cycle of war films. Telling is the genre-familiar invocation of the narratively crucial map, with its space-territorializing and scale-making mechanisms that I have tracked as a core part of the genre's semantics since *Dr. Hart*. Maps often intervene at key moments in a film's narrative to orient viewers in certain ways. They also manifest even wider-ranging spatial processes. *Fox*'s crucial meeting sequence opens with the general commanding the defense of France, von der Heinitz, standing in front of a massive map of the fateful front to come: the enormous, freestanding map images northern France, the English Channel, and all the United Kingdom with the amassing Allied forces carefully inscribed on it. This particular map temporally locates the viewer in the milieu of spring 1944, in the run-up to the Allied invasion of France—as one review notes, Hartmann's Heinitz seems to invoke Commanding General Carl-Heinrich von Stülpnagel.[30] But the map also conjures a conventional battlefront, with its clearly drawn sides, geographical/Channel obstacle, and coming conflict. A slow push in introduces General von der Heinitz not so much studying the map as mulling its ominous implications, with a mien hinting at problems to come (figure 6.1).

The subsequent tension in the meeting becomes clear when Heinitz's underling Quade presents the map to Toller. Heinitz articulates that the plans to defend the coast are futile and will result in tens of thousands of needless casualties. Toller, however, represents the perspective of the führer's headquarters, in deliberately emphatic, even fanatical tones: the enemy must be met full on as soon as they cross the Channel, and the hesitation of the Wehrmacht command in France reflects a defeatist tendency to pointless bean counting. He declares, against Heinitz and Quade, that headquarters back in Berlin will not reconsider, let alone revise, the plans criticized by the local commanders.

This discussion among officers about both battle tactics and campaign strategy locates the film squarely in the war genre: it spells out, writ large, the kind of landscape-to-territorial struggles and national-scaled affective geography that have been part and parcel of the genre since its beginnings. But it also manifests the older modes of military thinking, here concerning the long-awaited Allied invasion, from which defense theorists in the 1950s were distancing themselves. With its conspicuous 1950s agenda, *Fox* is foregrounding the kind of disagreements that could divide commanders, here concerning the largest amphibious invasion of all time. The film's very postwar and late-cycle implication is clear: the führer's representative Toller is fanatically insisting on pointless deaths in a self-proclaimed "dynamic attack strategy" that hardly amounts to a considered defense. In this critique of wartime leaders and their misguided planning, *Fox* recalls one of the key elements of the genre's syntax that I track throughout: the distance of the commander from fighting forces and its consequences for effective scaling for the individual soldier to the unity and nation. Heinitz invokes this (physical and psychological) distance back to Hitler's headquarters versus the local facts on the ground to advocate reconsidering the current, doomed plans. The führer (present here only in portrait) sends a minion to dispatch any dissent from a tellingly detached distance. Here, as in

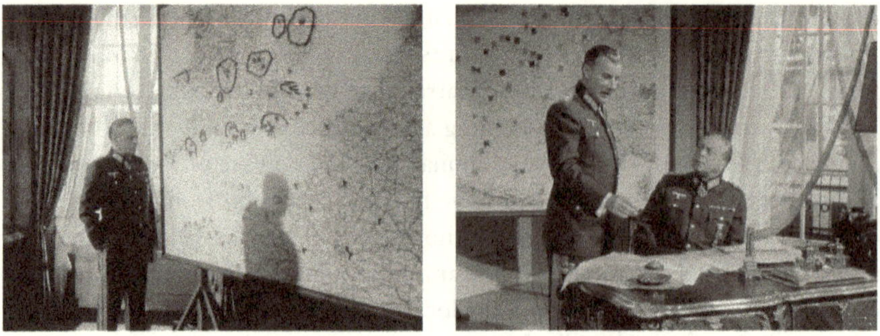

FIG. 6.1 Contrasting maps of the front versus of the occupied nation, *Fox*. Digital frame enlargement.

Westfront, the distance of the commander signals a psychological detachment from realities on the territorial ground as well as the ultimate subversion of scale at the core of the genre.

After Toller makes clear the distant führer's inflexibility, the camera revealingly follows Heinitz and Quade as they retreat from the meeting room to Heinitz's private office (the office has a telling contrasting map). The use of a hidden back room was a staple of the detective and espionage genres in the 1920s—perhaps above all in Fritz Lang's labyrinthine spaces winding their ways throughout his work, hidden spaces that abruptly open up, literally, a whole other dimension of the ever-twisting plots. Here, however, the back room, trapdoor sort of space is used to underscore not clandestine complexity but the moral goodness of generals turning increasingly into spies. Heinitz expresses to Quade his despair about the current plans and Toller's intransigent position on them. Heinitz has been unable to sleep, thinking about the tens of thousands about to die and how they not just are soldiers but "have wives, mothers, families." He lies awake at night, listening to all the church bells and clock towers of Paris and thinking and contemplating all this: both *denken* and *nachdenken*, the dialogue underscoring a recurring theme as well from *Canaris*, the need for those serving not only to think about but to contemplate their actions. As with *Canaris*, the film is conspicuously invested in rehabilitating select top commanders as considerate and caring of their underlings—here in the body of one of the Nazis' war genre's most celebrated actors. If the führer's distance is leading them down a deathly rabbit hole, Heinitz/Hartmann's on-site proximity to his underlings, including Quade and other soldiers with whom he is consistently imaged, yields the appropriate rumination on, and regret about, their portentous circumstance.

In this deviation from the commanders back in Berlin, the maps are, as so often in the genre, particularly telling for the emergence of a second affective geography. The larger map with which the sequence begins and that Quade presents to the plenum suggests the traditional wartime and war genre kind of calculable topographic space, with easily discernible boundaries, predictable conflicts, and clearly drawn sides. As Heinitz confesses his doubts in his private office, however, viewers may notice how he is framed with a noticeably different map—namely, a more detailed one of France that pushes the issue of the opposing side, clear border, and looming, legible front to the obscure periphery. The map with which he is now framed instead shows the internal positions and murky networks within France itself, emphasizing the internal complexities of the space of the occupied country, internal complexities that, rather than the obvious battles to come, eventually dominate and determine *Fox*'s espionage plot. Instead of clear and fixed scales, Heinitz's private map reflects how the film's affective geography resembles the spiderweb network of topological space rather than the clearly drawn topographies of most war films.[31] A space of "completely mixed up scales" is symptomatic of what Latham emphasizes is topological—a space to remake the war genre and its concomitant scaling and mapping.[32] Above all, such topological spaces support the precariousness of traditional hierarchies and conventional scaling—exactly those hierarchies that will wobble and loosen to allow for soldiers to become double agent spies.

The film's first major sequences, covering the film's opening fourteen minutes, barely involve the young protagonist in any substantive way. These opening sequences instead sketch a spatial context for him to be transformed from a conventional soldier into a newfangled spy. Although he is briefly introduced to Colonel Toller, the emissary from Berlin, Fürstenwerth's main contribution in these opening fifteen minutes is not to have shot at the French resister André. Rather than focusing on Fürstenwerth (or offering his focalization, narratively speaking), those first fourteen minutes show how this war film offers a very different setting—namely, a topological city space of confusing cafés and back rooms, of intertwined interests and conflicting networks: the visually pleasing street café has intelligence services working at cross-purposes—surveilling, evading, abruptly arresting—while the war has begun to rend the ranks of occupying German officers, now debating, deriding, and secretly scheming. The first appearance of Fürstenwerth in the Lutetia lobby reveals that he does not yet comprehend the complexity of this refigured wartime geography after his years on the eastern front. Fürstenwerth's second substantive experience, however, demonstrates how the tourist urge with which the film opens, and on which it clearly banks for viewers, intersects this topologically complex geography—indeed, his tourist experiences eventually pull him inextricably into such topology's troubling webs.

After Heinitz confesses his private doubts to Quade in a back room away from the Berlin contingent, and Quade confesses his anti-Berlin machinations to Heinitz, the film cuts to Fürstenwerth in broad, exterior daylight, now in a civilian suit, enjoying the grounds of Versailles as a tourist. As Carter has noted of *Canaris*, the apparel of the soldiers in the 1950s underscores the reformed vision for a citizen-soldier.[33] In *Canaris*, this refigured military kit entailed a cardigan, highlighting Canaris's older, wiser, and more contemplative ways.

With Fürstenwerth, as a younger, more flexible spy, it will be the civilian suit that allows him to submerge himself into the French capital, a soldier-tourist going civilian-native. In both cases, the long-standing generic semantics of the soldier's uniform register the passing of time. Fürstenwerth's apparel and different, more cosmopolitan sensibility are immediately underscored, as May frames the smartly dressed young captain with another Wehrmacht soldier passing by, although this one is in full uniform and does not seem nearly as engaged with the picturesque, historical surroundings (figure 6.2).

The images of Fürstenwerth with uniformed Germans enjoying the palace and its enormous garden offer viewers the tourist pleasures of the famed sight as well as the distinction being drawn between Fürstenwerth and his uniformed comrades. In fact, when he happens to see a child fall into one of the enormous garden fountains, viewers watch him sprint away from his comrades, literally and figuratively.

Upon saving the boy, Fürstenwerth is approached by an appreciative young woman who, rather inexplicably, was riding around the Versailles grounds in a horse-drawn carriage. *Fox* thus introduces the last main principal, Yvonne (Marianne Koch, with French-accented German), at the very moment that Fürstenwerth has divided himself from his comrades, both physically (sprinting away) and narratively (it is not clear why no other soldiers rush to help the drowning child). In gratitude, Yvonne brings the soaked Fürstenwerth back to her family's nearby château for a dry suit, but the château turns out to double as a base for the French resistance. With his rescue of the French boy, Fürstenwerth has been pulled back into the network that the film introduced in its café opening, treading upon labyrinthine spaces that will eventually spell his doom. When Yvonne's family realizes that Fürstenwerth is German, they regret offering to help him, since "there has never been a German in this house," and they "don't love his fellow Germans." But at the paterfamilias's insistence, they extend the promised hospitality, giving Fürstenwerth a dry suit, one from Yvonne's dead brother Marcel, who was killed fighting the Germans. The film's initial theme of (Wehrmacht) uniform versus (civilian) suit (one familiar from the 1950s genre) has now been extended to the new, Francophile identity that Fürstenwerth will unfold along with his costume change. Hans will not only draw close to this family but also eventually become party to their political machinations: the resistance officer André enters, with Hans recognizing him immediately from his Hotel Lutetia flight from German authorities.

In May's framings of Fürstenwerth in this château and then increasingly in other interiors, Fürstenwerth is imaged with mirrors around him, mirrors that evoke not only Versailles but also the malleability of identity amid the topological spaces that *Fox* carefully cultivates. This new identity open to the natives allows his uncle, General Quade, to propose to his nephew utilizing these new connections to the French resistance—not least the mutual attraction he and Yvonne clearly feel—to give the Allied forces the Wehrmacht's plans for coastal

FIG. 6.2 Versailles tourism in a civilian suit, *Fox*. Digital frame enlargement.

defense. Quade's ploy to leak the plans for coastal defense so that they would be abandoned lacked a convincing way to deliver them credibly to the opposite side—the Allies would have suspected the leaking of bogus, misleading plans. But Fürstenwerth's new, more flexible identity will permit him to pass them on convincingly. Fürstenwerth comes to dub himself the eponymous *Fox*, an untamed and free agent amid the city's topological spaces. If Quade needs Fürstenwerth to pass the plans to the Allies in convincing fashion, Fürstenwerth seems only too happy to participate, not least because it fosters his links to the French and especially to Yvonne. The solid soldier / loyal nephew from the eastern front now operates between the increasingly blurred fronts as they are manifest amid the novel urban geography.

When approached with General Quade's plan—a recruitment to clandestine conspiracy—Hans initially declares he prefers an "enemy in front of me": resisting the back-channel modes of espionage amid the underground forces in favor of conventionally clear conflicts of topographic space familiar from the war genre (and the film's earlier, now obsolete maps). But Hans soon finds himself at an André-arranged rendezvous with a British agent who has parachuted in just to meet him, emphasizing the flexible front and foldable spaces of the topological worlds of espionage. In short order, Fürstenwerth is fleeing his own surveilling comrades. In fact, this war film's second, and last, shooting conflict comes when Fürstenwerth uses his pistol to destroy a searchlight his German countrymen are using to scour the countryside for the resistance of which he now finds himself part. He is careful to avoid shooting his Kameraden, but he does subvert their surveillance that the film has been exploring from early in the plot: the syntax of the genre has shifted from the clear battle lines to a German shooting at his own comrades to head off his side's own surveillance. Moreover, Hans has soon come to occupy the subject position of André's: a repeat of the film's opening café scene has Hans delivering plans with German field airports to Yvonne at a street café, an explicit parallel to André's café visit in the film's opening. As he approaches the café, however, Hans is framed with Notre Dame in the background, recalling the tourist overtones with which the film experience started. This time, however, he, like André, is the subject of surveillance, and the same SD agents from the opening scene arrest him in the café, to the horror of Yvonne.

With this repetition and variance of the film's café/surveillance opening—with Fürstenwerth's passing on real plans and arrested for it—the fate of *Fox*'s young protagonist is sealed. Although he hopes that his uncle, General Quade, will bail him out, Fürstenwerth learns that he has been pulled even more deeply into the conspiracy than he could have fathomed: not only were the plans for the field airports real but also those for the entire coastal defense. Quade cannot confess that he helped recruit his nephew for these purposes because it would lead to scores of arrests and executions of the Wehrmacht officer corps. It is subsequently hinted that Quade himself commits suicide for his part in the plot and in his nephew's death. On both counts—Quade's suicide and the implication that many were resisting Hitler—the film is, as in *Canaris*, confirming the myth of Wehrmacht honor, widely affirmed in the 1950s, although the recruitment of an unsuspecting soldier-nephew does leave a bad taste in one's moral mouth.

Fox's concluding messages are clear: the back-channel, clandestine operations of Paris's topological affective geographies, which have turned loyalties inside out, claim both the general and the Francophile captain turned spy. The film's working through the identity of the soldier who has deliberately retooled himself—taken off his uniform to don a smart French suit, so to say—is enforced in the very downbeat end sequences of Fürstenwerth in his cell. The prison spaces here contrast to the tourist spaces offered at the beginning: this end negates the visual and affective pleasures of the tourism with which the film plays for most of its plot. As opposed to the broad expanses, high angle, and deep-space urban compositions of Paris—or the affective thrill of meeting a love interest in the urban masses—May shoots Fürstenwerth's cell as a shallow space and at an extremely low angle reminiscent of Expressionist classic's most stylized sequences. The goal would seem to be to convey the existential circumstances in which Fürstenwerth now finds himself—existentialist subjectivity very much à la mode at the time but, in this genre context, deliberately detaching the despairing soldier from the scales of the war film to relocate him amid the topological affective geographies of the 1950s espionage city.

Rommel Calls Cairo: Revoking the War Genre

Our spy in Cairo is the greatest hero of them all.

—attributed to Erwin Rommel, 1942[34]

Fox's complex western front, however, was not the only laboratory in which to reforge soldierly subjectivity for the postwar. Conventional war genre semantics arise even earlier on, and faster, in Schleif's 1959 *Cairo*. The film was a critical success, even remade in 1959, with some of the same footage, in the United Kingdom as *Foxhole in Cairo*. Set on the African "southern front" of the war, the film opens, as it declares, in "Afrika April 1942" with a briefing room, into which sweeps Erwin Rommel in full uniform accompanied by multiple officers in the bright hues of the Wehrmacht's Afrika Korps uniforms. The 1950s choice of Rommel, rather than some other officer or general, to "call Cairo" is revealing and resonates with the ongoing "Rommel myth" in both wartime and postwar culture.[35] In a way similar to the mythos built up around World War I flying aces (discussed in chapter 4), Hitler and Goebbels had deliberately cultivated mass adoration for the general, with his full and conscious cooperation. He had won the pour le mérite as a young man on the Italian front in World War I; written a well-received and genre-busting book, the 1938 *Infantrie greift an* (*The Infantry Attacks*); and then established a reputation for battlefield brilliance in the northern Africa campaigns in 1941–1943 as the still famous "desert fox" (Wüstenfuchs).

This notoriety, however, was carefully fostered and managed by the regime, including via Goebbels's personnel involvement, the assignment of one of the Ministry of Propaganda's officials to Rommel's staff, and the innovative use of press conferences for the charismatic general.[36] It is no surprise, then, that the regime deployed the famous general to assuage anxiety about the imminent Atlantic invasion, assigning him supervision (if not command) of the Atlantic defenses, hoping that his mere presence would soothe German fears and inspire Allied terror. Rommel's place in the propaganda pantheon was such that Hitler did not feel he could have Rommel summarily executed when he suspected the latter's role in the July 1944 assassination attempt against the führer. Rommel was given the option of committing suicide to protect his wife, Lucie, and son, Manfred (the future long-term mayor of postwar Stuttgart), an option the general took in October 1944. True to propaganda form, the regime announced he had succumbed to wounds and gave him an elaborate state funeral that further exploited his image as probably the foremost military man of, and for, the regime.

Perhaps less well known but even more relevant for the present investigation of the 1950s is one of the stranger twists in the Rommel myth. Odd, indeed, is how British veterans and military historians took up the Nazi propaganda mantle and reburnished Rommel's image for the Cold War period and purposes. By the early 1950s, the Western Allies were becoming increasingly convinced that West Germany could serve as a bulwark against the expanding sphere of Soviet influence. In 1950, a very popular biography of Rommel appeared in the United Kingdom (*Rommel: The Desert Fox*, by Brigadier Desmond Young), followed by the well-known film *The Desert Fox* (1951), with James Mason as Rommel and Jessica Tandy as his wife, Lucie (Mason would even reprise his Rommel role in *The Desert Rats*, 1953). With the subsequent publication in England of the *Rommel Papers* (also 1953, edited by B. H. Liddell Hart), the postwar extension of the Rommel mythos had increasingly clear parameters: that, beyond any uncomfortable political questions, Rommel had been a great soldier and tactician, to be respected, even revered by the enemy. This was only enforced by the 1959 British remake of *Cairo* I mentioned above. It does seem that Rommel's forces treated their prisoners relatively well (the advantages of low expectations), but these British books and films suggest that he had wanted to stay out of Nazi politics entirely, and when the time came, he became an active participant in the conspiracy against Hitler. Most seemed to believe, in fact, that Hitler had forced him to commit suicide because he had actively participated in the assassination plot against the führer. But Rommel himself, his chief of staff (who was in on the plot), and even his son, Manfred, admitted that Rommel did not know any details of the famous assassination attempt ahead of time. It seems more likely that the celebrated general, although he had his doubts (one wonders who could not have), remained loyal to the regime that had made him one of the best-known generals in the world. After all, even his own chief of staff did not recruit him to the actual plot.

In the various versions of *The Desert Fox*, then, his active conspiring against Hitler is exaggerated considerably, and the obvious question has to be, Why, so soon after the war, would some British (writing for their own and American audiences) want to rehabilitate a general whom Hitler and Goebbels had celebrated above all others? The answer would seem to be the ongoing whitewashing of the Wehrmacht, which many believed would be crucial to rebuilding any armed forces for the young Federal Republic and welcoming it into the Cold War Western Alliance. If the Wehrmacht's abstention from, even resistance to, the Nazis' most nefarious crimes could be maintained—that is, its soldierly ability and loyalty cited above any politics—then the putative "honor" of the Wehrmacht could remain intact and the Cold War world order could assume its desired shape. In these ways, one finds in the contested figure of Rommel one of the starkest and most curious lines of continuity from the Nazi era to the 1950s Cold War: the abiding myth of a soldier's soldier who did his best to stay out of politics and who always remained loyal to his men. But, so the myth continues, when he had to become involved in an increasingly dire situation, he came down on the right side of the Hitler question and ended up a brutalized victim of the criminal regime. It is a trajectory, of course, that the Wehrmacht, most Germans, and apparently most of the Western Alliance wanted to believe of themselves.

The depiction of Rommel in *Cairo* confirms this mythic image and its Wehrmacht-sanitizing objectives. Schleif's 1950s Rommel is an approachable, very humble, and human individual popular with his underlings, a surprise for someone whose personnel file back in Berlin bulged with complaints about his overbearing, even bullying, manner.[37] Schleif's personally modest Rommel seems an explicit parallel to *Canaris*'s approach with another top (and highly compromised) officer to be rehabilitated for the reconstructive 1950s. Here, however, despite even more trappings of the conventional genre than *Canaris*, there is the deliberate passing of a generational baton to younger officers. If *Canaris*'s young spies provide ephemeral intrigues and passing visual attractions, *Rommel* builds its core narrative around such spies, agents whose operations are tailored to the Cold War 1950s. In its opening sequence, Rommel's command center does offer the familiar trappings from the conventional genre: broad spaces to entertain numerous staff officers, a well-lit meeting table, and surrounding maps that will, in short order, convey this film's curious territorial vagaries.[38] But Rommel almost immediately flags the challenge that will occasion the film's surprise espionage: he may be an old fox, he declares, but he is no magician, and they need to know more about the defenses of Libyan harbor-city Tobruk, about the British in the eyes of the Egyptians, and especially about the potential for an uprising against their colonial oppressors.

To address these intelligence gaps, he summons two Wehrmacht captains, Captains Almaszy and Eppler, who plan to infiltrate Cairo for reconnaissance.[39] Schleif is extending the Rommel myth in the direction of espionage with real-life characters whose stories Eppler published in book form (with no one to confirm its crucial Rommel details). Eppler's 1959 book of the same title offers a more extended account of the espionage support that he and his comrades offered Rommel, an account with telling differences. In fact, in one of the stranger turns of postwar, transnational culture—further confirming, much like the Rommel myth, the shared cultural legacy of the World Wars—these Wehrmacht officers became the espionage protagonists of Ken Follett's best-selling novel *The Key to Rebecca* (1980), and Almaszy, redubbed Almásy, became the center of Michael Ondaatje's *The English Patient* (1992; subsequently played by Ralph Fiennes in the celebrated 1996 Anthony Minghella film of the same name). Apparently, the attractions of border-defying, cosmopolitan spies and their ability to recast conventional war narratives abided throughout the Cold War and into the likewise transnational post-1989 era.

The Hungarian Almaszy is an expert on the northern Sahara and, in the 1959 German film, explains, via one of the briefing room's freestanding maps, not so much battle tactics or territorial objectives. Rather, Rommel and his staff use the maps to explore how they can deliver Eppler into the city of Cairo without the British knowing. Almaszy sketches how they will, counterintuitively, deliver him over the desolate lands from the south: circumventing the British fortified coast, they will drive him some 3,200 km across the Libyan and Egyptian deserts to the "million-person metropolis." As in *Fox*, the military map is used, at this particular historical juncture, to convey not so much the film's battle lines but a different affective geography that detaches this plot from the usual war genre mechanisms (figure 6.3).

Rather than highlighting a clearly drawn front and coming battle—recalling the topographical trajectories of Heinitz's initial map of the Normandy invasion in *Fox*—the map here sketches an alternative, topological space,

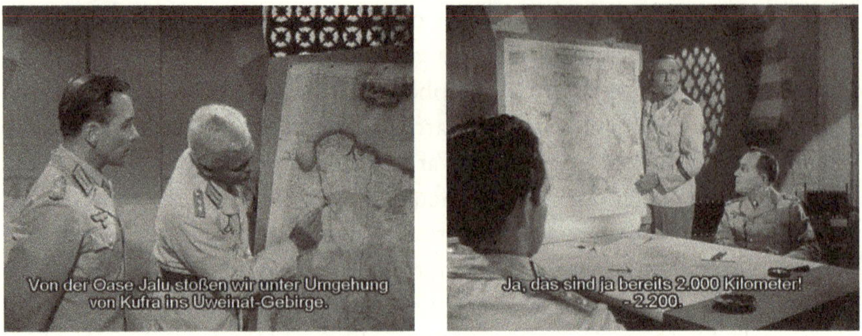

FIG. 6.3 A circuitous geography for the war-espionage hybrid, *Cairo*. Digital frame enlargement.

circumventing the enemy to enter the urban labyrinth as a spy. Despite its Rommel-referencing title and initial war genre semantics, the film opens, then, with an objective decidedly diverging from a conventional military mission: its objective is not the conquering of new territory but rather the placement of a single agent in the dense networks of the city.

This trajectory of the first few minutes underscores the late-cycle transformation of the popular 1950s war genre. The collective mission has now boiled down to two men, a descaling transformation then confirmed in another scene before Almaszy and Eppler hit the desert road. Before Schleif's camera tracks them across the broad, bright expanses of the desolate northern Sahara, Eppler visits his radio team to explain how, once delivered to Cairo, he will have difficulties making contact with Rommel. Cairo's urban, networked topological space, with its flexible hierarchies and foldable distances, foregrounds the importance but also unreliability of communications. But this recurring communications theme within the genre—stretching back at least to the command-control infrastructure on the hillside in the mid-1910s *Dr. Hart*—looms even larger in the espionage genre, since faltering communications with distant commanders yield useful autonomy for the increasingly free agent. Communications on both sides were certainly a central aspect of the desert war, especially since the British territories stretched across three continents and nine countries. Here, too, the hybrid genre mints a different kind of war film subjectivity: the communications theme and its uncertainty occasion a no-fault descaling of the individual agent from the collective, rendering contingent the sort of scaling that underpins the conventional war genre.

When, in his initial briefing, Rommel speculates on the delivery of Eppler to Cairo, he calls his young captain "an agent"—but then apologizes for doing so. This slip, however, underscores how the transformation in genre tracks the subjective trajectory of war films' young soldiers, much like Fürstenwerth in *Fox* and in parallel to Jameson's argument about the war-correspondent film emerging from the war genre in the 1970s/1980s.[40] Notably similar to *Fox*, the emergent spy in *Cairo* is played by another young actor who cut his filmic teeth in earlier, more mainstream works of the war genre. Austrian Adrian Hoven, a future actor in numerous Fassbinder classics (including, among others, *Fox and His Friends*, *Berlin Alexanderplatz*, and *Lili Marleen*), had his start, like Hardy Krüger, in a wartime war film. For Hoven, it was the 1944 Heinz-Rühmann-vehicle *Quax in Fahrt* (*Quax in Africa*), which was banned after the war by the Allies and then premiered widely in West Germany in 1953. He also appeared, as noted above, in one of the most famous war films of the 1950s, *Canaris*, as Captain Althoff, the admiral's closest espionage underling. As with the casting in *Fox*, *Cairo* extends a kind of war film star system—in fact, the actual military background of the actor playing Captain Almaszy, Peter van Eyck, was foregrounded in the publicity materials for *Cairo*, since he was a German émigré who had returned to Europe as an American citizen in the occupying forces.[41] The publicity materials for *Cairo* highlight van Eyck's peregrinations probably because they recall his character's diegetic shuttling, like Eppler's, between continents, here Europe and Africa.

The mobile, even transitional character of these soldierly subjectivities in the 1950s grows even clearer in another scenario familiar from the genre—namely, the confession-like conversation with a comrade the night before a major deployment (also important, for example, in early 1940s war films under the Nazis, like *Squadron Lützow*). Here Almaszy asks Eppler if he has really thought through his arrival in Cairo—Almaszy is asking, in his careful way, what it will mean for Eppler to be on his own in the British-controlled foreign metropolis, to become, instead of the unit-based soldier, the sort of agent Rommel correctly called him. Warming to this new mode of subjectivity, however, Eppler declares that he will be fine: Almaszy forgets that he is half Egyptian, "even full Egyptian in my hatred of the English," as he puts it. As a contemporary reviewer observed, with his Egyptian father and German mother, Eppler counts as much more than the usual Deutscher Landser populating these 1950s war films because he is "between two peoples."[42] Such is doubtless a new kind of hero for the late 1950s war film, an ethnically hybrid and border-crossing cosmopolitan of the sort that Krüger's Fürstenwerth only attains late in his Paris stay. Eppler shows how this late-genre war film will explore the identity and interiority of this soldier as he becomes, like the plot, increasingly hybrid. As a protagonist, Eppler embodies the generic transformation from the conventional war genre to a more individualistic, more open-ended cosmopolitan, refunctioning the genre's long-standing mobility and travel.

This mobility and travel aspect of the genre and the film are manifest in *Rommel*'s first thirty minutes, which follow the small convoy on its 3,000 km-plus journey, the same as the "distance from Madrid to Moscow." *Rommel*'s journey across the northern Sahara, to deliver Eppler to Cairo from the south, takes up over one-third of the ninety-minute film, reinforcing the travel aspect of the genre I have been tracing since the 1910s. The journey is noticeably abbreviated in Follett's novel, underscoring the links of tourism to the film genre in particular.[43] This travel aspect of the film was consistently highlighted in the reviews relating to the film. In the tent confessional during which Almaszy queries Eppler's preparation for his lonely journey to Cairo, Eppler asks Almaszy, in turn, why he is here, why Africa. Almaszy says nowadays everyone has to be fighting somewhere in the world and, for him, the African front is "more sporting" (figure 6.4).

As noted, some war films, particularly the Luftwaffe films (Luftwaffenfilme) of the Nazis, exploit the link between modern sports (like gliding or auto racing) and war. Eppler confirms this sporting observation of Almaszy and elaborates that, yes, espionage is also more sporting. The sort of sporting espionage remaking the genre is certainly manifest on this lengthy first-act journey, which resembles more a rally across the desert for the five-car convoy than the sort of mass mobilization familiar from the earlier genre. *Cairo*'s espionage retooling of war means this group is largely on its own—the 1930s and 1940s Luftwaffe films, after all, typically locate the flyers in a flight school or squadron that scaled easily to the nation. Here the nation seems (literally) farther and farther away.

One of the markers of espionage as it emerges in these war films, as noted above, is the plot's intensification of surveillance—as in *Fox*, surveillance, especially the paranoid experience of being surveilled, becomes increasingly important in *Cairo*. On this journey, Schleif begins to cut intermittently to an aerial point of view. Such extreme long shots of the convoy from a plane convey both striking desert landscapes and the possibility that they are all being watched, which Eppler, binoculars in hand, quickly diagnoses as "Tommies—I don't like it." The awareness of this surveillance inspires the film's next espionage motif: the facile adoption and then extended feigning of foreign identities, underscoring the transitional subjectivities in this period. Immediately after spotting the plane, Eppler asks his radio assistant, Sandy, how he would like to pass once they are in Cairo, perhaps as "a South African from Capetown" or as "an American whose hobby is Egyptian temple architecture"—it is easy to imagine how Germans in the 1950s might, indeed, want to playfully fantasize a different national identity or at least travel with one, given recent history (in one early postwar survey in Bavaria, for instance, a large percentage said they wanted to join the United States). Almaszy then briefs the larger group similarly: he lectures the bigger group about how, now that they are traveling in "Tommy" territory, they should remove their Nazi uniform insignia and don the beret of British kit—a fitting metaphor for the more malleable, less Nazi-defined identities that Germans were seeking in this period, seeking on the literal and metaphorical road.

The airborne points of view of these surveillance planes anticipate the film's next unexpected turn: locating viewers, for an unusual duration, with the purveyors of this surveillance, the Egypt-occupying British. Shortly after Eppler

FIG. 6.4 "Sporting" travel across the desert, *Cairo*. Digital frame enlargement.

has spotted the surveillance plane above and conjured new identities for all his men, the film cuts from the desolate desert to the Hotel Semiramis with the superimposed title "Cairo"—as with *Fox*'s famous Hotel Lutetia in Paris, foreign occupation affords a filmic opportunity to serve up tourist-like images of a luxury destination. In the broad and bright British offices of Hotel Semiramis, viewers watch Colonel Robertson study the aerial surveillance photos presumably taken by the plane in the previous sequence.

He also asks an officer recently returned from London, Kay Morrison, to inspect the photos, on which she immediately spots the five vehicles of the convoy. The depiction of the British here and in a following scene is one of professional competence and personal correctness, despite their control of colonial aerial surveillance in their Middle Eastern territories.[44] The British had been in Egypt since the nineteenth century, when they started to assert their interests in the local territories of the ailing Ottoman Empire (famously referred to in the period as "the sick man of Europe"). Even as the British claimed more and more sovereignty in the region around 1900 and up to World War I, Egypt remained nominally Ottoman. This interplay of the British and Ottoman empires highlights the slow but assiduous assertion of British control over the Middle East amid what was known as the Eastern Question—that is, what would happen to the Ottomans' expansive territories as their centuries-old empire faded. By the early 1940s, Egypt was a British "protectorate," a status that many Egyptian resented and that they had tried to curtail with a 1936 agreement limiting the number of British troops.[45] Those restrictions, however, were quickly ignored when Rommel's campaigns threatened Tobruk and then Egypt itself in 1941/1942. For these long-simmering and contingent reasons, the colonial tensions around the British were running particularly high in the period in which the film is set. In fact, many Egyptians saw the Afrika Korps' advances and German spies' presence in Cairo as an opportunity to promote their own interests against the British occupiers. It is an interplay between and among colonial domination, decolonizing hopes, and expansive war that we observed as early as *Dr. Hart*.

After studying a second set of photos from a lower altitude, Robertson declares that only Almaszy could be guiding the convey so deep into the desert, since only Almaszy and a former British colleague of his, Clayton, know the desert south of Jalu (now in eastern Libya) "like their own pockets." Robertson's theory manifests clear respect for Almaszy, whose prewar collaboration with Clayton highlights the randomness of who ended up on which side in the war. Besides the refiguring of geography familiar from the genre, this introduction in *Rommel* exemplifies one of the more remarkable, if not surprising, changes in the late genre—namely, these late war films' depiction of the enemy. Conventional war films tend not to spend much narrative time/focalization with the enemy. Certainly, there are some propaganda works that depict the enemy negatively, even noxiously, but the most popular war films generally prefer the positive affects and emotions of camaraderie and the thrill of mobile-combat-unto-territorial acquisition. Indeed, those films have proven more powerful in mobilizing their subject-citizens through love of friends/comrades, family, and home rather than hatred of enemy. Radicalizing this tendency, the late-cycle 1950s war genre offered considerable screen time, focalization, and ultimately empathy for wartime enemies, be they French, as in *Fox*, or British, as in *Rommel*—not a surprise given the new Cold War world order to which the films are contributing.

Robertson's obvious respect for Almaszy and Rommel only grows over the course of the film, underscoring the notion of a "sporting" front to the ravaging war. The film codes Robertson and Kay so positively that it gives Robertson, in the second conversation about the surveillance photos, one of the key lines of the film: in answering a query about how a small desert convoy could be a threat, Robertson ominously answers that "there are weapons more fatal than tanks and bombs," underscoring how this film self-consciously transitions from the genre that its *Rommel*-title promises to espionage. Robertson and Kay will figure more prominently as the plot unfolds in the second act, and that they are woven into the (German-generated and German-centered) narrative also departs from the technical approach of conventional war film editing. Their introduction comes by deliberate crosscutting between their hotel headquarters in Cairo and the "sporting" progress of the German desert convoy. In chapters 2 and 3, I explored how important crosscutting became even very early in the genre, especially to build suspense across the spatial distances that the genre repeatedly thematizes. In the silent era, the crosscutting between home and front played a central role in disparate films like *Dr. Hart* and *Inexpiable* as well as in the Weimar-era *Westfront*; in the Nazi era films, the distances covered by the Luftwaffe planes were contrasted both with other planes and with their nest-like home airports. In all those films, crosscutting was used, as Jameson puts it, to spatialize the narrative and its constitutive distances in specific ways, especially to integrate the home and front and to claim territory.[46] In *Rommel*'s increasingly espionage milieu, however, this crosscutting of homogenization and integration shifts to the cat-and-mouse game of suspense common to spy films. The genre often deploys space-traversing crosscutting between collective mobility and territorial target, but here it transpires between intensified surveillance and the individualistic mobility of the spy-protagonist. As in many war films, Eppler's movements—via unpredictable routes around and then within the mazelike Cairo—bring him closer to the puzzled British authorities. But the convergence results not so much in conquered and integrated territory as in intelligence that he and Sandy will radio out to Rommel.

Cairo introduces the setting promised in its title in a way that similarly contrasts the spatialization of the espionage genre to that of the war film. After some 3,000 km, Eppler (now posing as a French attaché) and his radio specialist, Sandy (an "American friend"), bid a sentimental farewell to Almaszy's convoy and make the final leg from Asyut to Cairo on their own. This final stage of their journey, like the crosscutting above, takes up a familiar aspect of the war film—the train station as the crucial venue for wartime mobilization. But it also alters the station's generic syntax. Here again, surveillance and the topological spaces of the city refigure the simpler, if central, function of the train station mobility noted above. As Colonel Robertson becomes more and more convinced that Almaszy has delivered an agent across the desert to Cairo, he demands that all train stations in Cairo be carefully monitored for arrivals from the south (figure 6.5).

Patrols should be seeking, he declares portentously, "Rommel's best man—personal details unfortunately unknown." The film then crosscuts, per the above cat-and-mouse editing, to the train station, where British soldiers prowl the platforms. This is a very different train station from that in the 1958 *Cairo Station* and from those mobilization-oriented stations appearing throughout the war genre, although the importance of the modern infrastructure of mobility abides. Eppler and Sandy have hired a local Egyptian boy to help them deliver their radio equipment to the city, so when they see the British surveillance set to greet their urban arrival, they dispatch the boy with the contraband and remain on the train without their luggage. The plan to arrive separate from their communications equipment works, and the questionable capacity of Robertson to exert surveillance control over the city becomes the main tension of the film's last hour. This shift from desert to urban surveillance exemplifies an observation that Edward Dimendberg made about urban films of the late 1940s and 1950s: as the more synoptic modes of imaging space (from, for example, airplanes) became fragmented and unreliable in the postwar period—true especially in the topographical maze of cities—there was a heightened sense of grassroots (i.e., lurking-around-every-corner surveillance).[47] It is precisely with this tension of urban surveillance—and a changing urban context—with which the rest of the film's city-set plot (and crosscutting within it) plays.

Compounding these political networks that galvanize much of the urban plot—with their repeated surveillance and hiding, then raids and ultimate arrests—*Rommel* also offers a romantic plot. But this romance's additional

FIG. 6.5 The war film train station refigured for the espionage milieu, *Cairo*. Digital frame enlargement.

complexity, hinted at as early as the tent confessional between Almaszy and Eppler, is also telling for the urban-set war film. *Fox* used its female love interest as a convenient entrée to the French resistance as well as the many tourist sites of Paris—establishing an erotically inflected affective geography for the city. *Rommel*, instead, locates Eppler in a peculiar but self-serving love triangle between a former Egyptian lover, Amina, and (surprisingly) the British officer Kay. Kay works in the counterintelligence office with Colonel Robertson that is actively seeking Eppler as the spy leaking British defensive plans to Rommel. The film, however, revealingly introduces Amina first, when it introduces the city of Cairo, because, as in *Fox*, the local foreign woman is the sexist key(hole) to the exotic, now erotic city. If the World War I films staged parallel mobilizations for their female characters, these 1950s films deploy their women as entrées to the tourist experiences of a foreign city. Right after Eppler and Sandy's first radio transmission back to command, Rommel is delighted, but he also tempers his enthusiasm with the observation that "it will take [Eppler] some three weeks to establish [intelligence] contacts" in Cairo—to which the film cuts to Amina's belly dancing in a nightclub, hinting somewhat lewdly that Eppler already has long-established "contacts."

This Cairo nightclub stages the orientalist "tourist gaze" that John Urry describes, as a Western-style club full of European tourists as well as Western-dressed Egyptians watching Amina's "native" dance.[48] As in *Fox*, *Rommel*'s local woman offers viewers an extended sequence, with the musical and dance charms of the foreign city. The press around the film highlights this gendered entry to the foreign city by featuring actor Leila Iman extensively, including her visit to Berlin for the shooting of interiors. They report, for example, that she changed hotels repeatedly, landing on the third because *three* is a lucky Egyptian number. She also apparently learned some of the German language, with the *Spandauer Volksblatt* claiming provocatively that her first phrase was "ish liebe dish [*sic*]."[49] Her use in the film and in the publicity materials underscores the tourist function of the Cairo locations as well as the coincidence of the tourist gaze with the male gaze. This male tourist gaze is carefully staged in the nightclub scene, with the camera and viewers dovetailing with the admiring looks of both Eppler and the British Major Smith. In fact, Amina will later seduce Major Smith to secure military plans for Eppler. The staging of the male tourist gaze is all the more telling because the Eppler book favors not this triangle with Amina but rather his infatuation with a Jewish woman, Edith, an assignation that allows him to express his dismay about the Nazis' concentration camps. The film keeps things considerably simpler, and decidedly lighter, in its more touristy affective geography of the city.

Paralleling Yvonne's showing Hans the Paris sights, Amina introduces Eppler to another useful tourist destination amid the foreign geography, the scenic Nile houseboats of Cairo. She lives in such a floating abode and suggests he rent one as well, which he promptly does, not least because it offers better radio reception for Sandy. Notably, in the book, they stumble on this communications insight on their own without Eppler and Amina's amorous intrigues. The lap dissolve from these picturesque houseboats—a famed riverscape to within the historic cityscape—to Eppler's stalking the inner streets emphasizes both the diversity of Cairo's different communities and the labyrinthine alleys where the Egyptian nationalist liberation forces are dug in.

Eppler goes to a trinket shop, uses an encoded password with the shopkeeper, and is soon led to a concealed back room where the leader of the liberation promises to assist him against the occupiers. There was in these years a political underground resisting the British occupation, especially as the British had violated their 1922 and 1936 agreements promising greater Egypt sovereignty. Among the ranks of these anti-British underground operatives was the young officer Anwar Sadat, who did, indeed, welcome German inroads into Egypt in the early 1940s. Sadat would be one of the key leaders in the 1952 uprising against the British and in subsequent reforms. As Eppler recounts in his book, Sadat was among those taking up contact with German spies: the future Egyptian leader would later be arrested and imprisoned for his work with the Germans.

In the film's simplified version of these underground contacts, the resistance leader provides Eppler a tailor to make him a British uniform—a tailor who also offers him additional intelligence about locally amassing Australian forces. Soon, Eppler pops up on the golf course in his French attaché identity, playing with Amina's admirer from the nightclub, Major Smith. While at the golf club, he meets Robertson and Kay for the first time, commencing a flirtation with the latter that lasts throughout the film and that creates the tense, politically charged love triangle with Amina. Given their immediate transnational affinity, Eppler also has to be careful that Kay does not recognize him when he infiltrates the colonial hotel headquarters in British kit and mustached disguise. In his book, the real Eppler emphasizes that the size and complexity of the city itself was the best protection against British surveillance: his almost picaresque experiences in these very different spaces of the colonial capital—including

Nile-lining houseboats, old-city back rooms, liberation-movement fronts, golf clubs, hotel headquarters—emphasize the topological nature of city space. It is a confusing but thrilling topological geography requiring that he, with a different uniform-disguise in almost every scene, navigates with multifaceted and malleable identities. This is a very different kind of uniform-unbound soldier, one tailor-made, so to say, to a spy for these very different wartime spaces.

Cairo begins with Wehrmacht military commanders in their desert headquarters planning another large-scale campaign against Tobruk, the strategic harbor in contemporary Libya, but quickly transitions to an espionage mission given to two men in the enemy-occupied foreign metropolis. Eventually, even those modest numbers of soldiers are whittled down to just two agents, operating in multiple disguises in the British-occupied capital of Egypt—it is a generic descaling typical, I am suggesting, for the film's postwar and increasingly Cold War moment. At a little over an hour, however, the film does relate this streamlined mission back to the conventional war genre: Sandy transmits the intelligence that Eppler has gathered at British headquarters back to Rommel, who cheerfully changes his plans from provisionally surrounding Tobruk to summarily conquering it. Historians generally regard this plan to conquer Tobruk—central as the city was to German supply lines in its Afrika Korps offensive—to have been in Rommel's approach for some time, but the film makes his more forward-leaning strategy pivot on the plans that Eppler and Sandy radio from deep within Cairo.[50] The film cuts from Rommel's abrupt reconsideration of his plans to stock footage of the subsequent desert battle scenes, scenes that return the film abruptly to the war genre. Suddenly—after forty minutes of Cairo's streets, houseboats, and hotels—viewers watch the Afrika Korps' military mobilization conquering and converting scenic (here desert) landscape into German territory (the same footage is also used in the 1951 British, Mason-as-Rommel *Desert Fox*).

With this attack, the film also returns, rather circuitously, to the familiar scaling of the genre, from the individual soldier-protagonist (Eppler, with sidekick Sandy) to the national-collective and territorial implications of his actions. Notably, however, in that familiar scaling of the individual to the nation, there is no unit to which the individual is first scaled—the film cuts quickly back to the individuals in the city's mazelike topology of both identities and spaces. The abrupt war sequence seemed intended to address a concern raised in a number of the film's reviews that complained that the film invokes the war genre but does not fully deliver on its marketing of Rommel in the title.[51] Interestingly, the script actually offers a much longer sequence relating to this famous victory in Tobruk—considered the high point of the Afrika Korps campaign—with Rommel giving a rousing victory speech shortly after conquering the port.[52] But the final film omits this scripted scene, opting simply instead for stock footage and then a cut back to Cairo, where the core of the action and heart of this late-cycle war-spy film rest anyway.[53]

This topological scaling of the individual agent to the upper echelons of the nation is typical for the espionage genre, a scaling that realizes the communicative "call" of the title. Rommel calls Cairo because the famed general was never able to conquer the place, despite his farfetched plans of conquering Egypt all the way to the Suez Canal. The increasingly espionage-focused film substitutes, at this postwar moment, radio communications for relinquished territorial conquest, and with this spatial shift, a newly minted topological geography replaces more traditional battlefield landscapes of the war genre—this conventional conversion and integration of landscape is foregone for tourism. Such communications as conquest help structure, fundamentally, the late-cycle war-espionage hybrid and do so via a novel form of urban soldierly subjectivity: such subjectivity allows for the individual actions of the soldier-spy to scale directly to the national and transnational. Such direct scaling of the individual (spy) to the nation foreshadows the popular Cold War espionage cycles like those of James Bond or even Indiana Jones. In this way, the sudden plot arrival at a conventional battle in the seventieth minute highlights a telling transformation for the war genre: information produced in the foreign city now has the ability to influence, on the national/transnational scale, the sort of air and ground war that previously structured experience in general. Such generic mechanisms underscore the accelerating shifts in cities around this time. The postwar city would increasingly become, as Manuel Castells has described, a "space of flows," where knowledge and communication would more and more drive urban economy, society, and culture within larger and larger networks.[54] As the city converts conventional spaces, and the phenomenological experience of them, to the kind of topological compression charted above—to the ubiquitous networks, foldable spaces, multiple hierarchies of topology—Castells suggests that flows remade the city, above all, through knowledge and its communication, both of which increasingly dominate and structure the spaces of the postwar city.

In light of these topological and communicative geographies of the postwar city, the film's final act (concluding third) is not spent, like so many earlier war films, in a climactic, extended battle sequence. Rather, *Cairo* finishes with a final, twenty-minute act focusing on Eppler's struggle with cracked codes, bad transmissions, and the defensive "einmauern" (walling in) of Sandy's last radio signals. Even as Eppler's daring, disguised infiltrations of the Brits' Cairo headquarters yield more intelligence, Rommel's people begin to fear that the British have cracked the code by which the intelligence is reaching them. Unable to evaluate the veracity of the intelligence getting through to them, they "wall in" Sandy—that is, isolate him and Eppler communicatively. This strangely communicative-technical development, one that dominates the drama of the film's last fifteen minutes, takes them out of the topological urban network in which they have functioned so adeptly. Falling out of this network generates the terror of a communicative fate written squarely on their increasingly haunted faces—their ghostlike visages remake the cheerful, sunny disposition of the earlier espionage.

Eventually—and unsurprisingly, given the looming importance of communications here at the narrative climax—Colonel Robertson traces Sandy's radio transmissions to their houseboat base, a literal space of flow. Matching the spies' mobility, Robertson deploys not with large-scale armed forces but rather in a cramped truck with map and radiomen, a parody of a large-scale counterattack. This is a counterattack befitting the film's increasingly communicative content and works to apprehend Eppler and doom Sandy, who dies not on the battlefield but by his own hand, near his radio equipment on a luxury riverboat. The spy dies alone, effectively detaching death from the collective and meaning-laden symbolization that earlier films in the genre were so careful to cultivate (notably, he does not die in Eppler's book).

This lonely death is revealing for the remade war genre, but the film concludes instead with the plot's most important agent, Eppler, escorted in cuffs off the same houseboat, his covert identity unmasked by the British authorities. When Eppler is brought to British headquarters, he passes Kay in the hotel lobby, in one last foldable space of this neowar film. She subsequently begs Colonel Robertson to ask Churchill for mercy for the German-Egyptian agent. In fact, Churchill did appear in Africa shortly thereafter in part to buck up the British forces that would defeat Rommel at the battles of El Alamein. The real Eppler did live—not least to write the unverifiable account on which the film is based. This spy will have to die another day, not a surprise given the geopolitical subjectivity recast for these former soldiers. If *Fox*'s Hans was killed by his own comrades for his mobility cum flexibility with the French, then half-Egyptian Eppler is spared by the British. It is an ending fitting the new genre for its confirmation of West Germany's being spared in the Western Alliance—the cornerstone of a new Europe built on such conveniently malleable subjectivities.

In these three films, the war genre in its late-cycle manifests politically convenient transformations and the arc of postwar subjectivities: the changes in the genre enact the remarkable reworkings of collective psychologies in postwar West Germany. In these ways, a society's recurring and beloved genres demonstrate a culture's revealing structure of feeling as it transitions out of militarism and away from the collective war mode that had been so important to Wilhelmine and Nazi culture. This transitional structure of feeling yields a new modality of individualism, not least through tourism rather than mobilization, with this individual's body as the paramount strategy of accumulation—strategies of individual accumulation that one sees in the full-blown, late-capitalist espionage genre cycles of James Bond and Indiana Jones. But global genres like these emerged out of a specific context, as such structures of feelings are historically conditioned and always working with existing forms. They are engaged with traditions but also constantly transforming them—along with the people who uphold and sustain them. And it is these cultural forms and transforming people I investigate herein, in this remarkable period of 1950s transition for Germany, Europe, and the world.

7

Conclusion: Affective Geographies of the Fading Genre

(*The Boat*, 1981; *Downfall*, 2004)

When the director Helmut Käutner commented on Bernhard Wicki and his film *Die Brücke* (*The Bridge*, 1959)—"After this, further war films will be superfluous in this country"—his remark reveals, at the least, two notable aspects of the film genre at the center of *German Ways of War*.[1] First, as an important director of both the Nazi and postwar eras, Käutner is demonstrating how such key personnel think through genre in their relation to the industry overall and to individual films specifically. Genres are clearly important to how various constituencies comprehend films, comprehension not only by audiences—as we have seen through the reception of many of these films—but also by filmmakers themselves. Second, Käutner's comment demonstrates, pace Rick Altman and Steve Neale, the starkly diachronic aspect of genres that I have highlighted throughout this study. Genres have histories, of which those various industry constituencies are well aware, including how genres unfold and change over time, not least via certain genre-defining or, in the later films, genre-dismantling films. This study has undertaken a history of such genre-transforming films across five crucial decades in German history and culture. These were not just any five decades but rather decades of radical and repeated social, political, and cultural upheaval. Above all, I have focused on moments of generic transformation, rather than on mere types or typologies, to comprehend how genres are interwoven and mutually illuminating with cultural history generally.

With this interwoven history of generic transformations and culture more generally, *German Ways of War* has attempted to address the relative lack of genre study in European and especially German film and media studies. As Corrigan and White have noted, there is probably no theoretical notion more important in U.S. film studies than genre, but Anglophone German film studies, with a couple of notable exceptions like Johannes von Moltke's and Laura Hein's work, has largely shied away from engaging popular cinema through genre.[2] There has been, it seems to me, too little work to follow up the engagement with popular genres that scholars like Karsten Witte, Eric Rentschler, and Johannes von Moltke signaled. It is notable that in these cases, the generically informed work has focused on particular historical periods, a laudable approach but nonetheless one that the present study has attempted to depart to unfold a history that can traverse the traditional caesurae of German history (1914, 1918/1919, 1933, 1945, 1949, etc.). This transperiod study of generic transformation tries to open up history in different ways by tracing the vicissitudes within the abiding but ever-evolving genre. Finally, by tracing a genre across the conventional caesurae of German history, from the 1910s to the early 1960s, I have aimed to illuminate anew even canonical objects from conventional film histories, which, analyzed in isolation as they often are, appear quite different from within longer-term genres, such as the celebrated 1930 *Westfront* or the popular 1940 *Request Concert*. In these ways, I have attempted to read films, well known and not, midgeneric stream—to paraphrase Altman's historical emphasis on the ebbs and flows of genre—to understand them as part of an ever-coursing but also ever-changing history, with the currents eddying around certain works both typical and transformational.[3]

Alongside this historically minded study of the transformations of the genre, *Ways of War* has attempted to offer a new theory of war films on the basis of their intensified spatial mechanisms and what I have highlighted as their affective geographies. War films have not, even in Anglo-American contexts, been subjected to the extensive theorizations that other genres have enjoyed—as with melodrama, musicals, or horror—in part, I think, because there has been too much focus on violence and combat scenes. As I noted above, extreme violence is difficult to theorize and unfamiliar to most viewers, it is expensive in terms of production conditions and so often a (vast) minority of the films' broader durations, and finally, violence, even organized battles between two sides, is shared by any number of other genres—for example, horror and action.

Instead, I suggested looking to other aspects of the genre's syntax and semantics, especially war films' positive spatial and affective mechanisms. I have highlighted throughout that much of what the genre has to offer positively is the affectively arresting experience of movement and travel. Of course, such movement and affect-intensified travel have to take place somewhere, and critical geography and the affective turn it has engaged illuminate various aspects of the genre. Critical geography foregrounds the worlding of any text as well as the affective dynamics at work in its spatial mechanisms, and notions like landscape, territory, scale, network, and topological space help one grasp the generic transformations I have foregrounded throughout. With the recent "turns" in space and mobility studies, such an approach seems well warranted. Moreover, a rethinking of theories of the war film is occasioned by the recent burgeoning of critical military studies, with which *Ways of War* has also tried to engage.

Ways of War explores how this intimate, inextricable relation of the war genre to that of travel and tourism is borne out by both the early and later histories of the genre in Germany. Here, too, the present analysis sought to weigh in on what seems a gap in film studies in general. Although, within Anglo-American film studies, there has been more engagement with the importance of space and mobility, particularly in work on early cinema, the works in this direction have neglected to link the important early genres of travelogues and/or cultural films to the early war film. Such is a particularly mysterious omission, since the war film emerged in force at the same 1910s time that these earlier genres consolidated into longer narrative forms. By investigating the film-industrial impact of the onset of World War I, *Ways of War* argues that these early, travel-oriented genres—originating largely from other countries—were absorbed and repackaged in long-form war films. In fact, these war films were explicitly linked to a specific geographical imagination that built on the educational potential of early cinema, as both the films of the early and mid-1910s and the culture around them highlighted.

Theorists ranging from Karl Marx to David Harvey to Stephen Kern have observed how modernity transformed, especially "destroyed" and "compressed," space and time, which points *Ways of War* toward the fundamental importance of distance in war films.[4] Modern wars were, in fact, based on an entirely different relationship to distance, due partially to new technologies of mobility (e.g., mobile assemblages of the train, tank, or airplane) but also to modern artillery, bombing, and the communicative technologies surrounding them. Few are the genres that more rely on modern technologies and economies to remake spatial distance. For an example foregrounded above, distance munitions and remote communications completely remade centuries of defensive architecture—forts, city walls, and so on—and removed commanders from the fighting front, such that the commanders' distance from combat became key to affective geographies throughout the genre. As early as the 1917/1918 *Dr. Hart* and its Poland-based hillside, the commanders are able to deploy these new distancing technologies to their advantage, while the 1930 pacifist war film *Westfront* set its problematically detached commanders at the end of an arduous journey. If Nazi-era films humanized the commanding officer and kept him close both physically and emotionally to his troops even as the airplanes traversed greater and greater distances, the 1950s had a more complex relationship to the authority of the officer corps: commanders were initially close but then often problematically distanced from the plots, be they unfolding in Paris or Cairo. In its genre-transforming brutality, a film like Bernhard Wicki's *The Bridge* (1959) models the perils of this relationship in the randomness with which the boys' commander is killed—in his absence, his youthful charges are left unable to comprehend the changing combat conditions.

Similarly, the distance of the home front from the fighting front provides a key narrative challenge to be overcome throughout the films' affective geographies. Early on in the genre, a journey from the home to the front, a journey both physical and emotional, structures the films' plots, such that tracing this journey throughout the different moments of the unfolding genre underscores how differently this distance can be covered. Central to this journey structure is the negotiation of distance not only from the home front but also very often from conventional gender relations; it is remarkable—early on, at least—how the films overtly address female audiences members with wartime mobilizations of their own, either staged or thematized extensively (see *Dr. Hart* and *Inexpiable* in chapter 2). While distances—and, really, the duration to cover them—were generally "compressed," in the phenomenon observed by Marx, Harvey, and Kern, the spatial processes of homogenization and mobility to overcome such distances provide much of the plots' narrative tension. Exemplary in this kind of emptying and homogenization of the distance between the home front and the fighting front would be the Luftwaffe films of the Nazi period, in which the technologies of the air assemblage permit a near whimsical advance from the home to the front, as in *Medal of Honor* (1938) and *Squadron Lützow* (1941). It is noticeable, however, that even in such films, the struggle to maintain this space-homogenizing assemblage creates the core narrative challenges. For example, Ritter and Bertram build their plots with a number of very different airports in *Medal of Honor*, the fate of planes after crashes in *Squadron Lützow*, or the stuttering homeward mobility of the expats in *Above Everything in the World* (1941). This serial interplay of distance with homogenization unto mobility yields the affective geographies in films ranging from the 1910s *Dr. Hart* to the 1930s *Pour le Mérite* to the 1950s *Cairo*.

These manipulations of distance via mobility highlight perhaps the key narrative mechanisms of these films, their deployment of sundry spaces to scale individuals to the national and even transnational. If Basinger's theory of the soldier/unit/mission triad has been widely cited, a sensitivity to space foregrounds the production of scale, which this study regards as intensified in moments of fundamental technological change (like the early twentieth century as well as our own). It is not only that scale for sociopolitical acts exists but that it is, like space, constantly being produced socially and politically. And such production of scale consistently transforms the spaces and individuals so scaled or descaled. In fact, this scaling and descaling distinguish war films' violence and battles, which are broadly shared by other genres like horror, action, and Westerns. War films' traversal and conquering of distance serve almost always the genre's scaling mechanism—scaling that constitutes and reveals the films' politics. For example, in *Dr. Hart*, the private subjectivity indicated by the title—the film as the eponymous diary—is scaled to the national and transnational by transforming the film's key modes of transportation (from carriage to quiet train compartment to modern medical train) as well as transforming images of a private landscape into a collectively processed territory. These spatial transformations scale the formerly private spa doctor to the national and even to the transnational in a refigured cosmopolitanism by the film's end. It is noteworthy, to return to how space intersects gender relations, that female characters were, as in *Dr. Hart*, taken along on this scaling ride, even as they (misogynistically) embody the home front. In its more pessimistic turn, a film like *Inexpiable* deliberately scales between individual acts in the home-front factory and the combat front dependent on it.

In the Weimar antiwar films like G. W. Pabst's *Westfront 1918* (1930), however, contrary processes produce very different spatial assemblages. Antiwar films may criticize belligerent endeavors more, but they maintain a spatially intensified approach to their material—many of the pleasures of the viewing experience abide even as the criticism rises. In such works the wartime distances usually homogenized and overcome are reinstated as fragmented and labyrinthine. This alternative spatial assemblage emerges above all through the films' memorable and meandering journeys that act contrary to the homogenized and compressed distance between the home front and the fighting front mentioned above. The interplay of distance with compression or homogenization of it explains the import of the meandering journey marking many antiwar films: they manage to lodge a macabre critique of some of the genre's underlying spatial syntax. In terms of such films' scalar operations, individual bodies—and, in particular, private memories at that personal scale—end up affectively intensified to detract from the normative scaling of war. Here affective thrills are achieved not so much by mobility, as in many pro-war films, but by touch registered by the individual suffering soldiers. It is notable that these late Weimar meandering journeys that reestablish distance reemerge in the late 1940s rubble films, which invoke the mobile assemblage in the Nazi-era films discussed above but then allow their Heimkehrer to wander aimlessly. In these rubble films, the Heimkehrer's meandering peregrinations also reestablish distances, to demobilize from the affective thrills of the Nazis' blitz speeds and mobility. The 1950s war films—made for a recovering West Germany full of veterans—also alter the scaling of the wartime genres, with hybrid war-espionage films like *Canaris* (1955), *Fox* (1957), and *Cairo* (1959) shifting increasingly to an individual scale anticipating the postwar neoliberal body as a strategy of accumulation, as Harvey has tracked. The politics of such films work altogether differently even as the affective mechanisms of movement and mobility abide. It is noticeable, in terms of gender and space, that the foreign women in these postwar films augment, rather than participate in, the affective intensities of travel.

Such scales and the films' production of them transform the spaces in which the films traffic more than other genres. War films fundamentally remake older spaces imbricated in the prewar cultures that the films are geared to alter. In the 1917/1918 *Dr. Hart*, the refigured mobility remakes private landscapes with the nationalized mythoscape of Hermann, a remaking that also recasts the private spa and aristocratic castle into the modern battlefield and nationalized hospital. In the 1941 *Squadron Lützow*, an entirely new community is forged out of the refugees that the Luftwaffe planes spot and save with their precision targeting. Across the genre, these are often contradictory engagements with city space, as both home front and combat settings. Many of these spatial transformations relate to the economics that war and its scaling intensify: for example, in *Sword and Hearth* (1916) as well as in *Inexpiable* (1917), the economic aspects of the war come to the foreground in the fate of older farms and factories. In *Inexpiable*, a film of flawed or failing scaling, the factory is effectively descaled from the national by the presence and then protests of the Fremde (stranger), who cultivates a rowdy public sphere in the pub against the war's reordering (i.e., scaling) of the civilian economy. Nationalist films of the Nazi era like *Medal of Honor* and *Above Everything in the World* both subvert civilian economics (Prank's unsatisfying working in a Weimar-era garage in *Medal of Honor*, the expats' ultimately perilous private positions abroad in *Über alles*) as they scale their labor anew to the nation. In antiwar films, such spatial transformations are problematized: *Westfront* refunctions a church as a field hospital that serves as a ghostly reminder of prewar humanity, or similarly, *Ways into Twilight* (1949) reconsecrates a church in the late 1940s that points to the demobilized soldiers rebuilding of their private lives, descaled, away from the unit.

Many of these spatial and affective mechanisms express themselves in recurring aspects of film style, in both the generic syntax and the generic semantics of the genre. From the beginning of the genre, the semantics of faraway exterior locations (or recreations in the studio) are central to the genre's spatial mechanisms: landscape, travel, and distance serve both semantics and syntax. Likewise, the semantics of uniforms, weapons, and nationalized spaces like airports all help scale the stakes of the genre's violence and recovery from it—they, in fact, are more reliant predictors of genre than violence or battles. (What other significant genre builds in more train stations, airports, and airfields?) Syntactically, the centrality of space and scale to the genre manifests itself in the recurring importance of crosscutting in the various films' editing. Such crosscutting was central to the consolidation of long-form narrative cinema in the 1910s—it helped maintain interest and suspense over the films' increasingly long durations—and seems a natural fit both for the genre's inclination to travel and its negotiation of distance. Recalling Griffith and his disturbing but arresting films, such editing strategies, in fact, help visualize the modern dialectic of space between homogenization and fragmentation that I have foregrounded in the introduction, following David Harvey's formulation. For example, in Karl Ritter's renowned Querschnitt (cross/diagonal cutting), the modern simultaneity of the Nazis' revolution compresses space and celebrates speed—in blitz fashion, it destroys distance and homogenizes spaces across a new affective geography of Europe. On the other hand, crosscutting in films like *Inexpiable* (between/among the failing factory, the riotous pub, and the failing front) and in *Westfront* (between Karl's troubled trip home and deadly combat) highlights the fragmentation of disparate spaces that were supposed to be linked and successfully scaled. By the 1950s, the crosscutting of the war-espionage films was revealingly transmogrified: in these hybrid films, the cat-and-mouse crosscutting is very often between authorities surveilling and undercover agents disappearing into labyrinthine city spaces, highlighting transformed urban settings and anticipating postwar modes of subjectivity.

Moving Forward and Inward: Scaling Spaces in More Recent German War Films

More contemporary war films work with these semantics and syntax of the genre, underscoring the genre's abiding entwinement of intensified space with ubiquitous mobility. For example, Wolfgang Petersen's *Das Boot* (*The Boat*, 1981), the top-grossing German film ever in the United States, has proven, as Hester Baer has observed, a "remarkable blindspot in German Film Studies"[5]—one that can be elucidated, I think, by its generic operations and peculiar affective geographies. It revealingly negates many of the above war film elements while building on others. Crosscutting between or among distant places proves markedly absent for *The Boat*—at least until a tellingly late suspense sequence—because the film deliberately compresses the spaces of the war film. In that way, *The Boat* telescopes virtually the entire war to one memorable mode of transportation, reducing its spaces to the eponymous submarine. Primarily, over the many hours of the film, the sub is shot at (via depth changes) rather than shooting or discharging its lovingly polished torpedoes, highlighting a discourse of German suffering that Brad Prager has convincingly foregrounded.[6] In order to negotiate, and largely negate, the guilt of its soldier-sailors, the film manages to avoid the territorial mechanisms above while still deliberately milking life below for the embodied, affective rich mobility that I have highlighted throughout the genre.

Locating almost the entire (long) film within the submarine abstracts the soldier-sailors from both wartime territory and guilt—a careful abstraction and extraction from their complex war context. Its nautical navigation circumvents all controversial battles of its day—for example, the blitz overrunning of Belgium, the brutal occupation of France, and the merciless aerial attacks on Britain. And certainly, it stays emphatically far away from the eastern front—for example, the Barbarossa invasion of the Soviet Union, Schnellbrief orders, giving cover to mobile killing units, and so on, all of which would have transpired or been unfolding by the film's autumnal 1941 plot. It is, to say the least, a convenient circumnavigation, far out and under the sea. Even the suspect 1950s war films, as detailed above, took aboard some of these ample controversies. With those 1950s works, there might have been notably self-serving plot twists—aiding French resistance in brutally occupied Paris, assisting postcolonial struggle in Egypt while falling for a British agent—but at least there were revealing spatial contexts that point toward historical events and the complexities of complicity.

The Boat manages the disturbing trick of delivering the pleasures of the war film highlighted above—technological mobility, perceptual luxuries, the embodied affect of both—while keeping it almost entirely abstracted from actual places and events. When the ship finally surfaces at Vigo, Spain, for instance, the main conflict is notably with other, more führer-following Germans, not with the land-based locals, whom viewers hardly see. Indeed, this film materializes what we noted above about almost perfectly homogenized space—namely, that such mechanisms render the spaces that they homogenize as empty and abstract. The memorable overture image at the beginning of the film—of the submarine suspended, levitating-like, in brackish green water—reworks the conventional establishing shot in exactly this mode: this is not a world of landscapes and their concomitant territorial jousting but an utterly abstracted seascape where meticulous world creation in the sub, not expansive world engagement, is the rule of the day.

This spatial abstraction in *The Boat*, as has been true throughout the present study, narrowly tracks the scaling operations of the film. There is an emphatic command structure in the eponymous boat—of the calm captain above his largely infantile charges—but it is a hierarchy almost entirely cut off from the scaling so often undertaken in the war genre. As Prager notes, this interrupts the links back to headquarters, further attenuating any attribution of guilt to the soldier-sailors.[7] It is a mechanism that I have traced above in the 1950s, for example, with Paul Hartmann's France-occupying forces in *Fox* wishfully, even wistfully, cut off from the brutality of the Führerhauptquartier (Hitler's headquarters). *Cairo* similarly highlights the changed guilt mechanisms of scaling after the war, with its German-Egyptian agent Eppler operating almost entirely on his own. Rommel has to call Eppler because he is far away and barely reachable, let alone controllable, thus truly out of network. In *The Boat*, even more starkly than in the 1950s, the world in self-serving miniature cuts the submarine command and crew off from the criminally compromised higher-ups. In what could be a time capsule—or mobile bomb shelter—the single vociferous embodiment of Nazi ideology within the sub is the young first officer (conveniently from Mexico), who is more and more ostracized by the stronger and stronger bonds of the ersatz subfamily. It is a family defined against, not scaled to, the Nazi leadership hierarchy. So here, too, space produces scales: the submarine's spatial abstraction from territory activates the scalar dismantling, carefully keeping the captain (almost never seen in any kind of uniform) from the taint of his official superiors and the crew from any collectivized guilt.

Going Global via Tunneling Out

An even more recent German war blockbuster likewise manages to avoid a telling conquering of territory: Oliver Hirschbiegel's (and Bernd Eichinger's) *Der Untergang* (*Downfall*, 2004) unfolds at the ground zero of Nazism, in Hitler's Berlin bunker, staging battle experiences without absorbing new territory. This unusual strategy proved highly successful both commercially and critically: it had circa five million visitors in Germany and $92 million in the global box office—which is substantially more than the contemporary Oscar-winners *Lives of Others* (2005) or *Pan's Labyrinth* (2006). In terms of its reception, in his review for the industry trade *Hollywood Reporter*, Eric Hansen declared *Downfall* "one of the best war films of all time." Hansen's review notably casts its superlative in an intellectual idiom of genre that hardly ever comes up in the sprawling scholarly literature on *Downfall*.[8] It is remarkable how much of the scholarship focuses on questions of historical representation, on the depiction of the Nazis—and how little it discusses genre. To grasp its revealing generic operations, I would highlight two of the mechanisms of the historical genre detailed above—namely, its scaling mechanisms and its telling manipulation of wartime spaces, here in the city.

Like *The Boat*, the basic spatial arc of the film relies on both the thrill of sudden upscaling to the nation and the perils of rapid descaling in defeat. First, the film's second scene of Traudl Junge applying for her position with Hitler at the Wolfschanze complex highlights Basinger's diversity of a unit and its being integrated into the mission. Here, however, it is a diverse military unit not of soldiers from different corners of the Reich but rather of would-be secretaries and servants, as they will stand in the place of the individual soldiers throughout much of the film. The familiar syntax of the diverse unit is secretarially remade to avoid the guilt of the film's protagonist, Traudl. Much of the surprise and curiosity of the scene has to do with the dizzying negotiation of scale, a mechanism shared with many of the war films discussed above. Suddenly, Traudl is very close to these commanders, with her and our viewer curiosity about the distance and proximity of officers immediately engaged in the film.

Later, however, the film relies on dizzying descaling, even if many of the war film pleasures abide. Probably the film's most famous sequence—that which became the grist for the endless mill of memes—is that of Hitler's briefing (Lagebesprechung) on April 22, 1945, in which both maps and descaled sense of space play such central roles. It is notable that Eichinger and Hirschbiegel focus on this particular briefing, in which Hitler's orders become increasingly erratic and eventually nonsensical—ultimately resulting in a fit of rage, on which both Joachim Fest and Junge report in their written accounts. It is telling, I think, how Eichinger and Hirschbiegel stylize the scene. If one examines the source material, the filmed sequence elaborates on the record, particularly in making the assembled military commanders even more grovelingly subservient than Fest and Junge report them to be—not to defend these commanders but just to note the generic stylization with the maps and Hitler's famous color pencils, thus generic gestures doubtless contributed to the scene's so-called spreadability as a viral internet meme.[9] It is not only that *Downfall* has violence and battles but also these additional aspects of generic semantics that underscore its late-cycle negotiation of genre. If maps usually serve as an important means to upscale a film's specific spaces—to relate the specific filmic instance to the larger scale of national war—here they become a baroque parody of Hitler's fading reach. As we have seen since *Dr. Hart*, the genre repeatedly deploys both maps and the delivery of orders, but as Cawelti suggests, the genre familiarity permits the film—and then so many hundreds of later meme makers—to play with the form in a critical yet reaffirming mode.[10]

The history of the genre has demonstrated that travel and a concomitant tourist gaze have been indispensable sources of viewer pleasure in war films. Such films, repeatedly and emphatically, upscaled these itinerant phenomena, like the map, to the nation and national struggle. As the genre continued to unfold, especially in the 1940s under the Nazis, the pleasures of urban modernity and what Denis Cosgrove has called the "Apollinian perspective" on the city continued to offer key pleasures of the war film[11]—one has only to think of the opening sequences of *Request Concert* (1940) and the city-based geography of *The Great Love* (1942), both among the highest-grossing titles of the regime. By the 1950s, one of the abiding pleasures indulged in ostensibly antiwar films was the touristic pleasure of foreign cities (in films like *Der Stern von Afrika* [*The Ace of Africa*, 1957], *Fox*, and *Cairo*).

Downfall parallels these 1950s genre-reaffirming war films, films that are aware of a duty to mint a new political message while also tapping the genre for its long-term cinematic pleasures. The marketing and reception of Eichinger's film confirm this urban aspect: many reviews linked *Downfall* to curiosity about Berlin's last days and about the now buried führer bunker, with some reviews even helpfully including diagrams and maps of central Berlin then and now. The importance of the city in war films also helps explain one of the plot particularities of the film—namely, the amount of time, some thirty minutes in its final act, that it spends after Hitler's suicide. This meandering journey that offers panoramas of ruins once the erstwhile faithful soldier or servant is descaled serves an important function in the history of antiwar films—for example, in Pabst's 1930 classic *Westfront* or Wicki's 1959 *The Bridge*. The extended scenes of their breakaway groups from the bunker seem geared primarily to offer the viewers the spectacle of the vanquished city.

The use of the city in these antiwar films, however, also creates an escape route for *Downfall*'s young protagonist, Traudl, by capitalizing on another cinematic pleasure and potentiality of the modern city. Cities offer the malleability of identity and the promise of a productive transformation for one lucky, invariably young protagonist. I have noted the importance of the discourse and debates about youth and generation in Germany's coming to terms with the past after the war, which created depictions that *Downfall* seems to cite at various moments.[12] For example, the Peter Kranz subplot quotes familiar father-son conflicts from various rubble films like Wolfgang Staudte's *Rotation* (1949). In the late 1950s Stalingrad film *Hunde, wollt ihr ewig leben?* (*Dogs, Do You Want to Live Forever?*, 1959), the chaos of the city in decline permits the sympathetic young character to change identities (literally) like uniforms. Its disillusioned young lieutenant (tellingly named Wisse) actually dons a Russian uniform to survive the bedlam of battle and to line up for some simple food and drink. The anonymity of the city has always allowed people to reinvent themselves, and this was a particular pleasure elaborated in the films of the 1920s, 1950s, and post-1989/1990 eras.

In the last act of *Downfall*, Traudl leaves her troupe behind by distancing herself from the uniformed contingent, and soon she, like *Dogs*'s lieutenant Wisse, indulges another long-term pleasure of the spatial multiplicity of the city—namely, the possibility of a chance encounter to help redefine one's self and one's relations. Chance encounters for pleasure and ultimate self-benefit had been a key aspect of the city in the city films of the 1920s, something definitely exploited in the 1940s and 1950s war films. Vulnerable out in the chaotic city streets, Traudl runs into a young, now orphaned Peter Kranz, whom she does not know but who helps her, unprompted, flee through enemy lines before riding off at the end of the film with her. These films that exploit modern space and mobility for their pleasures build repeatedly on the city as a homogenized space and foster affectively intensive movement unto the new social encounter in designing the modern measure. In both 1959's *Dogs* and 2004's *Downfall*, the city offers this panorama of destruction as well as the saving grace of both malleable postwar identities and the redeeming chance encounter with a stranger sharing the solidarity of wartime suffering.

All these aforementioned films confirm that, pace Virilio's influential expression in his *War and Cinema*, there did emerge a "watching machine" alongside the modern war machine. But *German Ways of War* has sought to demonstrate how that influential insight unfolds within broader mechanisms drawing on modern spatial contexts and the mobility on which they rely. For example, the coup d'oeil available from the airplane (and assorted 1920s cultural films) does not reveal much about war or its sociopolitical consequences without the spatial and affective ends to which it is put, as the peculiar targeting in *Squadron Lützow* suggests: that film's pilots seek and find "targets of opportunity" but end up building a colony for ethnic Germans in the east. Critical military studies has foregrounded the influence and sheer force of militarism within the wider culture, and this study aims to demonstrate that the audiovisual media, particularly in the genre of the feature film, manifest certain spatio-affective tendencies that can be traced across time even into recent war films.[13] This can be done at the scales of the national and transnational. For example, the different eras construct and scale their soldiers according to very different models of what we can contemplate as modern cosmopolitanism. Both *Dr. Hart* and *Über alles* offer antiquated modes of cosmopolitanism (aristocratic and peripatetic, respectively), which they then aim to remake, while *Westfront*, *Cairo*, and even a more recent film like *The Boat* all point their postwar Germans toward a war-wearier cosmopolitanism for their more individualized but still border-crossing futures.

Acknowledgments

This project has been a long time in the making and has relied on the kindness of friends, family, and colleagues throughout. At Rutgers University Press, I would like to thank Daniel Leonardo Bernardi, the series editor for War Culture, and Nicole Solano, executive editor, for their steadfast support for the project and guidance throughout. For the research for the project, I am grateful to the staff at the Deutsche Kinemathek and Die Deutsche Film- und Fernsehakademie Berlin library, including especially to Cordula Döhrer, Lisa Roth, and Gerrit Thiess, as well as to the staff at the Bundesarchiv—Filmarchiv in Berlin and Klaus Volkmer at the Filmmuseum in Munich. This research was supported in different phases by time on site by the University of California Education Abroad Program and by grants from the Academic Senate of the University of California, Davis (UC Davis) as well as from the Alexander-von-Humboldt Foundation.

Sincerest thanks go to Nora Alter for her intervention at a crucial phase of the manuscript and her tireless work on it. I want to express my gratitude to the graduate students at UC Davis who participated (during a pandemic!) in a seminar on the topic of this book, including Jesse Archbold, Stephen Armstrong, Adam Davis, Katrina Katzenbach, Evan Martens, Nick Petry, and Seva Shinde—their insights were a constant source of stimulation and inspiration. Various research assistants offered indispensable research along the meandering way, including especially Erin Altman. I am grateful to Eric Rentschler for his advice and guidance throughout the time it took me to complete it. A thank-you goes as well to Gerd Gemünden, Johannes von Moltke, and Jim Walker at Camden House for supporting the collection *Generic Histories* and its exploration of questions of genre in German cinema. Peter Hohendahl was unflaggingly supportive throughout the project, Anton Kaes offered consistently engaging insights, and early illuminating discussions were had as well with David Bathrick, whose influence is to be found on every page, while the shortcomings are entirely my own.

This study entailed many delightful stays in Berlin, where I had the good fortune to land with or near Joan Murphy, Uli Nowka, and Francis and Julie Nowka-Murphy. In Berlin, too, Lutz Artmann offered both his insights and his feedback, while Dorothea Schmidt and Jens Kempf hosted me in Kiel at a watershed moment in my research. Many productive conversations were had there on the project and on the topic in general with Philipp Stiasny, and to him, I am grateful. In Vienna, Gerald Posselt engaged with many of the topics of the project, especially on the intersection of language and violence. I feel fortunate to have met Brad Prager and Mike Richardson a(n incredibly!) long time ago and to have remained in both productive and amusing dialogue with both ever since. Brad was kind enough to read much of the manuscript and made typically helpful comments, while Mike offered helpfully skeptical scrutiny every time I would see him. I would also like to thank Jennifer Kapczynski, who was generous with both her time and her insights in reading the manuscript. Tom Clyde was always ready with a kind word and perspicacious thought. Here at UC Davis, I am grateful to my colleagues in the German department, including Carlee Arnett, Gail Finney, Sven-Erik Rose, Chunjie Zhang, and especially Elisabeth Krimmer, who worked in inspiring ways on these topics long before I did. My colleagues in UC Davis's Cinema and Digital Media Department and elsewhere, including Kris Fallon, Jeff Fort, Tim Lenoir, Susette Min, and Kriss Ravetto, were consistently helpful and supportive, while Caren Kaplan and Eric Smoodin offered incisive insights as well as good-humored company throughout.

The study was helped along by various colleagues at pivotal points. Harald Höbusch was kind enough to host me in Lexington, Kentucky, at the excellent foreign language conference there, where I enjoyed invaluable feedback on the project. That trip also introduced me to Mark Gagnon, who was incredibly giving in his insights about the project. Chris Young at Cambridge and Hanneke Grootenboer at Oxford generously arranged visiting lectures that had a decisive impact on the direction of the manuscript. Paul Reitter kindly hosted me at the Ohio State University to discuss this work and much more. Stefan Keppler-Tasaki invited me to present parts of the manuscript in both Berlin and in Tokyo, and to him, as well as to Seiko Keppler-Tasaki, I am grateful for both much intellectual dialogue and many convivial times. A renewed sense of enthusiasm for the project was found on a memorable trip to the Museum of Military History in Vienna with John Barbieri, when we were shocked to turn a corner and see Franz Ferdinand's uniform and infamously wayward car parked in a lonely room.

My parents, Jackie Yang Fisher and Randy Fisher, were unswervingly supportive, helping us here in California, en route to Europe through Massachusetts—and especially my mother, Jackie, in Berlin and Vienna, even when she did not feel like another trip. I feel indescribably graced (in a secular way) to have undertaken this endeavor with Jacqueline Berman, with whom I am fortunate to share a household, parenting, and all intellectual undertakings. She is a rigorous interlocutor and constant inspiration. We faced many marvelous, as well as sometimes trying, times while working on this project, and it was/is all unimaginable without her. Our son, Noah, has kept everything in perspective, in the most surprising ways. This study is dedicated to our dear daughter, Alexandra, whose good humor and heartfelt support have carried me through the many years of this study. She put up with many hours of film watching, book reading, and debate having, for which I am forever grateful.

Notes

Chapter 1 Introduction

1 George Mosse, *Fallen Soldiers: Reshaping the Memory of the World Wars* (Oxford: Oxford University Press, 1991), 213. Much of the recent wave of critical military studies also foregrounds how militaristic techniques and technologies have colonized the wider culture. See, for example, Roger Stahl, *Through the Crosshairs: War, Visual Culture, and the Weaponized Gaze* (New Brunswick, N.J.: Rutgers University Press, 2018), 17–18.

2 Two exceptions that will be important herein are Philipp Stiasny, *Das Kino und der Krieg, Deutschland 1914–1929* (Munich: edition text + kritik, 2009); and Bernadette Kester, *Film Front Weimar: Representations of the First World War in German Films of the Weimar Period (1919–1933)* (Amsterdam: Amsterdam University Press, 2003). Paul Cooke and Marc Silberman's anthology *Screening War: Perspectives on German Suffering* (Rochester, N.Y.: Camden House, 2010) also addresses war films to a certain extent, although it tends to explore historical dramas and melodramas more than films that would be classified as war films, with Kapczynski's and Koeppen's essays as notable exceptions. See Jennifer Kapczynski, "Armchair Warriors: Heroic Postures in the West German War Film," in Cooke and Silberman, *Screening War*, 17–35; and Manuel Koeppen, "The Rhetoric of Victim Narratives in West German Films of the 1950s," in Cooke and Silberman, *Screening War*, 56–78. The volume also does not really engage questions of genre.

3 The association of shooting and looking, of attacking and watching, is a core element of critical military studies and is based especially on Paul Virilio's *War and Cinema: The Logistics of Perception* (New York: Verso, 1991). Even very recent, and rich, work (like Allison's and Stahl's) continues to work through this intersection, which, although undoubtedly important, also tends to reduce the effects of audiovisual media to sight, which the affective turn has largely problematized.

4 W. J. T. Mitchell, *Picture Theory: Essays on Verbal and Visual Representation* (Chicago: University of Chicago Press, 1995), 15.

5 See Jaimey Fisher, "Film and Affect, Theories Entwined: The Case of the War Genre in *Saving Private Ryan* (Steven Spielberg, 1998)," in *The Palgrave Handbook of Affect*

Studies and Textual Criticism, ed. Donald R. Wehrs and Thomas Blake (New York: Palgrave, 2018), 509–537.

6 See Pansy Duncan, *The Emotional Life of Postmodernism: Affect Theory's Other* (London: Routledge, 2016), 16; Eugenie Brinkema, *The Forms of the Affects* (Durham, N.C.: Duke University Press, 2014), 43.

7 Nigel Thrift, *Non-representational Theory: Space, Politics, Affect* (London: Routledge, 2007), 91.

8 See, for instance, Wendy Kozol, *Distance War Visible: The Ambivalence of Witnessing* (Minneapolis: University of Minnesota Press, 2014); or McKenzie Wark, *Virtual Geographies: Living with Global Media Events* (Bloomington: Indiana University Press, 1994).

9 Liz Bondi, Joyce Davidson, and Mick Smith, "Introduction: Geography's 'Emotional Turn,'" in *Emotion, Place, Culture*, ed. Liz Bondi, Joyce Davidson, and Mick Smith (London: Routledge, 2016), 3.

10 See Derek Gregory, *Geographical Imaginations* (Oxford: Blackwell, 1994), 12: "Geography in this expanded sense is not confined to any one discipline, or even to the specialized vocabularies of the academy; it travels instead through social practices at large and is implicated in myriad topographies of power and knowledge. We routinely make sense of places, spaces, and landscapes in our everyday lives—in different ways and for different purposes—and these 'popular geographies' are as important to the conduct of social life as our understandings of (say) biography and history."

11 See Stahl, *Through the Crosshairs*, 13, 16–17.

12 Lauren Goodlad, *Victorian Geopolitical Aesthetic: Realism, Sovereignty, and Transnational Experience* (Oxford: Oxford University Press, 2015), 25–29; John Marx, *Geopolitics and the Anglophone Novel, 1890–2011* (Cambridge: Cambridge University Press, 2012), 10–11.

13 See David Harvey, *Consciousness and the Urban Experience* (Oxford: Blackwell, 1985), 28; and David Harvey, *Spaces of Capital: Towards a Critical Geography* (New York: Routledge, 2002), 54.

14 See Brinkema, *Forms of the Affects*, 37, on close reading.

15 Fredric Jameson, *The Geopolitical Aesthetic: Cinema and Space in the World System* (Bloomington: Indiana University Press, 1992), 3–4.

16 Jameson, 74–75.

17 Interestingly, although most of his *Geopolitical Aesthetic* focuses on the paranoid psychological thrillers of the 1960s–1980s, Jameson does turn to the conventional war genre at one point. In fact, he draws a telling—and, to me, inspirational—contrast. For him, what he calls the "guerilla-war correspondent film" diverges from the "older war-film genre" even as it retains some of the older genre's trappings (notably, I would say), its travel and "exotic" settings. Jameson, 29–30. For Jameson, the relation of the character to the collective is most tellingly transformational: if the older genre were able to balance the character with the collective—very often (as he notes) in a kind of bildungsroman—in these newer films, the protagonist is a "journalist-witness" who takes the collective as its object. Jameson, 40. If the collective indicates the films' attempts to comprehend and work with social totality, then these later films, within the context of war, demonstrate a disjuncture between the individual and the collective. It is a typically elegant reading, but it suggests the payoff to be found in reading historically, with the specifics of genre that can, over time, register revealing cultural shifts, revised contexts, and new and telling structures of feeling.

18 Fredric Jameson, *Valences of the Dialectic* (New York: Verso, 2010), 32–36; Kevin Lynch, *The Image of the City* (Cambridge, Mass.: MIT Press, 1960).

19 See Thrift, *Non-representational Theory*, and Bondi, Davidson, and Smith, *Emotion, Place, Culture*.

20 Klaus Kreimeier, *The Ufa Story* (1992; repr., Berkeley: University of California Press, 1999), 274, 275.

21 Timothy Corrigan and Patricia White, with Meta Mazaj, *Critical Visions in Film Theory: Classic and Contemporary Readings* (Boston: Bedford / St. Martin's, 2011), 443.

22 See Jaimey Fisher, *Generic Histories of German Cinema: Genre and Its Deviations* (Rochester, N.Y.: Camden House, 2013).

23 See Gerd Gemünden, "Film and Media Studies," *German Studies Review* 39, no. 3 (October 2016): 541–551.

24 See, for instance, Jeanine Basinger, *The World War II Combat Film: Anatomy of a Genre* (1986; repr., Middletown, Conn.: Wesleyan University Press, 2003); J. David Slocum, *Hollywood and the War, the Film Reader* (New York: Routledge, 2006); Douglas A. Cunningham and John Nelson, eds., *A Companion to War Films* (Malden, Mass.: Wiley, 2016); Tanine Allison, *Destructive Sublime: World War II in American Film and Media* (New Brunswick, N.J.: Rutgers University Press, 2018); and Stahl, *Through the Crosshairs*.

25 See, for instance, Marco Abel, *Violent Affect: Literature, Cinema, and Critique after Representation* (Lincoln: University of Nebraska Press, 2007); and Richard Langston, *Visions of Violence: German Avant-Garde after Fascism* (Evanston, Ill.: Northwestern University Press, 2008).

26 Jeffrey Ruoff and Alexandra Schneider, eds., *Virtual Voyages: Cinema and Travel* (Durham, N.C.: Duke University Press, 2006); Jennifer Lynn Peterson, *Education in the School of Dreams: Travelogues and Early Nonfiction Film* (Durham, N.C.: Duke University Press, 2013); Julia Hallam and Les Roberts, eds., *Locating the Moving Image: New Approaches to Film and Place* (Bloomington: Indiana University Press, 2013); Lynne Kirby, *Parallel Tracks: The Railroad and Silent Cinema* (Durham, N.C.: Duke University Press, 1997).

27 Timothy Lenoir and Luke Caldwell, *The Military-Entertainment Process* (Cambridge, Mass.: Harvard University Press, 2018).

28 See, for instance, Konrad Jarausch, *After Hitler: Recivilizing Germans, 1945–1995* (Oxford: Oxford University Press, 2008); and Konrad Jarausch and Michael Geyer, *Shattered Past: Reconstructing German Histories* (Princeton, N.J.: Princeton University Press, 2003).

29 See Fisher, *Generic Histories*.

30 Rick Altman, *Film/Genre* (1999; repr., London: British Film Institute, 2002), 89.

31 Altman, 89.

32 Altman, 49.

33 Steve Neale points out that structuralism tended to reduce genre to society's timeless oppositions (see Steve Neale, *Genre and Hollywood* [London: Routledge, 2000], 4–5), while Altman problematizes its tendency to "surround" genres with "pagan rituals, native ceremonies, undated traditional texts, and descriptions of human nature" to render genre a "rabbit hole" for archetype and myth. Altman, *Film/Genre*, 49. For Altman, looking back from the late 1990s and stating it starkly, "two generations of genre critics have done violence to the historical dimensions" of genre. Altman, 49. These points have helped steer genre study in a new direction, although

it should be observed that both John G. Cawelti and Thomas Schatz did address the evolution of genres. See, for instance, John G. Cawelti, *Adventure, Mystery and Romance: Formula Stories as Art and Popular Culture* (Chicago: University of Chicago Press, 1976); John G. Cawelti, "*Chinatown* and Generic Transformation in Recent American Film," in *Film Genre Reader III*, ed. Barry Keith Grant (1997; repr., Austin: University of Texas Press, 2003); and Thomas Schatz, *Hollywood Genres: Formulas, Filmmaking and the Studio System* (New York: Random House, 1981), 13.

34 Altman, *Film/Genre*, 65.

35 Neale, *Genre and Hollywood*, 39–40. This wide field would include, at the least, the "public discourse of press, television, radio." Neale, 39.

36 See Janet Staiger, "Hybrid or Inbred: The Purity Hypothesis and Hollywood Genre History," in Grant, *Film Genre Reader III*.

37 Andrew Tudor, "Genre," in Grant, 3–11.

38 For example, J. David Slocum's anthology *Violence and American Cinema* (London: Routledge, 2001) largely passes over the war film. While it offers chapters on Westerns, noirs, and action films—and even one on slapstick—the volume does not have any sustained essay on, or investigation of, war films. Similarly, in his *Fascination of Film Violence* (New York: Palgrave, 2015), Henry Bacon offers a general theory of the history of violence on the screen, but it does not adequately distinguish the war genre from other forms of violence. For example, there is no section on war films, and in discussing a film like Godard's *Le Petit Soldat* (*The Little Soldier*, 1963), he pairs it not with other films about the French-Algerian war or even other war films but instead with *Breathless* (*A bout de souffle*, 1959), offering an auteurist rather than generic approach. On this challenge of working through violence in the war film, cf. Lisa Haegele, "Violence," in *The Berlin School Glossary: An ABC of the New Wave in German Cinema*, ed. Roger Cook et al. (London: Intellect, 2013).

39 Andrew Tudor uncovered the now often-cited notion of an "empiricist dilemma" in most genre theories and histories. See Tudor's chapter "Genre," from his *Theories of Film*, reprinted in Grant, *Film Genre Reader III*, 5. Tudor observes that scholars analyzing a genre invariably begin by examining a given set of films to ascertain what "indefinable 'X'" the films share that qualifies them for that particular genre. Tudor, 3.

40 Neale arrives at such a definition by commencing with a more audience-oriented inquiry: he follows John Ellis in asking what the "narrative image" of a genre is—that is, what people imagine when they hear the name of a given genre. Neale, *Genre and Hollywood*, 39.

41 Steven Shaviro, *Post-cinematic Affect* (Winchester, U.K.: Zero Books, 2010), 3–4.

42 Carl Plantinga, *Moving Viewers: American Film and the Spectator's Experience* (Berkeley: University of California Press, 2009), 54–56.

43 See Lauren Berlant, "Cruel Optimism: On Marx, Loss and the Senses," *New Formations*, no. 63 (Winter 2007): 33–51; and Ben Anderson, "Affective Atmospheres," *Emotion, Space and Society* 2, no. 2 (December 2009): 77–81.

44 Julian Hanich, *Cinematic Emotion in Horror Films and Thrillers: The Aesthetic Paradox of Pleasurable Fear* (New York: Routledge, 2010), 102–103.

45 Hanich, 102–103.

46 Alexander Watson, *Ring of Steel: German and Austria-Hungary in World War I* (New York: Basic Books, 2014), loc. 5220–5224 of 20422, Kindle.

47 See especially John Urry, *Mobilities* (Cambridge: Polity, 2007).

48 Jameson, *Geopolitical Aesthetic*, 15.

49 See Ruoff and Schneider, *Virtual Voyages*; and Peterson, *School of Dreams*.

50 Hanich points out that films favor affects and emotions that viewers would be familiar with, even when conveying unconventional setups. Hanich, *Cinematic Emotion*, 106.

51 John David Rhodes and Elena Gorfinkel, eds., *Taking Place: Location and the Moving Image* (Minneapolis: University of Minnesota Press, 2011).

52 See John Keegan, *The First World War* (1998; repr., New York: Vintage, 2000), loc. 481–484 of 8961, Kindle: "Submerged, also, below the surface of Europe's civil geography was a secondary, military geography of corps and divisional districts. France, a country of ninety administrative departments, created by the First Republic to supplant the old royal provinces with territorial units of approximately equal size, named for the most part after the local river—Oise, Somme, Aisne, Marne, Meuse (names to which the First World War would give a doleful fame)—was also divided into twenty military districts, comprising four or five departments." I will develop this idea of a second geography further in chapter 3, as a number of authors (e.g., Caren Kaplan) write about it in the context of the military mapping of society.

53 Thomas Lekan and Thomas Zeller, eds., *Germany's Nature: Cultural Landscape and Environmental History* (New Brunswick, N.J.: Rutgers University Press, 2005), 5.

54 See, for example, Michael Heffernan, "Fin de siècle, fin du monde? On the Origins of European Geopolitics, 1890–1920," in *Geopolitical Traditions: Critical Histories of a Century of Geopolitical Thought*, ed. David Atkinson and Klaus Dodds (New York: Routledge, 2000); and Bruno Schelhaas and Ingro Hönsch, "History of German Geography: Worldwide Reputation and Strategies of Nationalization and Institutionalization," in *Geography: Discipline, Profession and Subject since 1870, an International Survey*, ed. Gary S. Dunbar (Dordrecht: Kluwer, 2001).

55 See Colin Flint, *Introduction to Geopolitics* (London: Routledge, 2017), 4.

56 Henri Lefebvre, *The Production of Space*, trans. Donald Nicholson-Smith (Cambridge: Blackwell, 1991), 49, 234–236.

57 Geoffrey Parker, *Western Geopolitical Thought in the Twentieth Century* (Sydney: Croom Helm, 1985), 55.

58 Mary Gilmartin and Eleonore Kofman, "Critically Feminist Geopolitics," in *Mapping Women, Making Politics: Feminist Perspectives on Political Geography*, ed. Lynn A. Staeheli, Eleonore Kofman, and Linda Peake (London: Routledge, 2004), 113–126, here 113.

59 Flint, *Introduction to Geopolitics*, 11.

60 For skepticism about the role of geopolitics in the regime, see Mark Bassin, "Race contra Space: The Conflict between German *Geopolitik* and National Socialism," in *Hitler's Geographies: The Spatialities of the Third Reich*, ed. Paolo Giaccaria and Claudio Minca (Chicago: University of Chicago Press, 2015); and Gearóid Ó Tuathail, *Critical Geopolitics* (Minneapolis: University of Minnesota Press, 1996). Although they effectively argue that the U.S. media exaggerated Haushofer as being some kind of policy mastermind behind Hess and Hitler, I do not think the insights of Bassin and Ó Tuathail into U.S. histrionics detract from these ideas being part of the intellectual context in Germany at the time.

61 Shelley Baranowski, *Nazi Empire: German Colonialism and Imperialism from Bismarck to Hitler* (Cambridge, Mass.: Harvard University Press, 2011), 141–142; cf. 177–179.

62 Lefebvre, *Production of Space*, 32–33.

63 Donna J. Haraway, "Situated Knowledges: The Science Question in Feminism and the Privilege of Partial Perspective," *Feminist Studies* 14, no. 3 (Autumn 1988): 575–599, here 581.

64 Heffernan, "Fin de siècle?," 29.

65 See Caren Kaplan, *Aerial Aftermaths: War from Above* (Durham, N.C.: Duke University Press, 2018), loc. 6 of 8915, Kindle, where she discusses an early theorist of the hot-air balloon as speculating on its potential to breach fortress walls.

66 See Caren Kaplan, "The Balloon Prospect: Aerostatic Observation and the Emergence of Militarised Aeromobility," in *From Above: War, Violence, and Verticality*, ed. Peter Adey, Mark Whitehead, and Alison J. William (London: Hurst, 2013), 28–29.

67 Yar Mintzker, *The Defortification of the German City, 1689–1866* (Cambridge: Cambridge University Press, 2012), 239.

68 Harvey, *Consciousness*, 13.

69 Harvey, 13.

70 Harvey, 13.

71 I use the notion of ensemble (as a variation on what Gilles Deleuze and Félix Guattari term "assemblage"/*agencement*) to convey a collection of elements that underscore the contingency of their collection: "We will call an assemblage every constellation of singularities and traits deducted from the flow—selected, organized, stratified—in such a way as to converge (consistency) artificially and naturally: an assemblage, in this sense, is a veritable invention." Gilles Deleuze and Félix Guattari, *A Thousand Plateaus*, trans. Brian Massumi (London: A&C Black, 2004), 448. They describe how the "man-horse-bow" assemblage, for example, demonstrates the way assemblages cross organic-inorganic lines, certainly an important constellation for war. In its contingency, such a notion should complicate any facile structural understanding. I regard spaces, especially for the purposes of film and film interpretation, along these lines of an assemblage, constellation, or ensemble rather than structure.

72 David Harvey, *Spaces of Hope* (Berkeley: University of California Press, 2000), 97–116.

73 Manuel Castells, *The Rise of the Network Society* (Oxford: Blackwell, 1996), 453–469.

Chapter 2 Land into Landscape, Landscape into Territory

1 W. Warstat, "Der Kinematograph im Felde," *Lichtbild-Bühne* 8, no. 17 (1915): 26–36.

2 Steve Neale, *Genre and Hollywood* (London: Routledge, 2000), 39–40.

3 Cf. Philipp Stiasny, *Das Kino und der Krieg, Deutschland 1914–1929* (Munich: edition text + kritik, 2009), 42.

4 See Klaus Kreimeier, *The Ufa Story* (1992; repr., Berkeley: University of California Press, 1999), 21–23, for the founding of BUFA and then Ufa under the star of increasing militarization in the late war. Kreimeier sees *The Diary of Dr. Hart* as among the most important of BUFA's circa fifteen long-form features.

5 Warstat, "Der Kinematograph im Felde," 26.

6 Thomas Elsaesser, "Early German Cinema: A Second Life?," in *A Second Life: German Cinema's First Decades*, ed. Thomas Elsaesser and Michael Wedel (Amsterdam: Amsterdam University Press, 1996), 13–14.

7 Warstat, "Der Kinematograph im Felde," 26.

8 I have in mind here, as I discussed in the introduction, the geopolitical aesthetic that Jameson sketches in his *The Geopolitical Aesthetic: Cinema and Space in the World System* (Bloomington: Indiana University Press, 1992).

9 A. Mellini, "Die Politik und der Film," *Lichtbild-Bühne* 7, no. 56 (August 29, 1914): 1. Cf. Elsaesser, "Early German Cinema."

10 "Mars regiert die Stunde," *Der Kinematograph*, no. 397 (August 5, 1914).

11 Stiasny, *Das kino und der krieg*, 27.

12 Stiasny, 27.
13 "Deutsche Kriegsfilms [*sic*] ins Ausland," *Der Kinematograph*, no. 475 (February 2, 1916).
14 In terms of such adjustments, see "Mars regiert die Stunde," 3–4.
15 "Zeitgemässe Kinobetriebe," *Der Kinematograph*, no. 402 (September 9, 1914); "Das Programm in Kriegszeiten," *Der Kinematograph*, no. 406 (September 30, 1914).
16 Jennifer Lynn Peterson, *Education in the School of Dreams: Travelogues and Early Nonfiction Film* (Durham, N.C.: Duke University Press, 2013), loc. 1500 of 8661, Kindle.
17 Julius Becker, "Der Kampf gegen die ausländischen Films," *Lichtbild-Bühne* 7, no. 62 (September 19, 1914): 8.
18 Distributor ads in both *Der Kinematograph* and *Lichtbild-Bühne* reflect this tendency in these years.
19 As noted in the introduction, just because the films were propagandistic does not mean that they were not influential or are not worth analyzing—something particularly true of the films under the Nazi regime, since many propaganda films were among the demonstrably most popular and, as I shall argue, were influential even after 1945.
20 Stiasny, *Das kino und der krieg*; Kester's book, *Film Front Weimar*, more pertains to the Weimar era, but she addresses war films made during World War I in the early parts of the book.
21 Jeffrey Ruoff and Alexandra Schneider, eds., *Virtual Voyages: Cinema and Travel* (Durham, N.C.: Duke University Press, 2006); Peterson, *School of Dreams*.
22 W. Richter, "Landschaftskinematographie," *Der Kinematograph*, no. 360 (November 19, 1913): 3.
23 Richter, 3.
24 For instance, "Die Untersee-Kinematographie," *Der Kinematograph*, no. 405 (September 30, 1914): 1, discusses incorporating ethnographic materials from border regions into the new film programs.
25 "Krieg und Kino," *Der Kinematograph*, no. 397 (August 5, 1914). Various articles from before and then during the war observe the achievements of foreign filmmakers, especially those with French and Italian firms, in travel and landscape films and exhort German producers and filmmakers to do similarly. See "Quo Vadis," *Der Kinematograph*, no. 394 (July 15, 1914); and Alfred Rosenthal, "Landschaftsnovellen im Film," *Der Kinematograph*, no. 534 (March 21, 1917).
26 "Krieg und Kino."
27 "Kinematographie in Kriegszeiten," *Der Kinematograph*, no. 398 (August 12, 1914): 1.
28 "Zeitgemässe Kinobetriebe."
29 Hans Bourquin, "Die Kinematographie von Landschaften," *Der Kinematograph*, no. 461 (October 27, 1915).
30 Leni became a well-known director in the Weimar era. He directed such films as *Waxworks* (*Wachsfigurenkabinett*, 1923/1924).
31 See, for instance, Thomas Brandlmeier, "Die polnische Karte: Anmerkungen zu Paul Lenis Film Das Tage Buch des Dr. Hart," in *Studien zur Kulturgeschichte des deutschen Polenbildes 1848–1939*, ed. Hendrik Feindt (Wiesbaden, Germany: Harrassowtiz Verlag, 1995), 156–164.
32 The film depicts how German troops will liberate Poles from Russia and thereby contribute to a Poland of its own. Of course, this normative trajectory to nationhood was not true in either World War I or World War II. What we understand as Poland today had been (and would be again) repeatedly partitioned, carved up primarily

among Russia, Prussia, and Austria-Hungary. For instance, Kalisz's proximity to Prussia had brought it considerable commercial prosperity but also made it one of the first targets in Germans' eastern front campaign: the *Berliner Tageblatt* reported the German occupation of Kalisz as early as August 3, 1914, just one day after M1, or the first day of mobilization. See D. E. Moraht, "Deutsche Infanterie in Kalisch," *Berliner Tageblatt*, August 3, 1914.

33 The difficult history of Poland (its multiple partitions, rising national consciousness under Napoleon, failed uprisings, etc.) had, in effect, left this region with a palimpsest of different territories that amounted to no actual Poland as of 1914. This territorial fantasy of the film had specific reasons, in both 1914 and 1917/1918: throughout the war, the three powers (Austria-Hungary, Russia, and Prussia/Germany) self-servingly kept Poland partitioned, much as they had vied for Polish loyalty and troops throughout the nineteenth century, a competition the film makes manifest even as *Dr. Hart* seems to spin a private tale. Given its complicated history, a remapping along national-ethnic lines remained the goal of many ethnic Poles. Some Poles within each territory saw their own governing power (Austria-Hungary, Prussia, or Russia) as the most likely geopolitical ticket to an autonomous and unified Poland, even though all three powers had been consistently brutal in pursuing their own self-interest against the Poles.

34 See Fredric Jameson, *The Geopolitical Aesthetic: Cinema and Space in the World System* (Bloomington: Indiana University Press, 1992), 13–15, where he describes the spatialization of narrative.

35 See, for instance, Charles Musser, *Before the Nickelodeon: Edwin S. Porter and the Edison Manufacturing Company*, The UCLA Film and Television Archive Studies in History, Criticism, and Theory (Berkeley: University of California Press, 1991), 108–113.

36 Peterson, *School of Dreams*, loc. 533 of 8661.

37 I shall elaborate on this issue more in chapter 2, but the references here and there are to Julian Hanich, *Cinematic Emotion in Horror Films and Thrillers: The Aesthetic Paradox of Pleasurable Fear* (New York: Routledge, 2010).

38 See Hans-Michael Bock, *Paul Leni: Grafik, Theater, Film* (Frankfurt: Deutsches Filmmuseum, 1986).

39 W. J. T. Mitchell, "Imperial Landscape," in *Landscape and Power*, ed. W. J. T. Mitchell (1994; repr., Chicago: University of Chicago Press, 2002), 27.

40 Mitchell, 19.

41 Mitchell, 19.

42 Mitchell, 14; W. J. T. Mitchell, "Preface to the Second Edition of *Landscape and Power*: Space, Place, and Landscape," in Mitchell, *Landscape and Power*.

43 Mitchell, "Imperial Landscape," 10.

44 Tom Gunning, "Landscape and the Fantasy of Moving Pictures: Early Cinema's Phantom Rides," in *Cinema and Landscape*, ed. Graeme Harper and Jonathan Rayner (Chicago: University of Chicago Press, 2010), 36–37; cf. Wolfgang Schivelbusch, *Railway Journey: The Industrialization of Time and Space in the Nineteenth Century* (1977; repr., Berkeley: University of California Press, 1986).

45 Joel Snyder, "Territorial Photography," in Mitchell, *Landscape and Power*.

46 Gunning, "Landscape," 44–45.

47 Gunning, 52–54.

48 Peterson, *School of Dreams*, loc. 535 of 8661. Cf. John Urry, *Mobilities* (Cambridge: Polity, 2007), 19.

49 Peterson, *School of Dreams*, loc. 3350 of 8661. Cf. Giorgio Bertellini, *Italy in Early American Cinema: Race, Landscape, and the Picturesque* (Bloomington: Indiana University Press, 2009), 3–4.
50 Peterson, *School of Dreams*, loc. 3354 of 8661.
51 Schivelbusch, *Railway Journey*, 66.
52 See the introduction for the usage of *assemblage* and *ensemble*.
53 Gunning, "Landscape," 35–36.
54 Malcolm Andrew, *Landscape and Western Art* (Oxford: Oxford University Press, 1999), 44.
55 Gillian Rose, *Feminism and Geography: The Limits of Geographical Knowledge* (Minneapolis: University of Minnesota Press, 1993), 160.
56 Mitchell, "Preface," vii.
57 See Jaimey Fisher, "Exploding the Cosmopolitan and Treating the Foreigners' Foreignness: Paul Leni's *The Diary of Dr. Hart*," in *Refocus: The Films of Paul Leni*, ed. Erica Tortolani and Martin F. Norden (Edinburgh: Edinburgh University Press, 2021).
58 Urry, *Mobilities*, 10, 13, 38, 50; the transition from embodied to technologized mobility is one of the key themes of his study.
59 Simon Schama, *Landscape and Memory* (New York: Vintage, 1996), 100–101.
60 Schama, 120–121.
61 Schama, 110.
62 See Mitchell, "Imperial Landscape," 24, 26, on the serpentine path as well as the depth of landscape composition in Peterson, *School of Dreams*, loc. 3736 of 8661.
63 The next sequence, of Hart among his comrades to celebrate the mobilization, tellingly locates the body of Hart in this kind of imagistic depth: he himself seems to occupy the space of the boldness-inspiring monument (for example, with Hart's holding up his fist in an echo of the raised sword of Hermann's monument). Viewers are guided through a deep-space frame, past soldiers and flags, to a charismatic speaker in what will become an iconographic image of a leader.
64 Alexander Watson, *Ring of Steel: German and Austria-Hungary in World War I* (New York: Basic Books, 2014), loc. 3339–3342 of 20422, Kindle.
65 Holger H. Herwig, *The First World War: Germany and Austria, 1914–18*, 2nd ed. (London: Bloomsbury, 2014), loc. 367 of 13356, Kindle.
66 Watson, *Ring of Steel*, loc. 3520–3525 of 20422.
67 Urry, *Mobilities*, 24, 47–48, 54–55; Gunning, "Landscape," 35–38, 48, 56.
68 Paul Virilio, *War and Cinema: The Logistics of Perception* (New York: Verso, 1991), 3. See also Robert Stam's account of how a kind of prosthetic vision emerges in the fusion of media with military surveillance. Robert Stam, "Mobilizing Fictions: The Media, the Gulf War, and the Recruitment of the Spectator," *Public Culture* 2 (1992): 102–103.
69 Herwig, *First World War*, loc. 1557 of 13356, citing Nachlass Schlieffen, N 43, vol. 101, "Der Krieg in der Gegenwart." Schlieffen later published his views in the *Deutsche Revue* (January 1909): 13–24, quoted in Herwig, *First World War*, loc. 1560 of 13356.
70 Bruno Latour, "Recalling ANT," *Sociological Review* 47, no. 21 (1999): 17–18.
71 See Doreen Massey, "Power-Geometry and Progressive Sense of Place," in *Mapping the Futures: Local Cultures, Global Change*, ed. John Bird et al. (London: Routledge, 1993), 40–70; and Doreen Massey, *For Space* (London: SAGE, 2005).
72 David Delaney, *Territory: A Short Introduction* (Oxford: Wiley-Blackwell, 2005), 12, 16–17.

73 Martin Creveld, *The Transformation of War* (New York: Free Press, 1991), 115.

74 Henri Lefebvre, *The Production of Space*, trans. Donald Nicholson-Smith (Cambridge: Blackwell, 1991), 45. It is noticeable that the horse is a central part of this circulating entity (as it was throughout World War I): the point is the forms of mobility and spaces they make rather than just the celebration of modern transportation.

75 For abstract space, see Lefebvre, *Production of Space*, 49, 234–236; and for homogenized space, see David Harvey, *Consciousness and the Urban Experience* (Oxford: Blackwell, 1985), 32.

76 Tom Conley, *Cartographic Cinema* (Minneapolis: University of Minnesota Press, 2007), loc. 450, 452, 650, 651 of 4225, Kindle.

77 Conley, loc. 384–385 of 4225.

78 Harvey, *Consciousness*, 12–13.

79 Lefebvre, *Production of Space*, 85–86.

80 See Heide Schlüppmann, *The Uncanny Gaze: The Drama of Early Cinema*, trans. Inge Pollmann, with a foreword by Miriam Hansen (1990; repr., Urbana: University of Illinois Press, 2010), 8–9.

81 Michel Foucault, "Of Other Spaces: Utopias and Heterotopias," *Diacritics* 16, no. 1 (Spring 1986): 22–27.

82 Warstat, "Der Kinematograph im Felde."

83 Alexander Watson, *Enduring the Great War: Combat, Morale and Collapse in the German and British Armies, 1914–1918* (Cambridge: Cambridge University Press, 2008), loc. 190–192 of 8871, Kindle.

84 In advertisements by the film's distributor, National-Film, it was listed as a Kriegsdrama. See *Lichtbild-Bühne*, October 6, 1917.

85 Maria Del Mar Azcona, *The Multi-protagonist Film* (Hoboken: Wiley-Blackwell, 2010).

86 Watson, *Ring of Steel*, loc. 1841–1844 of 20422.

87 Lefebvre, *Production of Space*, 77–79.

88 See, for instance, "Die Programme der Berliner Theater: Besprechungen," *Der Film* 1, no. 2 (January 13, 1917): 32–33.

89 Roger Chickering, *Imperial Germany and the Great War, 1914–18*, 3rd ed. (Cambridge: Cambridge University Press, 2014), 80–81.

90 Stiasny, *Das kino und der krieg*, 87.

91 Stiasny, 82. The strikes in March–April 1917 were large-scale strikes against munitions manufacturing, said to have involved some three hundred thousand workers. Stiasny describes how a Spartakus pamphlet shared some of the same wording used in the film to describe the Fremde.

92 Stiasny, 87.

93 Stiasny, 82.

94 Chickering, *Imperial Germany*, 77–79; see also Roger Chickering, "Total War: Use and Abuse of a Concept," in *Anticipating Total War: The German and American Experiences, 1871–1914*, ed. Manfred F. Boemeke, Roger Chickering, and Stig Förster (Cambridge, 1999).

95 Chickering, *Imperial Germany*, 82.

96 Harvey, *Consciousness*, 13–14.

97 Walter Benjamin, "The Paris of the Second Empire in Baudelaire," in *Selected Writings*, ed. Michael Jennings and Gary Smith, vol. 4, *1938–1940* (Cambridge, Mass.: Harvard University Press, 2006), 3–92.

98 Watson, *Ring of Steel*, loc. 7221–7225 of 20422.
99 Robert G. Moeller, "Dimensions of Social Conflict in the Great War: The View from the German Countryside," *Central European History* 14, no. 2 (June 1981): 152.
100 Watson, *Ring of Steel*, loc. 7231 of 20422.
101 Watson, loc. 1622–1623 of 20422.
102 Christopher Clark, *The Sleepwalkers: How Europe Went to War in 1914* (New York: HarperCollins, 2012), 165.
103 Chickering, *Imperial Germany*, 31.
104 Chickering, 72.
105 Watson, *Ring of Steel*, loc. 6688, 6751 of 20422.
106 Chickering, *Imperial Germany*, 94.
107 Watson, *Ring of Steel*, loc. 7226, 7256 of 20422.
108 Kevin Lynch, *Image of the City* (Cambridge, Mass.: MIT Press, 1960), 64.
109 Watson, *Ring of Steel*, loc. 3279–3281 of 20422.
110 Bastian Heinsohn, "Film as Pedagogy in Late Weimar and Early Nazi Cinema: The Role of the Street in Mobilizing the Spectator," in *Continuity and Crisis in German Cinema 1928–1936*, ed. Barbara Hales, Valerie Weinstein, and Mihaela Petrescu (Rochester, N.Y.: Camden House, 2016), 51–71; Todd Herzog, "Crime Stories: Criminal, Society and the Modernist Case History," *Representations* 80, no. 1 (2002): 34–61.
111 See Doreen Massey, "Flexible Sexism," *Environment and Planning D: Society and Space* 9, no. 1 (1991): 31–57.
112 Watson, *Ring of Steel*, loc. 4373 of 20422; Roger Chickering, *The Great War and Urban Life in Germany: Freiburg, 1914–1918* (Cambridge: Cambridge University Press, 2007), 372–390.
113 Jürgen Habermas, *The Structural Transformation of the Public Sphere: An Inquiry into a Category of Bourgeois Society* (Cambridge, Mass.: MIT Press, 1990), 27–33.
114 Watson, *Ring of Steel*, loc. 6863 of 20442.
115 Detlev Peukert, *The Weimar Republic: Crisis of Classical Modernity* (London: Penguin, 1991); Jaimey Fisher, *Disciplining Germany: Youth, Reeducation, and Reconstruction after the Second World War* (Detroit: Wayne State University Press, 2007).
116 Watson, *Ring of Steel*, loc. 7322–7324 of 20422; see also Watson, loc. 14167 of 20422.
117 The failure of the Hindenburg Program was clear by spring 1917; see Chickering, *Imperial Germany*, 82–83.
118 Watson, *Ring of Steel*, loc. 7498 of 20422.
119 Watson, loc. 4541 of 20422.

Chapter 3 Landscapes of Death and Memories of the Human

1 "Erfolg der *Westfront 1918*," *Der Film* 14, no. 21 (May 24, 1930): 1 (cover). An earlier version of this chapter was published in Jaimey Fisher, "Landscapes of Death: Sound, Space, and Commemoration in G. W. Pabst's *Westfront 1918* (1930)," in *The Many Faces of Weimar Cinema: New Approaches to Weimar Film*, ed. Christian Rogowski (Rochester, N.Y.: Camden House, 2010), 268–285.
2 "Erfolg der *Westfront 1918*," 1 (cover).
3 "Erfolg der *Westfront 1918*," 1 (cover).
4 Pierre Nora, "General Introduction: Between Memory and History," in *Realms of Memory: Rethinking the French Past*, ed. Pierre Nora (New York: Columbia University Press, 1996), 7.

5 Alison Landsberg, *Prosthetic Memory: The Transformation of American Remembrance in the Age of Mass Culture* (New York: Columbia University Press, 2004), 120–121.

6 Jay Winter, "Sites of Memory and the Shadow of War," in *Cultural Memory Studies: An International and Interdisciplinary Handbook*, ed. Astrid Erll and Ansgar Nünning (Berlin: de Gruyter, 2008), 64. Nora also makes similar points about collective and personal memory in his "General Introduction."

7 Michael Geisler, "The Battleground of Modernity: *Westfront 1918* (1930)," in *The Films of G. W. Pabst: An Extraterritorial Cinema*, ed. Eric Renschler (New Brunswick, N.J.: Rutgers University Press, 1990), 91–102.

8 Bernd Hüppauf, "Langemarck, Verdun, and the Myth of a New Man in Germany after the First World War," *War and Society* 6, no. 2 (1988): 70–103.

9 Kaes convincingly disputes Kracauer's still-predominant yet reductive psychological model. See Anton Kaes, *Shell Shock Cinema: Weimar Culture and the Wounds of War* (Princeton, N.J.: Princeton University Press, 2010), 4–6. For Kaes, the cutting of this trauma across genres proves telling, while in my own examination, I focus on how the war genre self-consciously took up the matter of memory in its personal and/versus collective forms.

10 Jeffrey Olick, "From Collective Memory to the Sociology of Mnemonic Practices and Products," in *Cultural Memory Studies: An International and Interdisciplinary Handbook*, ed. Astrid Erll and Ansgar Nünning (Berlin: de Gruyter, 2008), 152.

11 Jeanine Basinger, *The World War II Combat Film: Anatomy of a Genre* (1986; repr., Middletown, Conn.: Wesleyan University Press, 2003).

12 Neil Smith, "Contours of a Spatialized Politics: Homeless Vehicles and the Production of Geographical Scale," *Social Text* 33 (1992): 54–81.

13 Sallie A. Marston, "The Social Construction of Scale," *Progress in Human Geography* 24, no. 2 (2000): 219–242.

14 Smith, "Contours."

15 Sallie A. Marston, J. P. Jones III, and K. Woodward, "Human Geography without Scale," *Transactions of the Institute of British Geographers*, n.s., 30, no. 4 (2005): 416–432. See Andrew Herod, *Scale* (London: Routledge, 2011), 33.

16 Marston, "Social Construction," 219–242.

17 Henri Lefebvre, *On the State* (Paris: Gallimard, 1976), 2:69. See, for this historicization of scales in Lefebvre, Neil Brenner, "The Urban Question as a Scale Question: Reflections on Henri Lefebvre, Urban Theory and the Politics of Scale," *International Journal of Urban and Regional Research* 24, no. 2 (June 2000): 361–378.

18 See Fredric Jameson, *The Geopolitical Aesthetic: Cinema and Space in the World System* (Bloomington: Indiana University Press, 1992).

19 The French character in the film is referred to as Yvette in the opening credits, but the student addresses her, quite audibly, as Jacqueline.

20 Jameson, *Geopolitical Aesthetic*, 74–75.

21 Jameson, 15. This notion of a character coming upon a secret second map is crucial to the cognitive mapping that Jameson traces in *Geopolitical Aesthetic*, for example: "Archetypal journeys back beyond the surface appearance of things are also dimly reawakened, from antiquity and Dante . . . , redeemed for once only by the possibility of turning the tables, when the hero is able to tap into the circuits and bug the buggers, abolishing space with his own kind of simultaneity by scrambling all the symptoms and producing his messages from all corners of the map at the same time." Jameson, 15; or "But the narrative by which [*Videodrome*] seeks to achieve this reality-effect remains one in which the individual subject of the

protagonist somehow manages to blunder into the collective web of the hidden social order." Jameson, 33.

22 Keegan describes, as cited in the introduction, a submerged geography of wartime that is parallel to civilian geographies. John Keegan, *The First World War* (1998; repr., New York: Vintage, 2000), loc. 481–484 of 8961, Kindle. Kaplan recounts how a number of new technologies changed senses of space to such a degree that they seemed to conjure entire new geographies. See Caren Kaplan, *Aerial Aftermaths: War from Above* (Durham, N.C.: Duke University Press, 2018), loc. 1611 of 8915, Kindle; see also her writings on the way that GPS created new geographies.

23 Kurt Pinthus, "*Westfront 1918*," *Das Abendblatt*, May 24, 1930.

24 Siegfried Kracauer, "*Westfront 1918*," *Frankfurter Zeitung*, May 27, 1930, https://www.filmportal.de/node/8133/material/678941.

25 Shooting script for *Westfront 1918*, Münchner Filmmuseum, p. 65.

26 Alison Landsberg, *Engaging the Past* (New York: Columbia University Press, 2015), 86–88.

27 Julian Hanich, *Cinematic Emotion in Horror Films and Thrillers: The Aesthetic Paradox of Pleasurable Fear* (New York: Routledge, 2010), 106.

28 See Jaimey Fisher, "Film and Affect, Theories Entwined: The Case of the War Genre in *Saving Private Ryan* (Steven Spielberg, 1998)," in *The Palgrave Handbook of Affect Studies and Textual Criticism*, ed. Donald R. Wehrs and Thomas Blake (New York: Palgrave, 2018), 509–537.

29 Hanich, *Cinematic Emotion*, 102–103.

30 Shooting script for *Westfront*, p. 13.

31 Wolfgang Schivelbusch, *Railway Journey: The Industrialization of Time and Space in the Nineteenth Century* (1977; repr., Berkeley: University of California Press, 1986), 31–32, 64; Giuliana Bruno, *Streetwalking on a Ruined Map: Cultural Theory and the City Films of Elvira Notari* (Princeton, N.J.: Princeton University Press, 1993).

32 See Walter Benjamin, "Theories of German Fascism," in *Selected Writings*, ed. Michael Jennings and Gary Smith, vol. 2, *1927–1934* (Cambridge, Mass.: Belknap Press of Harvard University Press, 1999); and Walter Benjamin, "Little History of Photography," in Jennings and Smith, *Selected Writings*, 2:518.

33 Benjamin, "Theories of German Fascism," 317–318.

34 Benjamin, 318.

35 Benjamin, 318.

36 Kracauer, "*Westfront 1918*."

37 Benjamin, "Little History of Photography," 518.

38 Benjamin, 518.

39 Walter Benjamin, "The Work of Art in the Age of Mechanical Reproduction," in *Selected Writings*, ed. Michael Jennings and Gary Smith, vol. 4, *1938–1940* (Cambridge, Mass.: Harvard University Press, 2006), 255.

40 Benjamin, "Little History of Photography," 518.

41 Kracauer, "*Westfront 1918*."

42 Hüppauf, "Langemarck," 70–103. For additional details on the Langemarck myth, see George Mosse, *Fallen Soldiers: Reshaping the Memory of the World Wars* (Oxford: Oxford University Press, 1991); Herbert Lehnert, "'Der gute Krieg ist es, der jede Sache heiligt': Das Innere Reich, Langemarck und moralische Konsequenzen," in *Im Dialog mit der Moderne: Zur deutschsprachigen Literatur von der Gründerzeit bis zur Gegenwart*, ed. Roland Jost and Hansgeorg Schmidt-Bergmann (Frankfurt: Athenäum, 1986), 311–321; and Herbert Lehnert, "Langemarck—historisch und symbolisch," *Orbis Litterarum* 42 (1987): 271–290.

43 Reinhart Koselleck, "War Memorials: Identity Formation of the Survivors," in *The Practice of Conceptual History: Timing History, Spacing Concepts*, trans. and ed. Todd Presner (Stanford, Calif.: Stanford University Press, 2002), 297, 308.
44 Maureen Turim, *Flashbacks in Film: Memory and History* (New York: Routledge, 1989), 2.
45 Hans Siemsen, "Kameradschaft," *Welt am Montag*, November 23, 1931, Bundesarchiv (BA) 8520/I.
46 Siemsen.
47 "G. W. Pabst zu seinem *Kameradschaft*," *Reichsfilmblatt*, November 7, 1931, BA 8520/I. Much of this material repeats in "G. W. Pabst über K," *Mein Film*, no. 316 (1932): 6.
48 Siegfried Kracauer, "Kameradschaft," *Frankfurter Zeitung*, November 21, 1931, BA 8520/I.
49 Jameson, *Geopolitical Aesthetic*, 15, 74–75.
50 "G. W. Pabst zu *Kameradschaft*," *Neue Pariser Zeitung*, February 4, 1931, BA 8520/I.

Chapter 4 Combat Films and Their Aerial Spaces under the Nazi Regime

1 Erich Maschke, "Der geopolitsche Film," *Zeitschrift für Geopolitik* 3 (1928): 276.
2 Derek Gregory, *Geographical Imaginations* (Oxford: Blackwell, 1994).
3 Maschke, "Der geopolitsche Film," 276.
4 Maschke, 276.
5 Karsten Witte, *Lachende Erbe, toller Tag: Filmkomödie im Dritten Reich* (Berlin: Vorwerk 8, 1995); Eric Rentschler, *The Ministry of Illusion* (Cambridge, Mass.: Harvard University Press, 1997); Linda Schulte-Sasse, *Entertaining the Reich: Illusions of Wholeness in Nazi Cinema* (Durham, N.C.: Duke University Press, 1996); Sabine Hake, *Popular Cinema of the Third Reich* (Austin: University of Texas Press, 2001); Mary-Elizabeth O'Brien, *Nazi Cinema as Enchantment: The Politics of Entertainment in the Third Reich* (Rochester, N.Y.: Camden House, 2004); Laura Heins, *Nazi Film Melodrama* (Urbana: University of Illinois Press, 2013).
6 Jay W. Baird, *The Mythical World of Nazi Propaganda, 1939–1945* (Minneapolis: University of Minnesota Press, 1975); David Welch, *Propaganda and the German Cinema 1933–1945* (London: I. B. Tauris, 1983).
7 Both O'Brien, *Nazi Cinema as Enchantment*, and Heins, *Nazi Film Melodrama*, for instance, highlight melodrama.
8 Heins, *Nazi Film Melodrama*, 1.
9 Various contemporary reviews of *Wunschkonzert*, for instance, make this clear: although the film is characterized as an Episodenfilm, it is clear how the goal, with the film's various narrative strands, was to bring the militaristic episodes into concert (so to say) with the romantic plot.
10 Matthias Rogg, "Die Luftwaffe im NS-Propagandafilm," in *Krieg Und Militär Im Film des 20: Jahrhunderts*, ed. Matthias Rogg and Wolfgang Schmidt Bernhard Chiari (Munich: Oldenbourg Wissenschaftverlag, 2003), 143.
11 Various scholars address the centrality of airpower to modern and contemporary war, including the following: Caren Kaplan, "Precision Targets: GPS and the Militarization of US Consumer Identity," *American Quarterly* 3 (2006): 693–713; Caren Kaplan and C. Kelley, "Dead Reckoning: Aerial Perception and the Social Construction of Targets," *Vectors Journal* 2, no. 2 (2006), http://vectors.usc.edu/projects/index.php?project=11; Peter Adey, *Aerial Life: Space, Mobilities, Affects*, ed. Royal Geographical Society with IBG (Malden, Mass.: Wiley-Blackwell, 2010),

Kindle; Peter Adey, Mark Whitehead, and Alison J. Williams, eds., *From Above: War, Violence, and Verticality* (London: Hurst, 2013); Saulo Cwerner, "Introducing Aeromobilities," in *Aeromobilities*, ed. S. Kesselring, John Urry, and Saulo Cwerner (New York: Routledge, 2009), 1–21; and Tim Cresswell, *On the Move: Mobility in the Modern West* (New York: Routledge, 2006). See also, for example, Rogg, "Luftwaffe im NS-Propagandafilm," and a brief discussion in Peter Fritzsche, *A Nation of Fliers: German Aviation and the Popular Imagination* (Cambridge, Mass.: Harvard University Press, 1992).

12 For example, see O'Brien, *Nazi Cinema as Enchantment*, 122, 128ff.

13 Henri Lefebvre, *The Production of Space*, trans. Donald Nicholson-Smith (Cambridge: Blackwell, 1991), 351.

14 Adey, *Aerial Life*, loc. 534 of 9406.

15 See, for instance, Wulf Siewert, "Flugzeug und Erdraum," *Zeitschrift für Geopolitik* 8 (1935): 508–516.

16 See Edward Soja, *Thirdspace: Journeys to Los Angeles and Other Real-and-Imagined Places* (New York: Blackwell, 1996).

17 See Klaus Kreimeier, *The Ufa Story* (1992; repr., Berkeley: University of California Press, 1999), 274; and William Gillespie, *Karl Ritter: His Life and "Zeitfilms" under National Socialism* (Chicago: Germanfilms.net, 2012), 93.

18 Kreimeier, *Ufa Story*, 279.

19 For more about this complex relationship, see Kreimeier, 346–347.

20 Although it is certainly understandable, this somewhat reductive approach to the multiplicity of propaganda content does not necessarily help comprehend its mechanisms or popularity. Kreimeier, 275: "Wherever political propaganda was on the agenda, it was attended with technical perfection and aesthetic uniformity. Artistic individualism and cinematic originality were detrimental here." Welch, *Propaganda*, also analyzes in this sometimes reductive way.

21 Susan Tegel, *Nazis and the Cinema* (London: Continuum, 2007), 102–105; Welch, *Propaganda*, 188–191. Kreimeier, *Ufa Story*, 279–280, also foregrounds this anti-Semitism but notes (also in the direction of acknowledging the diversity of propaganda productions) that he, although personally more anti-Semitic than most Ufa directors, did not seem to be interested in making anti-Semitic films.

22 See Kaplan, "Precision Targets," 695–698, as well as Fritzsche, *Nation of Fliers*, 82, which highlights the putative chivalry of the pilot. For the Nazi context and thinking about the subjectivity of pilots through a racial lens, see Siewert, "Flugzeug und Erdraum," 508–516.

23 William H. McNeill, *Keeping Together in Time: Dance and Drill in Human History* (Cambridge, Mass.: Harvard University Press, 1995), 65.

24 McNeill, 152.

25 Julian Hanich, *Cinematic Emotion in Horror Films and Thrillers: The Aesthetic Paradox of Pleasurable Fear* (New York: Routledge, 2010), 102–103.

26 Shooting script for *Pour le Mérite*, Deutsche Kinemathek, script no. 391, p. 3.

27 Stephen Kern, *The Culture of Time and Space, 1880–1918* (Cambridge, Mass.: Harvard University Press, 1983), 240. This notion was then popularized by David Harvey in his *The Condition of Postmodernity: An Enquiry into the Origins of Cultural Change* (1989; repr., Malden, Mass.: Blackwell, 1992).

28 W. Luthardt, "Der Verkehrsflug in der Reich- und Landesplanung," *Zeitschrift für Geopolitik* 8 (August 1935): 516–522.

29 Alexander Watson, *Ring of Steel: German and Austria-Hungary in World War I* (New York: Basic Books, 2014), loc. 5220–5224 of 20422, Kindle.

30 Fritzsche, *Nation of Fliers*, 82.

31 See Christopher Clark, *The Sleepwalkers: How Europe Went to War in 1914* (New York: HarperCollins, 2012), 179–180.

32 Fritzsche, *Nation of Fliers*, 93–94.

33 See, for instance, Günther Schwark, "Gerhard Ritters *Pour le Mérite*," *Illustrierter Film-Kurier* 20, no. 300 (December 23, 1938).

34 Tom Gunning, "Landscape and the Fantasy of Moving Pictures: Early Cinema's Phantom Rides," in *Cinema and Landscape*, ed. Graeme Harper and Jonathan Rayner (Chicago: University of Chicago Press, 2010), 51–53.

35 See Paul Virilio, *War and Cinema: The Logistics of Perception* (New York: Verso, 1991), 20:

> Since the battlefield has always been a field of perception, the war machine appears to the military commander as an instrument of representation, comparable to the painter's palette and brush. . . . The pilot's hand automatically trips the camera shutter with the same gesture that releases his weapon. *For men at war, the function of the weapon is the function of the eye.* It is therefore quite understandable that after 1914, the air arm's violent cinematic disruption of the space continuum, together with the lightning advances of military technology, should have literally exploded the old homogeneity of vision and replaced it with the heterogeneity of perceptual fields.

36 Tom Gunning, "Cinema and the New Spirit in Art within a Culture of Movement," in *Picasso, Braque and Early Film in Cubism* (New York: Pace Wildenstein, 2007).

37 Brian Massumi, *Parables for the Virtual: Movement, Affect, Sensation* (Durham, N.C.: Duke University Press, 2002), 252.

38 See the interview with Ritter in Herman Hacker, "Film Beobachter: *Pour le Mérite*," *Völkischer Beobachter*, no. 346 (December 12, 1938): 8.

39 Adey, *Aerial Life*, loc. 1107–1110 of 9406. For the German context, see Wulf Siewert, "Flugzeung und Erdraum," *Zeitschrift für Geopolitik* 8 (August 1935): 508–516; and Luthardt, "Der Verkehrsflug."

40 John Keegan, *The First World War* (1998; repr., New York: Vintage, 2000), loc. 481–484 of 8961, Kindle.

41 See Marc Augé, *Non-places: Introduction to an Anthropology of Supermodernity* (1995; repr., London: Verso, 2006).

42 Shooting script for *Pour le Mérite*, p. 6, "Schauplätze der Handling."

43 See Fritzsche, *Nation of Fliers*, 107.

44 The script labels the secretaries as such—Ritter was detailed about their appearance. Shooting script for *Pour le Mérite*.

45 Welch, *Propaganda*, 190.

46 See "Film im Werden: Im Kampf mit Sonne, Wolken und Regen, Karl Ritter dreht auf der Wasserkuppe Außenaufnahmen zu 'Pour le merite,'" *Filmkurier*, August 18, 1938.

47 Fritzsche, *Nation of Fliers*, 93–94.

48 For a magisterial reading of this victimization discourse between the wars and in the Nazi regime, see Omer Bartov, "Defining Enemies, Making Victims: Germans, Jews, and the Holocaust," *American Historical Review* 103, no. 3 (1998): 771–816.

49 See Fritzsche, *Nation of Fliers*, 109.

50 Fritzsche, 112.

51 Fritzsche, 110.

52 Jeffrey Herf, *Reactionary Modernism: Technology Culture and Politics in Weimar and the Third Reich* (Cambridge: Cambridge University Press, 1984).

53 Shooting script for *Pour le Mérite*, p. 6, "Schauplätze."
54 Shooting script for *Pour le Mérite*, shots 243–244.
55 Michel Chion, "The Acousmêtre," in *Critical Visions in Film Theory: Classic and Contemporary Readings*, ed. Timothy Corrigan and Patricia White, with Meta Mazaj (Boston: Bedford / St. Martin's, 2011), 160.
56 Tegel, *Nazis and the Cinema*, 103; Welch, *Propaganda*, 191.
57 "Mit dem Pour le mérite Stab in Beeskow, Tag der Verkundung der Wehrfreiheit," *Filmkurier*, August 9, 1938.
58 "Feuilletonheft," *Pour le Mérite*, Deutsche Kinemathek 3582.
59 Rudolf Metzler, "Ein Abenteur der Lüfte," *Süddeutsche Zeitung*, February 26, 1989.
60 Adey, *Aerial Life*, loc. 534 of 9406.
61 "Kampfgeschwader Lützow: Werbeheft," Tobis, BA 8539/I, pp. 11–12.
62 Shooting script for *Kampfgeschwader Lützow*, Deutsche Kinemathek, file no. 8502, "Scene IV: 3."
63 "Kampfgeschwader Lützow: Werbeheft," 17.
64 "Kampfgeschwader Lützow: Presseheft," BA 8539/I.
65 Paul Ickes, *Programm von Heute, Zeitschrift für Film und Theater*, no. 1735, BA 8539/I.
66 See Bartov, "Defining Enemies, Making Victims." See also Bill Niven, ed., *Germans as Victims* (Basingstoke, U.K.: Palgrave Macmillan, 2006); and Paul Cooke and Marc Silberman, *Screening War: Perspectives on German Suffering* (Rochester, N.Y.: Camden House, 2010).
67 Richard Evans, *Third Reich at War, 1939–45* (London: Penguin, 2008), loc. 394, 746 of 21698, Kindle.
68 "Kampfgeschwader Lützow: Werbeheft," 21.
69 Caren Kaplan discusses Clausewitz's use of this concept; see Kaplan, *Aerial Aftermaths: War from Above* (Durham, N.C.: Duke University Press, 2018), loc. 1309 of 8915, Kindle.
70 Samuel Weber, *Targets of Opportunity: On the Militarization of Thinking* (New York: Fordham, 2005), loc. 134–136 of 2765, Kindle. He also notes the sense of seizing a fleeting moment, one that underscores the "mortality" of the target. Weber, loc. 115–118 of 2765.
71 "Kampfgeschwader Lützow," *Illustrierter Film-Kurier*, BA 8539/I.
72 Donna J. Haraway, *Simians, Cyborgs and Women: The Reinvention of Nature* (London: Free Association Books, 1991), 581.
73 See "Kampfgeschwader Lützow," BA 8539/I: "Die . . . polnischen Begleitmannschaften suchen Deckung und zwingen die Deutschen, die Zielscheibe zu spiel. Ein Meisterwerk der deutschen Bordschützen ist es, als sie die Polen wegjagen und empfindlich treffen, ohne daß einer der Volksdeutschen in Gefahr gerät" (The Polish auxiliaries look for cover and force the Germans to play the target. It's a masterwork of the German gunners that they hit and chase away the Poles without bringing the ethnic Germans into danger).
74 See Rey Chow, *The Age of the World Target: Self-Referentiality in War, Theory, and Comparative Work* (Durham, N.C.: Duke University Press, 2006), 31; and Kaplan, *Aerial Aftermaths*, loc. 707 of 8915.
75 Kaplan, "Precision Targets," 699–700.
76 See, for example, Doreen Massey, "Power-Geometry and Progressive Sense of Place," in *Mapping the Futures: Local Cultures, Global Change*, ed. John Bird et al. (London: Routledge, 1993), 40–70.
77 "Im Zeitalter der schnell entstandenen Autobahnen und einer immer stärkeren Motorisierung wuchsen die scharfen und schnellen neuen Waffen im

nationalsozialistischen Deutschland mit staunenswerter Geschwindigkeit und Präzision heran." "Presseheft," *Kampfgeschwader Lützow*, Deutsche Kinemathek, file no. DK/3709.

78 Cwerner, "Introducing Aeromobilities," 10.

79 Kaplan, *Aerial Aftermaths*, loc. 264 of 8915.

80 Shooting script for *Kampfgeschwader Lützow*, "Scene IV: 3, Bild 39," "Bild 73–74."

81 Shooting script for *Kampfgeschwader Lützow*, "Scene IV: 3, Bild 47."

82 Günther Schwark, "'*Über alles in der Welt*' in Posen Uraufgeführt: Ein Höhepunkt der Gaukulturtage des Warthegaus," *Illustrierter Film-Kurier* 23, no. 67 (March 20, 1921).

83 Dr. W., "Neues Aus Breslau: Kampfgeschwader Lützow festlich aufgeführt," *Illustrierter Film-Kurier* 23, no. 64 (March 17, 1941): 3.

84 Schwark, "*Über alles in der Welt*."

85 Schwark.

86 "*Über alles in der Welt*," *Illustrierter Film-Kurier*, no. 162 (July 13, 1940), BA 17432/I. See also *Illustrierter Film-Kurier*, no. 256 (October 31, 1940): 2, which describes the end of photography on the picture and reviewed its many settings.

87 "*Über alles in der Welt*," *Illustrierter Film-Kurier*, March 17, 1941, BA 17432/I.

88 Ulrich Beck, *The Cosmopolitan Vision* (Cambridge: Polity, 2006).

89 David Held, *Democracy and the Global Order: From the Modern State to Cosmopolitan Governance* (Cambridge: Polity, 1995), 233.

90 Zygmunt Bauman, *Globalization* (Cambridge: Polity, 1998), 87.

91 "Zeitgeschichte und Spielfilm: Besuch bei Karl Ritter in Heiligenblut," *Illustrierter Film-Kurier* 163 (July 15, 1940): 3, BA 17432/I.

92 Ritter analyzes cinema in relation to the *Hamburg Dramaturgy*, for example; see "Zeitgeschichte und Spielfilm," 3.

93 Benjamin Martin, *The Nazi-Fascist New Order for European Culture* (Cambridge, Mass.: Harvard University Press, 2016).

94 Caren Kaplan, "Mobility and War: The Cosmic View of US 'Air Power,'" *Environment and Planning A* 38, no. 2 (2006): 396.

95 Quoted in Adey, *Aerial Life*, loc. 106 of 9406.

96 Bauman, *Globalization*, 87.

97 See Allen Mitchell, *Nazi Paris: The History of an Occupation, 1940–1944* (New York: Berghahn, 2008), 12, 39–40.

98 Shooting script for *Über alles in der Welt*, Deutsche Kinemathek, script no. 7759, scene 49, p. 71, shot 143, "Negertanzerinnen zu Hot-Musik frech tanzend."

99 Shooting script for *Über alles*, scene 40, p. 65, "Über die beiden durch die Glaskanzel Blick auf Warschau in der Tiefe."

100 Caren Kaplan, "The Balloon Prospect: Aerostatic Observation and the Emergence of Militarised Aeromobility," in Adey, Whitehead, and William, *From Above*, 36.

101 Shooting script for *Über alles*, scene 118, shot 323, 155.

Chapter 5 Out of the War Mode

1 An earlier version of this chapter appeared in Jaimey Fisher, "Trains, Planes, and the Occasional Car: The Rubble-Film as Demobilization Film," in *German Postwar Films: Life and Love in the Ruins*, ed. William Rasch and Wilfried Wilms (New York: Palgrave Macmillan, 2008), 175–192, reproduced with permission of Palgrave Macmillan.

2 For details of the Filmpause, see Robert Shandley, *Rubble-Films: German Cinema in the Shadow of the Third Reich* (Philadelphia: Temple University Press, 2001).

3 I shall detail below the writings from which I derive this notion as well as some of its themes, but the main reference in this context is Fredric Jameson, *The Geopolitical Aesthetic: Cinema and Space in the World System* (Bloomington: Indiana University Press, 1992); and Fredric Jameson, "Spatial Systems in *North by Northwest*," in *Everything You Always Wanted to Know about Lacan but Were Afraid to Ask Hitchcock*, ed. Slavoj Zizek (New York: Verso, 1992).

4 Eric Rentschler outlines how very popular these two films were. Both were the most popular releases of their respective years, and *Request Concert*, with 26.5 million tickets sold, was considerably more popular than the nefariously well-visited *Jud Süss* (20.3 million tickets). *Request Concert*, in fact, had 2 million more tickets sold than the second-place film of its year and 6 million more than the third-place film. See Eric Rentschler, *The Ministry of Illusion* (Cambridge, Mass.: Harvard University Press, 1997), 250, 255, 258.

5 I have in mind here the transfiguration of place of which Jameson writes, such that this new approach to space as cognitively mapped entails rethinking the nature of place:

> We are given, in *North by Northwest*, a whole series or sequence of concrete spaces which are not too rapidly to be reduced to mere *places*. . . . Place and place name are only the starting points, the raw material, from which a rather different realization of concrete space is produced, which is no longer scene or backdrop for an action for actors, but includes those in some new, qualitative way. The vocation of these new space-signs is often so imperious as to master the individual episodes and to transform each into the occasion for a qualitatively distinct production.

Jameson, "Spatial Systems," 50.

6 Shandley, *Rubble-Films*; Hester Baer, *Dismantling the Dream Factory: Gender, German Cinema, and the Postwar Quest for a New Film Language* (New York: Berghahn, 2009).

7 I do not want to argue, of course, that there was no significant overlap between the militarization of Germany and the Nazis, but I do want to suggest that the specifically military experience of many Germans has been neglected in analyses of the early postwar period, with the notable exceptions of Robert Moeller, James Diehl, and Frank Biess.

8 For Frank Biess—quite rightly, in my opinion—the Wehrmacht's "fighting up until the very end" begs questions of both the pervasiveness of military ideology and the Wehrmacht's complicity with war crimes. Frank Biess, *Homecomings: Returning POWs and the Legacies of Defeat in Postwar Germany* (Princeton, N.J.: Princeton University Press, 2006), 3.

9 It is not that I do not think the usual focus on character and cast is unimportant—in fact, I have argued elsewhere that one of the most telling aspects of the films of the late 1940s is how they negotiated the star system they inherited from the Third Reich.

10 It is notable, in fact, that many reviews avoid calling them Kriegsfilme (war films), even as they admit the home and combat fronts are central to the plots. These reviews are attempting, pretty clearly, to broaden *Request Concert*'s appeal—for instance, one review makes a clear point that the film is not merely a "man's film." *Der Ufa-Film im Wort und Bild*, January 13, 1941.

11 Linda Williams, "Melodrama Revisited," in *Refiguring American Film Genres: History and Theory*, ed. Nick Browne (Berkeley: University of California Press, 1998).

12 Roberto J. González and Hugh Gusterson, *Militarization: A Reader* (Durham, N.C.: Duke University Press, 2019), especially the introduction, 6.

13 Paul Virilio, *War and Cinema: The Logistics of Perception* (New York: Verso, 1991), 17; Wolfgang Schivelbusch, *Railway Journey: The Industrialization of Time and Space in the Nineteenth Century* (1977; repr., Berkeley: University of California Press, 1986); Giuliana Bruno, *Streetwalking on a Ruined Map: Cultural Theory and the City Films of Elvira Notari* (Princeton, N.J.: Princeton University Press, 1993).

14 Schivelbusch, *Railway Journey*, 31.

15 Virilio, *War and Cinema*, 17.

16 Virilio, 2; see also Virilio, 7: "*The history of battle is primarily the history of changing fields of perception.*"

17 Jameson, "Spatial Systems."

18 Jameson, *Geopolitical Aesthetic*, 75; or, in Jameson's analysis of Hitchcock, "The vocation of these new space-signs is often so imperious as to master the individual episodes and to transform each into the occasion for a qualitatively distinct production." Jameson, "Spatial Systems," 50.

19 Williams, "Melodrama Revisited," 42–88.

20 On Jünger's cold gaze, see Anton Kaes, "The Cold Gaze: Notes on Mobilization and Modernity," *New German Critique* 20, no. 59 (1993): 105–117.

21 This notion of a character coming upon a secret second map is crucial to the cognitive mapping that Jameson traces in *Geopolitical Aesthetic*, for example:

> Archetypal journeys back beyond the surface appearance of things are also dimly reawakened, from antiquity and Dante. . . . This promise of a deeper inside view is the hermeneutic content of the conspiracy thriller in general, although its spatialization in *Condor* seems somehow more alarming than the imaginary networks of the usual suspects: the representational confirmation that telephone cables and lines and their interchanges follow us everywhere, doubling the streets and buildings of the visible social world with a secondary secret underground world, is a vivid, if paranoid, cognitive map, redeemed for once only by the possibility of turning the tables, when the hero is able to tap into the circuits and bug the buggers, abolishing space with his own kind of simultaneity by scrambling all the symptoms and producing his messages from all corners of the map at the same time.

Jameson, 15; or "But the narrative by which it seeks to achieve this reality-effect remains one in which the individual subject of the protagonist somehow manages to blunder into the collective web of the hidden social order." Jameson, 33.

22 Jameson, "Spatial Systems," 47–72.

23 Edward Soja, *Thirdspace: Journeys to Los Angeles and Other Real-and-Imagined Places* (New York: Blackwell, 1996). In "Spatial Systems," Jameson observes that over the course of the narrative, the film drives at an ultimate space of pure representation, Mount Rushmore.

24 Alon Confino, "Traveling as a Cultural Remembrance: Traces of National Socialism in West Germany, 1945–1960," *History and Memory* 12 (2000): 92–121.

25 See Jameson, *Geopolitical Aesthetic*, 33. For a well-known instance, toward the chaotic end of *Metropolis*, one could speak of the actantial shift from Freder and Maria to the masses rather than to any one character. What makes this actantial shift potentially revolutionary is another spatial aspect of the narrative scenario: the actantial shift

happens in the very same place rather than shifting to a different location. Of course, the film then activates to renegotiate the actantial shift—on the stairs of a cathedral nonetheless, dangerous as it might be to the existing social hierarchies.

26 Tellingly, Koch was even prepared to cede his desire for a fellow soldier he thought was engaged to Inge—camaraderie above all, his will to renounce his love with the same coldness as before.

27 James Diehl, *The Thanks of the Fatherland* (Chapel Hill: University of North Carolina Press, 1993), 46.

28 Diehl, 55.

29 For specific examples, see "Militarismus und Soldatentum," *Süddeutsche Zeitung*, p. 44; and the follow-up piece "Noch einmal: Militarismus und Soldatentum," *Süddeutsche Zeitung*, July 22, 1946, p. 59, which returns to discuss the earlier piece because the paper had received so much mail pertaining to it. For examples of pieces about former POWs and conditions in the camps, see Paul Herzog, "Heimkehr aus russischer Gefangenschaft," *Die Wandlung* 3, no. 1 (1948): 71–79; and Hermann Sinsheimer, "Heimkehr: Der Kriegsgefangenen aus England," *Deutsche Rundschau* 71, no. 6 (1948): 194–199. On the guilt question as it intersected militarism, see Helmut Lindemann, "Die Schuld Der Generale," *Deutsche Rundschau* 75, no. 1 (1949): 20–22; and Hermann von Müller, "Entartung Des Krieges," *Deutsche Rundschau* 75, no. 9 (1949): 800–806.

30 Diehl, *Thanks of the Fatherland*, 69.

31 Sinsheimer, "Heimkehr," 194.

32 Various reviews mention the Bahnhofsleben of the three veterans.

33 Schivelbusch, *Railway Journey*, 174.

34 Henri Lefebvre, *The Production of Space*, trans. Donald Nicholson-Smith (Cambridge: Blackwell, 1991), 49, 234–236.

35 For a good overview of the debates and anxiety about nihilism after the war, see Stephen Brockmann, *German Literary Culture at the Zero Hour* (New York: Camden House, 2004).

36 Gilles Deleuze, *Cinema 1: The Movement-Image* (Minneapolis: University of Minnesota Press, 1986), 220. In *Und über uns der Himmel*, for instance, the protagonist looks around a courtyard into the windows of his neighbors, each with their own story and suffering; Rossellini's *Germany Year Zero* is based on a series of such vignettes offered to the camera as it follows Edmund around, the underage protagonist who wanders from one symptomatic situation to the next.

37 See Virilio, *War and Cinema*, 9: "In her child's universe, the cinema [during the war] was a kind of 'perception luxury' (Bergson) quite distinct from other forms of spectacle and entertainment, an abstract weekly luxury which it would be hard for her to do without."

38 The sequences in which the veterans find their way to this town and eventually go to work are all contrasted to the industrial modernity of the film's first twenty minutes. Various reviews of the film make mention of it being shot in a cloister in the country, certainly an unusual setting for such a film about veterans but one that underscores the curious topography of postwar Germany: to shoot in cities like Hannover meant shooting among the rubble, whereas the country was usually spared the brunt of the bombing and afforded the impressive historical architecture that marked the cloister. The sequences in the town hall or the cloister garden where Stefan falls in love with Lukas's secretary all form a stark spatial contrast to the claustrophobic train station and the expressionistically shot ruined cathedral in the first twenty minutes.

39 The organ player's offering the lost soldiers guidance through the fog of war recalls the myth of Langemarck as well, in which soldiers sang "Deutschland über alles" to find one another and their way to battle.

40 Raymond Bellour, "The Obvious and the Code," in *Narrative, Apparatus, Ideology*, ed. Philip Rosen (New York: Columbia University Press, 1986), 98–99.

41 Although it should be noted that one of the three leaves his military uniform behind for, likely, prison garb: Peter is apprehended by the police at the end of the film for some activities that predated the group's dealing with Fleck, but even he seems blithely accepting of his fate, as if the film has proven to him the validity of postwar civilian law and authorities.

42 Although she expects to hear from Günther, as she had from Hans, all about happy childhood memories, she instead gets an earful of pain, suffering, and resentment of the war years. Hans informs her that, for them in Germany, even the stars became dangerous, an indisputable reference, despite many claims to the contrary, to the air war and the terror, justified or not, it brought to city inhabitants.

43 The film immediately arranges another demobilization scenario, one familiar from *Irgendwo in Berlin* (*Somewhere in Berlin*), in the way that it introduces Georg: by setting the scene for his return but then making the other principals wait for him. This technique invokes, obviously, the ubiquitous waiting for the release of POWs, a familiar experience for millions of their friends and families. In arranging its scenario of waiting, however, *Birds of Migration* foregoes the waiting at home of *Somewhere in Berlin* and favors instead those traveling veterans I tracked above.

44 The old couple who direct Wolfgang to Georg lament, "Such a young man, and always in the dark," a play on both Raddatz's age and the angry young veteran type.

45 Jennifer Kapczynski, *The German Patient: Crisis and Recovery in Postwar Culture* (Ann Arbor: University of Michigan Press, 2008), 69–74.

46 Herzog, "Heimkehr aus russischer Gefangenschaft," 71; Sinsheimer, "Heimkehr," 196.

Chapter 6 War in the Reconstructive 1950s

1 See Robert Moeller, "Victims in Uniform: West German Combat Movies from the 1950s," in *Germans as Victims*, ed. Bill Niven (Basingstoke, U.K.: Palgrave Macmillan, 2006), 43–61.

2 Jaimey Fisher, "Resisting the War (Film): Wicki's 'Masterpiece' *Die Brücke* and Its Generic Transformations," in *Generic Histories of German Cinema: Genre and Its Deviations*, ed. Jaimey Fisher (Rochester, N.Y.: Camden House, 2013), 114–116.

3 Omer Bartov, "Defining Enemies, Making Victims: Germans, Jews, and the Holocaust," *American Historical Review* 103, no. 3 (1998): 771–816; Moeller, "Victims in Uniform," 43–61.

4 Robert Moeller, *War Stories: The Search for a Usable Past in the Federal Republic of Germany* (Berkeley: University of California Press, 2001); Elizabeth Heineman, "The Hour of the Woman: Memories of Germany's 'Crisis Years' and West German National Identity," *American Historical Review* 101, no. 2 (April 1996): 354–395; Frank Biess, *Homecomings: Returning POWs and the Legacies of Defeat in Postwar Germany* (Princeton, N.J.: Princeton University Press, 2006); Jaimey Fisher, *Disciplining Germany: Youth, Reeducation, and Reconstruction after the Second World War* (Detroit: Wayne State University Press, 2007).

5 Moeller, "Victims in Uniform," 44.

6 Jennifer Kapczynski, "Armchair Warriors: Heroic Postures in the West German War Film," in *Screening War: Perspectives on German Suffering*, ed. Paul Cooke and Marc Silberman (Rochester, N.Y.: Camden House, 2010), 17–35.

7 Erica Carter, "Men in Cardigans: Canaris (1954) and the 1950s West German Good Soldier," in *War-Torn Tales: Representing Gender and World War II in Literature and Film*, ed. Danielle Hipkins and Gill Plain (Oxford: Peter Lang, 2007), 95–219; Mark Gagnon, "Making Citizens out of Soldiers: Rearming the Individual in Paul May's *08/15*," in *A Companion to War Films*, ed. Douglas A. Cunningham and John Nelson (Malden, Mass.: Wiley, 2016), 271–288; Moeller, "Victims in Uniform," 43–61.

8 Stephen Brockmann, *German Literary Culture at the Zero Hour* (New York: Camden House, 2004).

9 Moeller, "Victims in Uniform," 43–61; John G. Cawelti, "*Chinatown* and Generic Transformation in Recent American Film," in *Film Genre Reader III*, ed. Barry Keith Grant (1997; repr., Austin: University of Texas Press, 2003), 243–261.

10 Franziska Violet, "Vor der Leinwand notiert," *Süddeutsche Zeitung*, January 12, 1958; see also "Der Fuchs von Paris," *Neue Zürcher Zeitung*, July 13, 1958.

11 Janet Staiger, "Hybrid or Inbred: The Purity Hypothesis and Hollywood Genre History," in Grant, *Film Genre Reader III*, 85–299; Rick Altman, *Film/Genre* (1999; repr., London: British Film Institute, 2002), 185–299.

12 Gagnon, "Citizens out of Soldiers," 272–273.

13 Nicholas Koch, "Revolution des Wehrdenkens," *Zeitschrift für Geopolitik* 27, no. 5 (May 1956): 17–24.

14 Ernst van Loen, "Grenzen des Krieges," *Zeitschrift für Geopolitik* 27, no. 3 (March 1956): 29–31, which discusses Adalbert Weinstein, "Mut zur militärischen Wirklichkeit," *Frankfurter Allgemeine Zeitung*, February 4, 1956, 30.

15 See Carter, "Men in Cardigans."

16 Gagnon, "Citizens out of Soldiers," 271–273.

17 Carter, "Men in Cardigans," 196.

18 See Konrad Jarausch and Michael Geyer, *Shattered Past: Reconstructing German Histories* (Princeton, N.J.: Princeton University Press, 2003).

19 See Carter, "Men in Cardigans," 206.

20 See Carter, 204.

21 See Carter, 210.

22 See Carter, 206.

23 See Carter, 199.

24 Fredric Jameson, *The Geopolitical Aesthetic: Cinema and Space in the World System* (Bloomington: Indiana University Press, 1992), 74–75.

25 David Harvey, "The Body as an Accumulation Strategy," in *Spaces of Hope*, 97–116.

26 Wolfgang Schivelbusch, *Railway Journey: The Industrialization of Time and Space in the Nineteenth Century* (1977; repr., Berkeley: University of California Press, 1986), 134.

27 Walter Benjamin, *The Writer of Modern Life: Essays on Charles Baudelaire*, ed. Michael Jennings (Cambridge, Mass.: Harvard University Press, 2006), 72–73, 79.

28 Siegfried Kracauer, "The Hotel Lobby," in *The Mass Ornament: Weimar Essays*, trans. Thomas Y. Levin (1963; repr., Cambridge, Mass.: Harvard University Press, 1995), 173–186.

29 Interestingly, extensive preparations for the Allied invasion—including the construction of a large bunker and an anticipatory depository for luggage—did transpire at a hotel, but at the Hotel Majestic, not Lutetia. See Allan Mitchell, *Nazi Paris: The History of an Occupation, 1940–1944* (New York: Berghahn, 2008), 97–98.

30 Karena Niehoff, "Der Fuchs von Paris," *Der Tagesspiegel*, April 4, 1958.
31 Andrew Herod, *Scale* (London: Routledge, 2011), 230.
32 See Latham, "Retheorizing the Scale of Globalization: Topologies, Actor-Networks, and Cosmopolitanism," in *Geographies of Power: Placing Scale*, ed. Andrew Herod and M. W. Wright (Oxford: Blackwell, 2002), 115–144.
33 Carter, "Men in Cardigans," 209–212.
34 Quoted in Ken Follett, *The Key to Rebecca* (1980; repr., New York: Penguin, 2002), ii.
35 David T. Zabecki, "Rethinking Rommel," *Military History* 32, no. 5 (2016): 24–28; Maurice Philip Remy, *Mythos Rommel* (Munich: List, 2002).
36 See Jon Latimer, *Alamein* (Cambridge, Mass.: Harvard University Press, 2002), 28; and Charles Messenger, *Rommel: Leadership Lessons from the Desert Fox*, World Generals Series (Basingstoke, U.K.: Palgrave Macmillan, 2009), 110.
37 Zabecki, "Rethinking Rommel," 28.
38 In the script, maps pervade; see, for example, shooting script for *Rommel ruft Kairo*, Deutsche Kinemathek, script no. 950, scene 1, p. 2: "Bild: Vielen Generalstabpläne, Lageplaene, und Skizzen."
39 The characterization of Eppler offered in the script's stage directions highlights both his nonchalance and his youth—for example, it mentions his "offenes Hemd, Seidenschal, Muetze . . . kurze hosen . . . er duerfte kaum 30 jahre alt sein" (open shirt, cravat, cap, shorts—he can't be 30). It is notable that Hoven's depiction of Eppler in the film makes him more of a regular officer, with the shorts gone and his shirt not open more than normal.
40 Jameson, *Geopolitical Aesthetic*, 39–40.
41 See Tim Bergfelder, "The Passenger: Ambivalences of National Identity and Masculinity in the Star Persona of Peter van Eyck," in *Framing the Fifties: Fifties Cinema in Divided Germany*, ed. John Davidson and Sabine Hake (New York: Berghahn, 2007), 44–57.
42 "Rommel ruft Kairo," *Rheinischer Post*, February 28, 1959, BA 13977. About the adjustment to food while traveling, see "Rommel ruft Kairo." About a sandstorm but the amazing view of the pyramids after it, see A. M. S., "Blick ins Atelier: Der Mann, der 'Eppler' hieß," *Der Tag* (Berlin ed.), December 14, 1958.
43 Irene, "Wüstensand und Wassernot," *Spandauer Volksblatt*, December 19, 1958.
44 Caren Kaplan, "Desert Wars: Virilio and the Limits of 'Genuine Knowledge,'" in *Virilio and Visual Culture*, ed. John Armitage and Ryan Bishop (Edinburgh: Edinburgh University Press, 2013).
45 Robert Tignor, *Egypt: A Short History* (Princeton, N.J.: Princeton University Press, 2010), 240–243.
46 Jameson, *Geopolitical Aesthetic*, 74–75.
47 Edward Dimendberg, *Film Noir and the Spaces of Modernity* (Cambridge, Mass.: Harvard University Press, 2004), 211–212.
48 John Urry, *The Tourist Gaze*, 3rd ed. (Los Angeles: SAGE, 2011).
49 Irene, "Wüstensand und Wassernot."
50 See Latimer, *Alamein*, 24; and Messenger, *Rommel*, 89.
51 "+rommel—+—ruft kairo+," *Illustrierte Film-Bühne*, no. 466; "Presseheft," *Rommel ruft Kairo*, *Illustrierte Film-Bühne*, no. 466.
52 Shooting script for *Rommel ruft Kairo*, p. 178, "Bild 395–40."
53 Martin Kitchen, *Rommel's Desert War: Waging World War II in North Africa, 1941–1943* (Cambridge: Cambridge University Press, 2015), 242. The truth was that although it was celebrated as a great victory, it spelled the end to Rommel's southern successes. He was shortly thereafter halted at the First Battle of El Alamein and then

driven back across northern Africa in the Second Battle of El Alamein in November 1942.

54 Manuel Castells, *The Rise of the Network Society* (Oxford: Blackwell, 1996), 453–469.

Chapter 7 Conclusion

1 "Und was sagen die Berliner? ABEND-Blitzumfrage vor dem Zoo-Palast-Portal," *Der Abend*, November 5, 1959.

2 Timothy Corrigan and Patricia White, with Meta Mazaj, *Critical Visions in Film Theory: Classic and Contemporary Readings* (Boston: Bedford / St. Martin's, 2011), 443.

3 Rick Altman, *Film/Genre* (1999; repr., London: British Film Institute, 2002), 19–21.

4 Karl Marx, *Grundrisse* (London: Penguin Classics, 1993); David Harvey, *The Condition of Postmodernity: An Enquiry into the Origins of Cultural Change* (1989; repr., Malden, Mass.: Blackwell, 1992); Stephen Kern, *The Culture of Time and Space, 1880–1918* (Cambridge, Mass.: Harvard University Press, 1983).

5 Hester Baer, "*Das Boot* and the Cinema of Neoliberalism," *German Quarterly* 85, no. 1 (Winter 2012): 21.

6 Brad Prager, "Beleaguered under the Sea: Wolfgang Petersen's *Das Boot* (1981) as German Hollywood Film," in *Light Motives: German Popular Film in Perspective*, ed. Randall Halle and Margaret McCarthy (Detroit: Wayne State University Press, 2003), 238–239.

7 Prager, 242.

8 Eric Hansen, "Downfall (Review)," *Hollywood Reporter*, September 16, 2005.

9 On spreadability on the internet, see Henry Jenkins, Sam Ford, and Joshua Green, *Spreadable Media: Creating Value and Meaning in a Networked Culture* (New York: New York University Press, 2013), 7–9.

10 See John G. Cawelti, "*Chinatown* and Generic Transformation in Recent American Film," in *Film Genre Reader III*, ed. Barry Keith Grant (1997; repr., Austin: University of Texas Press, 2003), 243–261.

11 See Denis Cosgrove, *Apollo's Eye: A Cartographic Genealogy of the Earth in the Western Imagination* (Baltimore: Johns Hopkins University Press, 2001).

12 Jaimey Fisher, *Disciplining Germany: Youth, Reeducation, and Reconstruction after the Second World War* (Detroit: Wayne State University Press, 2007).

13 Roberto J. González and Hugh Gusterson, introduction to *Militarization: A Reader* (Durham, N.C.: Duke University Press, 2019), 7.

Selected Bibliography

Archives

Bundesarchiv (Berlin-Lankwitz)
Bundesarchiv Filmarchiv (Berlin)
Deutsche Kinemathek (Berlin)
Filmmuseum (Munich)
Hans Helmut Prinzler / Deutsche Kinemathek Library and Press Archive (Berlin)
Hochschule für Film und Fernsehen / Press Archives (Munich)

Secondary Sources

Abel, Marco. *Violent Affect: Literature, Cinema, and Critique after Representation*. Lincoln: University of Nebraska Press, 2007.

Adey, Peter. *Aerial Life: Space, Mobilities, Affects*. Edited by Royal Geographical Society with IBG. Malden, Mass.: Wiley-Blackwell, 2010.

Adey, Peter, Mark Whitehead, and Alison J. Williams, eds. *From Above: War, Violence, and Verticality*. London: Hurst, 2013.

Adorno, Theodor W. *Aesthetic Theory*. Translated by Robert Hullot-Kentor. New York: Continuum, 2004.

Allison, Tanine. *Destructive Sublime: World War II in American Film and Media*. New Brunswick, N.J.: Rutgers University Press, 2018.

Altman, Rick. *Film/Genre*. 1999. Reprint, London: British Film Institute, 2002.

Anderson, Ben. "Affective Atmospheres." *Emotion, Space and Society* 2, no. 2 (December 2009): 77–81.

Atwell, Lee. *G. W. Pabst*. Boston: Twayne, 1977.

Auge, Marc. *Non-places: Introduction to an Anthropology of Supermodernity*. 1995. Reprint, London: Verso, 2006.

Azcona, Maria Del Mar. *The Multi-protagonist Film*. Hoboken: Wiley-Blackwell, 2010.

Baer, Hester. "*Das Boot* and the Cinema of Neoliberalism." *German Quarterly* 85, no. 1 (Winter 2012): 18–39.

Baird, Jay W. *The Mythical World of Nazi Propaganda, 1939–1945*. Minneapolis: University of Minnesota Press, 1975.

Baranowksi, Shelley. *Nazi Empire: German Colonialism and Imperialism from Bismarck to Hitler*. Cambridge: Cambridge University Press, 2011.

———. *Strength through Joy: Consumerism and Mass Tourism in the Third Reich*. Cambridge: Cambridge University Press, 2004.

Bartov, Omer. "Defining Enemies, Making Victims: Germans, Jews, and the Holocaust." *American Historical Review* 103, no. 3 (1998): 771–816.

Basinger, Jeanine. *The World War II Combat Film: Anatomy of a Genre*. 1986. Reprint, Middletown, Conn.: Wesleyan University Press, 2003.

Bassin, Mark. "Race contra Space: The Conflict between German *Geopolitik* and National Socialism." In *Hitler's Geographies: The Spatialities of the Third Reich*, edited by Paolo Giaccaria and Claudio Minca, 110–137. Chicago: University of Chicago Press, 2015.

Bathrick, David. "Making a National Family with the Radio: The Nazi Wunschkonzert." *Modernism/Modernity* 4, no. 1 (1997): 115.

Bauman, Zygmunt. *Globalization*. Cambridge: Polity, 1998.

Bazin, André. *What Is Cinema?* Translated by Hugh Gray. Vol. 1. Berkeley: University of California Press, 1967.

Beck, Ulrich. *The Cosmopolitan Vision*. Cambridge: Polity, 2006.

Bellour, Raymond. "The Obvious and the Code." In *Narrative, Apparatus, Ideology*, edited by Philip Rosen, 98–99. New York: Columbia University Press, 1986.

Benjamin, Walter. *The Arcades Project*. Cambridge, Mass.: Belknap Press of Harvard University Press, 1999.

———. "Experience and Poverty." In *Selected Writings*, edited by Michael Jennings and Gary Smith, vol. 2, *1927–1934*, 732–736. Cambridge, Mass.: Belknap Press of Harvard University Press, 1999.

———. "Little History of Photography." In *Selected Writings*, edited by Michael Jennings and Gary Smith, vol. 2, *1927–1934*, 507–530. Cambridge, Mass.: Belknap Press of Harvard University Press, 1999.

———. "The Paris of the Second Empire in Baudelaire." In *Selected Writings*, edited by Michael Jennings and Gary Smith, vol. 4, *1938–1940*, 3–92. Cambridge, Mass.: Belknap Press of Harvard University Press, 2006.

———. "The Return of the Flâneur." In *Selected Writings*, edited by Michael Jennings and Gary Smith, vol. 2, *1927–1934*, 262–268. Cambridge, Mass.: Belknap Press of Harvard University Press, 1999.

———. "The Storyteller: Observations on the Works of Nikolai Leskov." In *Selected Writings*, edited by Howard Eiland and Michael Jennings, vol. 3, *1935–1938*, 143–166. Cambridge, Mass.: Harvard University Press, 2002.

———. "Theories of German Fascism." In *Selected Writings*, edited by Michael Jennings and Gary Smith, vol. 2, *1927–1934*, 312–321. Cambridge, Mass.: Belknap Press of Harvard University Press, 1999.

———. "The Work of Art in the Age of Mechanical Reproduction." In *Selected Writings*, edited by Michael Jennings and Gary Smith, vol. 4, *1938–1940*, 250–283. Cambridge, Mass.: Belknap Press of Harvard University Press, 2006.

———. *The Writer of Modern Life: Essays on Charles Baudelaire*. Edited by Michael Jennings. Cambridge, Mass.: Harvard University Press, 2006.

Bergfelder, Tim. *International Adventures: German Popular Cinema and European Co-productions in the 1960s*. New York: Berghahn, 2004.

———. "The Passenger: Ambivalences of National Identity and Masculinity in the Star Persona of Peter van Eyck." In *Framing the Fifties: Fifties Cinema in Divided Germany*, edited by John Davidson and Sabine Hake, 44–57. New York: Berghahn, 2007.

Berlant, Lauren. "Cruel Optimism: On Marx, Loss and the Senses." *New Formations*, no. 63 (Winter 2007): 33–51.

Bertellini, Giorgio. *Italy in Early American Cinema: Race, Landscape, and the Picturesque*. Bloomington: Indiana University Press, 2009.

Betz. "Der Kriegs-Tonfilm im Capitol: *Westfront 1918* (Vier von der Infantrie)." *Der Film* 21 (May 21, 1930).

Biess, Frank. *Homecomings: Returning POWs and the Legacies of Defeat in Postwar Germany*. Princeton, N.J.: Princeton University Press, 2006.

Blackbourn, David. "Fashionable Spa Towns in Nineteenth-Century Europe." In *Water, Leisure and Culture: European Historical Perspectives*, edited by Susan C. Anderson and Bruce H. Tabb, 9–22. New York: Berg, 2002.

Bock, Hans-Michael. *Paul Leni: Grafik, Theater, Film*. Frankfurt: Deutsches Filmmuseum, 1986.

Bondi, Liz, Joyce Davidson, and Mick Smith, eds. *Emotion, Place, Culture*. London: Routledge, 2016.

Brandlmeier, Thomas. "Die polnische Karte: Anmerkungen zu Paul Lenis Film Das Tage Buch des Dr. Hart." In *Studien zur Kulturgeschichte des deutschen Polenbildes 1848–1939*, edited by Hendrik Feindt, 156–164. Wiesbaden, Germany: Harrassowtiz Verlag, 1995.

Brinkema, Eugenie. *The Forms of the Affects*. Durham, N.C.: Duke University Press, 2014.

Brockmann, Stephen. *German Literary Culture at the Zero Hour*. New York: Camden House, 2004.

Bruno, Giuliana. *Streetwalking on a Ruined Map: Cultural Theory and the City Films of Elvira Notari*. Princeton, N.J.: Princeton University Press, 1993.

Burch, Noël. "Fritz Lang: German Period." In *Cinema: A Critical Dictionary*, edited by Richard Roud, 583–599. London: Secker & Warburg, 1980.

Carter, Erica. "Men in Cardigans: Canaris (1954) and the 1950s West German Good Soldier." In *War-Torn Tales: Representing Gender and World War II in Literature and Film*, edited by Danielle Hipkins and Gill Plain, 195–219. Oxford: Peter Lang, 2007.

Castells, Manuel. *The Rise of the Network Society*. Oxford: Blackwell, 1996.

Cawelti, John G. *Adventure, Mystery and Romance: Formula Stories as Art and Popular Culture*. Chicago: University of Chicago Press, 1976.

———. "*Chinatown* and Generic Transformation in Recent American Film." In *Film Genre Reader III*, edited by Barry Keith Grant, 243–261. 1997. Reprint, Austin: University of Texas Press, 2003.

Chickering, Roger. *The Great War and Urban Life in Germany: Freiburg, 1914–1918*. Cambridge: Cambridge University Press, 2007.

———. *Imperial Germany and the Great War, 1914–18*. 3rd ed. Cambridge: Cambridge University Press, 2014.

———. "Total War: Use and Abuse of a Concept." In *Anticipating Total War: The German and American Experiences, 1871–1914*, edited by Manfred F. Boemeke, Roger Chickering, and Stig Förster, 13–28. Cambridge: Cambridge University Press, 1999.

Chion, Michel. "The Acousmêtre." In *Critical Visions in Film Theory*, edited by Timothy Corrigan and Patricia White, with Meta Mazaj, 156–164. Boston: Bedford / St. Martin's, 2011.

Chow, Rey, *The Age of the World Target: Self-Referentiality in War, Theory, and Comparative Work*. Durham, N.C.: Duke University Press, 2006.

Clark, Christopher. *The Sleepwalkers: How Europe Went to War in 1914*. New York: HarperCollins, 2012.

Clover, Carol. *Man, Women, and Chain Saws: Gender in the Modern Horror Film*. Princeton, N.J.: Princeton, 1991.

Confino, Alon. "Memory and the History of Mentalities." In *Cultural Memory Studies: An International and Interdisciplinary Handbook*, edited by Astrid Erll and Ansgar Nünning, 77–84. Berlin: de Gruyter, 2008.

———. "Traveling as a Cultural Remembrance: Traces of National Socialism in West Germany, 1945–1960." *History and Memory* 12, no. 2 (2000): 92–121.

Conley, Tom. *Cartographic Cinema*. Minneapolis: University of Minnesota Press, 2007.

Conrad, Andreas. "Die Todsünde der Wehrkraftzersetzung: Nicht im Interesse der Bundeswehr: Frank Wisbars Stalingrad-Film 'Hunde, wollt ihr ewig leben?'" *Der Tagesspiegel*, January 31, 1993.

Cooke, Paul, and Marc Silberman. *Screening War: Perspectives on German Suffering*. Rochester, N.Y.: Camden House, 2010.

Corrigan, Timothy, and Patricia White, with Meta Mazaj. *Critical Visions in Film Theory: Classic and Contemporary Readings*. Boston: Bedford / St. Martin's, 2011.

Cosgrove, Denis. *Apollo's Eye: A Cartographic Genealogy of the Earth in the Western Imagination*. Baltimore: Johns Hopkins University Press, 2001.

Crane, Conrad C. *Bombs, Cities, and Civilians: American Airpower Strategy in World War II*. Lawrence: University Press of Kansas, 1993.

Cresswell, Tim. *On the Move: Mobility in the Modern West*. New York: Routledge, 2006.

Creveld, Martin. *The Transformation of War*. New York: Free Press, 1991.

Cunningham, Douglas A., and John Nelson, eds. *A Companion to War Films*. Malden, Mass.: Wiley, 2016.

Cwerner, Saulo. "Introducing Aeromobilities." In *Aeromobilities*, edited by S. Kesselring, John Urry, and Saulo Cwerner, 1–21. New York: Routledge, 2009.

Davidson, John, and Sabine Hake, eds. *Framing the Fifties: Fifties Cinema in Divided Germany*. New York: Berghahn, 2007.

Delaney, David. *Territory: A Short Introduction*. Oxford: Wiley-Blackwell, 2005.

Deleuze, Gilles. *Cinema 1: The Movement-Image*. Minneapolis: University of Minnesota Press, 1986.

———. *Cinema 2: The Time-Image*. Minneapolis: University of Minnesota Press, 1989.

Diehl, James. *The Thanks of the Fatherland*. Chapel Hill: University of North Carolina Press, 1993.

Dimendberg, Edward. *Film Noir and the Spaces of Modernity*. Cambridge, Mass.: Harvard University Press, 2004.

Duncan, Pansy. *The Emotional Life of Postmodernism: Affect Theory's Other*. London: Routledge, 2016.

Eisner, Lotte. *Fritz Lang*. 1976. Reprint, New York: De Capo, 1986.

Ek. "Bei Göttingen wird das Grauen wieder lebendig: General Heusinger meinte: 'zu Früh!'" *Abendpost*, February 4, 1959.

Elden, Stuart. *The Birth of Territory*. Chicago: University of Chicago Press, 2013.

Elias, Norbert. *The Civilizing Process: Sociogenetic and Psychogenetic Investigations*. Malden, Mass.: Blackwell, 1994.

Elsaesser, Thomas. "Early German Cinema: A Second Life?" In *A Second Life: German Cinema's First Decades*, edited by Thomas Elsaesser and Michael Wedel, 9–40. Amsterdam: Amsterdam University Press, 1996.

———. *Weimar Cinema and After: Germany's Historical Imaginary*. New York: Routledge, 2000.

Eppler, John. *Rommel ruft Kairo*. Gütersloh, Germany: Bertelsmann, 1959.

Erll, Astrid, and Ansgar Nünning, eds. *Cultural Memory Studies: An International and Interdisciplinary Handbook*. Berlin: de Gruyter, 2008.

Evans, Richard. *Third Reich at War, 1939–45*. London: Penguin, 2008.

Federle, Courtney. "Picture Postcard: Kracauer Writes from Berlin." In *Peripheral Visions: The Hidden Stages of Weimar Cinema*, edited by Kenneth Calhoon, 39–54. Detroit: Wayne State University Press, 2001.

Fisher, Jaimey. "Deleuze in a Ruinous Context: German Rubble-Film and Italian Neorealism." *Iris* 23 (Spring 1997): 53–74.

———. *Disciplining Germany: Youth, Reeducation, and Reconstruction after the Second World War*. Detroit: Wayne State University Press, 2007.

———. "Exploding the Cosmopolitan and Treating the Foreigners' Foreignness: Paul Leni's *The Diary of Dr. Hart*." In *Refocus: The Films of Paul Leni*, edited by Erica Tortolani and Martin F. Norden, 36–51. Edinburgh: Edinburgh University Press, 2021.

———. "Film and Affect, Theories Entwined: The Case of the War Genre in *Saving Private Ryan* (Steven Spielberg, 1998)." In *The Palgrave Handbook of Affect Studies and Textual Criticism*, edited by Donald R. Wehrs and Thomas Blake, 509–537. New York: Palgrave, 2018.

———. *Generic Histories of German Cinema: Genre and Its Deviations*. Rochester, N.Y.: Camden House, 2013.

———. "Introduction: Toward Generic Histories: Film Genre, Genre Theory, and German Film Studies." In *Generic Histories of German Cinema: Genre and Its Deviations*, 1–26. Rochester, N.Y.: Camden House, 2013.

———. "Landscapes of Death: Space and the Mobilization Genre in G. W. Pabst's *Westfront 1918* (1930)." In *The Many Faces of Weimar Cinema: Rediscovering Germany's Filmic Legacy*, edited by Christian Rogowski, 268–285. Rochester, N.Y.: Camden House, 2010.

———. "Resisting the War (Film): Wicki's 'Masterpiece' *Die Brücke* and Its Generic Transformations." In *Generic Histories of German Cinema: Genre and Its Deviations*, edited by Jaimey Fisher, 109–132. Rochester, N.Y.: Camden House, 2013.

Fisher, Jaimey, and Brad Prager. Introduction to *The Collapse of the Conventional: German Film and Its Politics at the Turn of the Twenty-First Century*, edited by Jaimey Fisher and Brad Prager, 1–38. Detroit: Wayne State University Press, 2010.

Flint, Colin. *Introduction to Geopolitics*. London: Routledge, 2017.

Follett, Ken. *The Key to Rebecca*. 1980. Reprint, London: Penguin, 2002.

Foucault, Michel. "Of Other Spaces: Utopias and Heterotopias." *Diacritics* 16, no. 1 (Spring 1986): 22–27.

Friedberg, Anne. *Window Shopping: Cinema and the Postmodern*. Berkeley: University of California Press, 1993.

Fritzsche, Peter. *Life and Death in the Third Reich*. Cambridge, Mass.: Belknap Press of Harvard University Press, 2008.

———. *A Nation of Fliers: German Aviation and the Popular Imagination*. Cambridge, Mass.: Harvard University Press, 1992.

Gagnon, Mark. "Making Citizens out of Soldiers: Rearming the Individual in Paul May's *08/15*." In *A Companion to War Films*, edited by Douglas A. Cunningham and John Nelson, 271–288. Malden, Mass.: Wiley, 2016.

Galt, Rosalind. *The New European Cinema: Redrawing the Map*. New York: Columbia University Press, 2006.

Geisler, Michael. "The Battleground of Modernity: *Westfront 1918* (1930)." In *The Films of G. W. Pabst: An Extraterritorial Cinema*, edited by Eric Rentschler, 91–102. New Brunswick, N.J.: Rutgers University Press, 1990.

Gemünden, Gerd. "Film and Media Studies." *German Studies Review* 39, no. 3 (October 2016): 541–551.

Gi. "Hunde, wollt ihr ewig leben?" *Evangelischer Film Beobachter* (190), April 16, 1959.

Giaccaria, Paolo, and Claudio Minca. "For a Tentative Spatial Theory of the Third Reich." In *Hitler's Geographies: The Spatialities of the Third Reich*, edited by Paolo Giaccaria and Claudio Minca, 19–44. Chicago: University of Chicago Press, 2015.

Gilmartin, Mary, and Elenoree Kofman. "Critically Feminist Geopolitics." In *Mapping Women, Making Politics: Feminist Perspectives on Political Geography*, edited by Lynn A. Staeheli, Eleonore Kofman, and Linda Peake, 113–126. London: Routledge, 2004.

Glaser, Herman. *Kulturgeschichte der Bundesrepublik Deutschland: Zwischen Kapitulation und Währungsreform, 1945–1948*. Munich: Hanser, 1985.

Gleber, Anke. *The Art of Taking a Walk: Flânerie, Literature, and Film in Weimar Culture*. Princeton, N.J.: Princeton University Press, 1999.

González, Robert J., Hugh Gusterson, and Gustaff Houtman, eds. *Militarization: A Reader*. Durham, N.C.: Duke University Press, 2019.

Goodlad, Lauren M. E. *Victorian Geopolitical Aesthetic: Realism, Sovereignty, and Transnational Experience*. Oxford: Oxford University Press, 2015.

Gregg, Melissa, and Gregory J. Seigworth, eds. *The Affect Theory Reader*. Durham, N.C.: Duke University Press, 2010.

Gregory, Derek. *Geographical Imaginations*. Oxford: Blackwell, 1994.

Gunning, Tom. "An Aesthetic of Astonishment: Early Film and the [In]Credulous Spectator." *Art and Text*, Fall 1989.

———. "Cinema and the New Spirit in Art within a Culture of Movement." In *Picasso, Braque and Early Film in Cubism*, 17–33. New York: Pace Wildenstein, 2007.

———. *The Films of Fritz Lang: Allegories of Vision and Modernity*. London: British Film Institute, 2000.

———. "Landscape and the Fantasy of Moving Pictures: Early Cinema's Phantom Rides." In *Cinema and Landscape*, edited by Graeme and Jonathan Rayner Harper, 31–69. Chicago: University of Chicago Press, 2010.

Habermas, Jürgen. *The Structural Transformation of the Public Sphere: An Inquiry into a Category of Bourgeois Society*. Cambridge, Mass.: MIT Press, 1990.

Haegele, Lisa. "Violence." In *The Berlin School Glossary: An ABC of the New Wave in German Cinema*, edited by Roger Cook, Lutz Koepnick, Kristin Kopp, and Brad Prager, 271–278. London: Intellect, 2013.

Hake, Sabine. *German National Cinema*. New York: Routledge, 2002.

———. *Popular Cinema of the Third Reich*. Austin: University of Texas Press, 2001.

Hallam, Julia, and Les Roberts, eds. *Locating the Moving Image: New Approaches to Film and Place*. Bloomington: Indiana University Press, 2013.

Hammond, Michael, and Michael Williams, eds. *British Silent Cinema and the Great War*. Basingstoke, U.K.: Palgrave Macmillan, 2011.

Hanich, Julian. *Cinematic Emotion in Horror Films and Thrillers: The Aesthetic Paradox of Pleasurable Fear*. New York: Routledge, 2010.

Hansen, Eric. "Downfall (Review)." *Hollywood Reporter*, September 16, 2005.

Haraway, Donna J. *Simians, Cyborgs and Women: The Reinvention of Nature*. London: Free Association Books, 1991.

———. "Situated Knowledges: The Science Question in Feminism and the Privilege of Partial Perspective." *Feminist Studies* 14, no. 3 (Autumn 1988): 575–599.

Hart, B. H. Liddell, ed. *The Rommel Papers*. Translated by Paul Findlay. New York: Harcourt, Brace, 1953.

Harvey, David. "The Body as an Accumulation Strategy." In *Spaces of Hope*, 97–116. Berkeley: University of California Press, 2000.

———. *The Condition of Postmodernity: An Enquiry into the Origins of Cultural Change*. 1989. Reprint, Malden: Blackwell, 1992.

———. *Consciousness and the Urban Experience*. Oxford: Blackwell, 1985.
———. *Spaces of Capital: Towards a Critical Geography*. New York: Routledge, 2002.
———. *Spaces of Hope*. Berkeley: University of California Press, 2000.
Heffernan, Michael. "Fin de siècle, fin du monde? On the Origins of European Geopolitics, 1890–1920." In *Geopolitical Traditions: Critical Histories of a Century of Geopolitical Thought*, edited by David Atkinson and Klaus Dodds, 27–51. New York: Routledge, 2000.
Heineman, Elizabeth. "Hour of the Woman: Memories of Germany's 'Crisis Years' and West German National Identity." *American Historical Review* 101, no. 2 (1996): 354–395.
Heins, Laura. *Nazi Film Melodrama*. Urbana: University of Illinois Press, 2013.
Heinsohn, Bastian. "Film as Pedagogy in Late Weimar and Early Nazi Cinema: The Role of the Street in Mobilizing the Spectator." In *Continuity and Crisis in German Cinema 1928–1936*, edited by Barbara Hales, Valerie Weinstein, and Mihaela Petrescu, 51–71. Rochester, N.Y.: Camden House, 2016.
Held, David. *Democracy and the Global Order: From the Modern State to Cosmopolitan Governance*. Cambridge: Polity, 1995.
Herf, Jeffrey. *Reactionary Modernism: Technology Culture and Politics in Weimar and the Third Reich*. Cambridge: Cambridge University Press, 1984.
Herod, Andrew. *Scale*. London: Routledge, 2011.
Herwig, Holger H. *The First World War: Germany and Austria, 1914–18*. 2nd ed. London: Bloomsbury, 2014.
Herzog, Todd. "Crime Stories: Criminal, Society and the Modernist Case History." *Representations* 80, no. 1 (2002): 34–61.
Hickethier, Knut. "The Restructuring of the West German Film Industry in the 1950s." In *Framing the Fifties: Fifties Cinema in Divided Germany*, edited by John Davidson and Sabine Hake, 194–209. New York: Berghahn, 2007.
Hüppauf, Bernd. "Experiences of Modern Warfare and the Crisis of Representation." In "Special Issue on Ernst Junger." Special issue, *New German Critique* 59 (Spring 1993): 41–76.
———. "Langemarck, Verdun, and the Myth of a New Man in Germany after the First World War." *War and Society* 6, no. 2 (1988): 70–103.
Ihering, Herbert. "'Westfront' und 'Cynkala.'" In *Von Reinhardt bis Brecht vier Jahrzehnte Theater und Film*, 308–309. Berlin: Aufbau, 1961.
Jameson, Fredric. *The Geopolitical Aesthetic: Cinema and Space in the World System*. Bloomington: Indiana University Press, 1992.
———. *Postmodernism, or The Cultural Logic of Late Capitalism*. Princeton, N.J.: Princeton University Press, 1992.
———. "Spatial Systems in *North by Northwest*." In *Everything You Always Wanted to Know about Lacan but Were Afraid to Ask Hitchcock*, edited by Slavoj Zizek, 47–72. New York: Verso, 1992.
———. *Valences of the Dialectic*. New York: Verso, 2010.
Jarausch, Konrad. *After Hitler: Recivilizing Germans, 1945–1995*. Oxford: Oxford University Press, 2008.
Jarausch, Konrad, and Michael Geyer. *Shattered Past: Reconstructing German Histories*. Princeton, N.J.: Princeton University Press, 2003.
Jenkins, Henry, Sam Ford, and Joshua Green. *Spreadable Media: Creating Value and Meaning in a Networked Culture*. New York: New York University Press, 2013.
Johnson, Mark. *The Body in the Mind*. Chicago: University of Chicago Press, 1990.
Kaes, Anton. "The Cold Gaze: Notes on Mobilization and Modernity." *New German Critique* 59 (1993): 105–117.
———. *M*. London: British Film Institute, 1999.

———. *Shell Shock Cinema: Weimar Culture and the Wounds of War*. Princeton, N.J.: Princeton University Press, 2010.

Kapczynski, Jennifer. "Armchair Warriors: Heroic Postures in the West German War Film." In *Screening War: Perspectives on German Suffering*, edited by Paul Cooke and Marc Silberman, 17–35. Rochester, N.Y.: Camden House, 2010.

———. *The German Patient: Crisis and Recovery in Postwar Culture*. Ann Arbor: University of Michigan Press, 2008.

Kaplan, Caren. *Aerial Aftermaths: War from Above*. Durham, N.C.: Duke University Press, 2018.

———. "The Balloon Prospect: Aerostatic Observation and the Emergence of Militarised Aeromobility." In *From Above: War, Violence, and Verticality*, edited by Peter Adey, Mark Whitehead, and Alison J. William, 19–40. London: Hurst, 2013.

———. "Desert Wars: Virilio and the Limits of 'Genuine Knowledge.'" In *Virilio and Visual Culture*, edited by John Armitage and Ryan Bishop, 69–85. Edinburgh: Edinburgh University Press, 2013.

———. "Mobility and War: The Cosmic View of US 'Air Power.'" *Environment and Planning A* 38, no. 2 (2006): 395–407.

———. "Precision Targets: GPS and the Militarization of US Consumer Identity." *American Quarterly* 3 (2006): 693–713.

Kaplan, Caren, and C. Kelley. "Dead Reckoning: Aerial Perception and the Social Construction of Targets." *Vectors Journal* 2, no. 2 (2006), http://vectors.usc.edu/projects/index.php?project=11.

Kearns, Gerry. *Geopolitics and Empire: The Legacy of Halford Mackinder*. Oxford: Oxford University Press, 2009.

Keegan, John. *The First World War*. 1998. Reprint, New York: Vintage, 2000.

Kern, Stephen. *The Culture of Time and Space, 1880–1918*. Cambridge, Mass.: Harvard University Press, 1983.

Kester, Bernadette. *Film Front Weimar: Representations of the First World War in German Films of the Weimar Period (1919–1933)*. Film Culture in Transition, edited by Thomas Elsaesser. Amsterdam: Amsterdam University Press, 2003.

Kirby, Lynne. *Parallel Tracks: The Railroad and Silent Cinema*. Durham, N.C.: Duke University Press, 1997.

Kitchen, Martin. *Rommel's Desert War: Waging World War II in North Africa, 1941–1943*. Cambridge: Cambridge University Press, 2015.

Kitses, Jim. *Horizons West*. London: Thames & Hudson, 1969.

Kitson, Simon. *The Hunt for Nazi Spies: Fighting Espionage in Vichy France*. Translated by Catherine Tihanyi. Chicago: University of Chicago Press, 2008.

Koeppen, Manuel. "The Rhetoric of Victim Narratives in West German Films of the 1950s." In *Screening War: Perspectives on German Suffering*, edited by Paul Cooke and Marc Silberman, 56–78. Rochester, N.Y.: Camden House, 2010.

Koselleck, Reinhart. "War Memorials: Identity Formation of the Survivors." In *The Practice of Conceptual History: Timing History, Spacing Concepts*, translated and edited by Todd Presner, 285–326. Stanford, Calif.: Stanford University Press, 2002.

Kozol, Wendy. *Distance War Visible: The Ambivalence of Witnessing*. Minneapolis: University of Minnesota Press, 2014.

Kracauer, Siegfried. "The Biography as an Art Form of the New Bourgeoisie." In *The Mass Ornament: Weimar Essays*, translated by Thomas Y. Levin, 101–106. 1963. Reprint, Cambridge, Mass.: Harvard University Press, 1995.

———. *From Caligari to Hitler: A Psychological History of the German Film*. Princeton, N.J.: Princeton University Press, 1947.

———. "The Hotel Lobby." In *The Mass Ornament: Weimar Essays*, translated by Thomas Y. Levin, 173–186. 1963. Reprint, Cambridge, Mass.: Harvard University Press, 1995.

———. "Those Who Wait." In *The Mass Ornament: Weimar Essays*, translated by Thomas Y. Levin, 129–140. 1963. Reprint, Cambridge, Mass.: Harvard University Press, 1995.

———. "Travel and Dance." In *The Mass Ornament: Weimar Essays*, translated by Thomas Y. Levin, 65–73. 1963. Reprint, Cambridge, Mass.: Harvard University Press, 1995.

———. "*Westfront 1918*." *Frankfurter Zeitung*, May 27, 1930. https://www.filmportal.de/node/8133/material/678941.

Kreimeier, Klaus. *The Ufa Story*. 1992. Reprint, Berkeley: University of California Press, 1999.

Krimmer, Elisabeth. "More War Stories: *Stalingrad* and *Downfall*." In *The Collapse of the Conventional: German Film and Its Politics at the Turn of the Twenty-First Century*, edited by Jaimey Fisher and Brad Prager, 81–108. Detroit: Wayne State University Press, 2010.

LaCapra, Dominick. *Representing the Holocaust: History, Theory, Trauma*. Ithaca, N.Y.: Cornell University Press, 1994.

Landsberg, Alison. *Engaging the Past: Mass Culture and the Production of Historical Knowledge*. New York: Columbia University Press, 2015.

———. *Prosthetic Memory: The Transformation of American Remembrance in the Age of Mass Culture*. New York: Columbia University Press, 2004.

Langer, Lawrence. *Holocaust Testimonies: The Ruins of Memory*. New Haven, Conn.: Yale University Press, 1991.

Langston, Richard. *Visions of Violence: German Avant-Garde after Fascism*. Evanston, Ill.: Northwestern University Press, 2008.

Latham, Andrew. "Retheorizing the Scale of Globalization: Topologies, Actor-Networks, and Cosmopolitanism." In *Geographies of Power: Placing Scale*, edited by Andrew. Herod and M. W. Wright, 115–144. Oxford: Blackwell, 2002.

Latimer, Jon. *Alamein*. Cambridge, Mass.: Harvard University Press, 2002.

Latour, Bruno. "Recalling ANT." *Sociological Review* 47, no. 21 (1999): 17–18.

Lefebvre, Henri. *The Production of Space*. Translated by Donald Nicholson-Smith. Cambridge: Blackwell, 1991.

Lehnert, Herbert. "'Der gute Krieg ist es, der jede Sache heiligt': Das Innere Reich, Langemarck und moralische Konsequenzen." In *Im Dialog mit der Moderne: Zur deutschsprachigen Literatur von der Gründerzeit bis zur Gegenwart*, edited by Roland Jost and Hansgeorg Schmidt-Bergmann, 311–321. Frankfurt: Athenäum, 1986.

———. "Langemarck—historisch und symbolisch." *Orbis Litterarum* 42 (1987): 271–290.

Lekan, Thomas, and Thomas Zeller, eds. *Germany's Nature: Cultural Landscape and Environmental History*. New Brunswick, N.J.: Rutgers University Press, 2005.

Lenoir, Timothy, and Luke Caldwell. *The Military-Entertainment Process*. Cambridge, Mass.: Harvard University Press, 2018.

Lindqvist, Sven. *A History of Bombing*. New York: New Press, 2000.

Lloyd, Christopher. *Collaboration and Resistance in Occupied France: Representing Treason and Sacrifice*. Basingstoke, U.K.: Palgrave Macmillan, 2003.

London, Kurt. "Musik und Tonübergragung." *Der Film* 21 (May 21, 1930).

Luthardt, W. "Der Verkehrsflug in der Reich- und Landesplanung." *Zeitschrift für Geopolitik* 8 (August 1935): 516–522.

Lynch, Kevin. *Image of the City*. Cambridge, Mass.: MIT Press, 1960.

MacKenzie, Donald. *Inventing Accuracy: A Historical Sociology of Nuclear Missile Guidance*. Cambridge, Mass.: MIT Press, 1990.

Marchall, Hanns. "*Westfront 1918*." *Reichsfilmblatt*, May 24, 1930.

Marston, Sallie A. "The Social Construction of Scale." *Progress in Human Geography* 24, no. 2 (2000): 219–242.

Martin, Benjamin. *The Nazi-Fascist New Order for European Culture*. Cambridge, Mass.: Harvard University Press, 2016.
Marx, John. *Geopolitics and the Anglophone Novel, 1890–2011*. Cambridge: Cambridge University Press, 2012.
Marx, Karl. *Grundrisse*. London: Penguin Classics, 1993.
Massey, Doreen. "Flexible Sexism." *Environment and Planning D: Society and Space* 9, no. 1 (1991): 31–57.
———. *For Space*. London: SAGE, 2005.
———. "Power-Geometry and Progressive Sense of Place." In *Mapping the Futures: Local Cultures, Global Change*, edited by John Bird, Barry Curtis, Tim Putnam, and Lisa Tickner, 40–70. London: Routledge, 1993.
———. *Space, Place, and Gender*. Minneapolis: University of Minnesota Press, 1994.
Massumi, Brian. *Parables for the Virtual: Movement, Affect, Sensation*. Durham, N.C.: Duke University Press, 2002.
McFarland, Stephen. *America's Pursuit of Precision Bombing, 1910–1945*. Washington, D.C.: Smithsonian, 2008.
McNeill, William H. *Keeping Together in Time: Dance and Drill in Human History*. Cambridge, Mass.: Harvard University Press, 1995.
Messenger, Charles. *Rommel: Leadership Lessons from the Desert Fox*. World Generals Series. Basingstoke, U.K.: Palgrave Macmillan, 2009.
Mintzker, Yar. *The Defortification of the German City, 1689–1866*. Cambridge: Cambridge University Press, 2012.
Mitchell, Alan. *Nazi Paris: The History of an Occupation, 1940–1944*. New York: Berghahn, 2008.
Mitchell, W. J. T. "Imperial Landscape." In *Landscape and Power*, edited by W. J. T. Mitchell, 5–34. 1994. Reprint, Chicago: University of Chicago Press, 2002.
———. *Picture Theory: Essays on Verbal and Visual Representation*. Chicago: University of Chicago Press, 1995.
———. "Preface to the Second Edition of *Landscape and Power*: Space, Place, and Landscape." In *Landscape and Power*, edited by W. J. T. Mitchell, vii–xiv. 1994. Reprint, Chicago: University of Chicago Press, 2002.
Moeller, Robert G. "Dimensions of Social Conflict in the Great War: The View from the German Countryside." *Central European History* 14, no. 2 (June 1981): 152.
———. "Victims in Uniform: West German Combat Movies from the 1950s." In *Germans as Victims*, edited by Bill Niven, 43–61. Basingstoke, U.K.: Palgrave Macmillan, 2006.
———. *War Stories: The Search for a Usable Past in the Federal Republic of Germany*. Berkeley: University of California Press, 2001.
Moraht, D. E. "Deutsche Infanterie in Kalisch." *Berliner Tageblatt*, August 3, 1914.
Moretti, Franco. *Atlas of the European Novel, 1800–1900*. New York: Verso, 1998.
———. *Graphs, Maps, Trees: Abstract Models for a Literary History*. New York: Verso, 2005.
Mortenson, Erik. *Ambiguous Borderlands: Shadow Imagery in Cold War American Culture*. Carbondale: Southern Illinois University Press, 2016.
Mosse, George. *Fallen Soldiers: Reshaping the Memory of the World Wars*. Oxford: Oxford University Press, 1991.
———. *Nationalism and Sexuality: Respectability and Abnormal Sexuality in Modern Europe*. New York: H. Fertig, 1985.
Munteán, László, ed. *Materializing Memory in Art and Popular Culture*. New York: Routledge, 2017.
Murphy, Davis Thomas. *The Heroic Earth: Geopolitical Thought in Weimar Germany, 1918–1933*. Kent, Ohio: Kent State University Press, 1997.

Murray, Williamson. *War in the Air: 1914–45*. London: Cassell, 1999.

Musser, Charles. *Before the Nickelodeon: Edwin S. Porter and the Edison Manufacturing Company*. The UCLA Film and Television Archive Studies in History, Criticism, and Theory. Berkeley: University of California Press, 1991.

Naremore, James. *More Than Night: Film Noir in Its Contexts*. Berkeley: University of California Press, 1998.

Neale, Steve. *Genre and Hollywood*. London: Routledge, 2000.

Nelson, Velvet. *An Introduction to the Geography of Tourism*. Plymouth, U.K.: Rowman & Littlefield, 2013.

Niven, Bill, ed. *Germans as Victims*. Basingstoke, U.K.: Palgrave Macmillan, 2006.

Nora, Pierre. "General Introduction: Between Memory and History." In *Realms of Memory: Rethinking the French Past*, edited by Pierre Nora, 1–20. New York: Columbia University Press, 1996.

O'Brien, Charles. "Film Noir in France: Before the Liberation." *Iris* 21 (Spring 1996): 7–20.

O'Brien, Mary-Elizabeth. *Nazi Cinema as Enchantment: The Politics of Entertainment in the Third Reich*. Rochester, N.Y.: Camden House, 2004.

Olick, Jeffrey. "From Collective Memory to the Sociology of Mnemonic Practices and Products." In *Cultural Memory Studies: An International and Interdisciplinary Handbook*, edited by Astrid Erll and Ansgar Nünning, 151–162. Berlin: de Gruyter, 2008.

Ondaatje, Michael. *The English Patient*. New York: Vintage, 1990.

Oppelt, Ulrike. *Film Und Propaganda Im Ersten Weltkrieg: Propaganda Als Medienrealität Im Aktualitäten- Und Dokumentarfilm*. Stuttgart: Steiner, 2001.

Ó Tuathail, Gearóid. *Critical Geopolitics*. Minneapolis: University of Minnesota Press, 1996.

Parker, Geoffrey. *Western Geopolitical Thought in the Twentieth Century*. Sydney: Croom Helm, 1985.

Peterson, Jennifer Lynn. *Education in the School of Dreams: Travelogues and Early Nonfiction Film*. Durham, N.C.: Duke University Press, 2013.

Peukert, Detlev. *The Weimar Republic: Crisis of Classical Modernity*. London: Penguin, 1991.

Pinthus, Kurt. "*Westfront 1918*." *Das Abendblatt*, May 24, 1930.

Plantinga, Carl. *Moving Viewers: American Film and the Spectator's Experience*. Berkeley: University of California Press, 2009.

Ponkie. "Hunde, wollt ihr ewig leben." *Abendzeitung*, May 13, 1959.

Prager, Brad. "Beleaguered under the Sea: Wolfgang Petersen's *Das Boot* (1981) as German Hollywood Film." In *Light Motives: German Popular Film in Perspective*, edited by Randall Halle and Margaret McCarthy, 237–258. Detroit: Wayne State University Press, 2003.

Pryce-Jones, David. *Paris in the Third Reich: A History of the German Occupation, 1940–1944*. London: William Collins, 1981.

Remy, Maurice Philip. *Mythos Rommel*. Munich: List, 2002.

Rentschler, Eric, ed. *The Films of G. W. Pabst: An Extraterritorial Cinema*. New Brunswick, N.J.: Rutgers University Press, 1990.

———. *The Ministry of Illusion*. Cambridge, Mass.: Harvard University Press, 1997.

Rhodes, John David, and Elena Gorfinkel, eds. *Taking Place: Location and the Moving Image*. Minneapolis: University of Minnesota Press, 2011.

Riding, Alan. *And the Show Went On: Cultural Life in Nazi-Occupied Paris*. New York: Alfred A. Knopf, 2010.

Robertson, Linda. *The Dream of Civilized Warfare: World War I Flying Aces and the American Imagination*. Minneapolis: University of Minnesota Press, 2003.

Rogg, Matthias. "Die Luftwaffe im NS-Propagandafilm." In *Krieg Und Militär Im Film des 20: Jahrhunderts*, edited by Matthias Rogg and Wolfgang Schmidt Bernhard Chiari, 343–348. Munich: Oldenbourg Wissenschaftverlag, 2003.

Rose, Gillian. *Feminism and Geography: The Limits of Geographical Knowledge*. Minneapolis: University of Minnesota Press, 1993.

Ruoff, Jeffrey, and Alexandra Schneider, eds. *Virtual Voyages: Cinema and Travel*. Durham, N.C.: Duke University Press, 2006.

Schama, Simon. *Landscape and Memory*. New York: Vintage, 1996.

Schatz, Thomas. *Hollywood Genres: Formulas, Filmmaking and the Studio System*. New York: Random House, 1981.

Schelhaas, Bruno, and Ingro Hönsch. "History of German Geography: Worldwide Reputation and Strategies of Nationalization and Institutionalization." In *Geography: Discipline, Profession and Subject since 1870, an International Survey*, edited by Gary S. Dunbar, 9–32. Dordrecht: Kluwer, 2001.

Schindler, Stephan, and Lutz Koepnick. "Against the Wall? The Global Imaginary of German Cinema." In *The Cosmopolitan Screen: German Cinema and the Global Imaginary, 1945 to the Present*, edited by Stephan Schindler and Lutz Koepnick, 1–21. Ann Arbor: University of Michigan Press, 2007.

Schivelbusch, Wolfgang. *Disenchanted Night: The Industrialization of Light in the Nineteenth Century*. Berkeley: University of California Press, 1995.

———. *Railway Journey: The Industrialization of Time and Space in the Nineteenth Century*. 1977. Reprint, Berkeley: University of California Press, 1986.

Schlüppmann, Heide. *The Uncanny Gaze: The Drama of Early Cinema*. Translated by Inge Pollmann, with a foreword by Miriam Hansen. 1990. Reprint, Urbana: University of Illinois Press, 2010.

Scholz, Anne-Marie. "The Bridge on the River Kwai (1957) Revisited: Combat Cinema, American Culture and the German Past." *German History* 26, no. 2 (2008): 219–250.

Schulte-Sasse, Linda. *Entertaining the Reich: Illusions of Wholeness in Nazi Cinema*. Durham, N.C.: Duke University Press, 1996.

Sebald, W. G. *On the Natural History of Destruction*. New York: Random House, 2003.

Shandley, Robert. *Rubble-Films: German Cinema in the Shadow of the Third Reich*. Philadelphia: Temple University Press, 2001.

Shaviro, Steven. *Post-cinematic Affect*. Winchester, U.K.: Zero Books, 2010.

Shaw, Tony. *British Cinema and the Cold War: The State, Propaganda and Consensus*. New York: I. B. Tauris, 2001.

Siewert, Wulf. "Flugzeung und Erdraum." *Zeitschrift für Geopolitik* 8 (August 1935): 508–516.

Simmel, Ernst. *Kriegs-neurosen und "psychisches trauma."* Munich: Otto Nemnich, 1918.

Sklar, Robert, and Charles Musser, eds. *Resisting Images: Essay on Cinema and History*. Philadelphia: Temple University Press, 1990.

Slocum, J. David. *Hollywood and the War, the Film Reader*. New York: Routledge, 2006.

Smith, Neil. "Contours of a Spatialized Politics: Homeless Vehicles and the Production of Geographical Scale." *Social Text* 33 (1992): 54–81.

Sobchack, Vivian. *The Address of the Eye: A Phenomenology of Film Experience*. Princeton, N.J.: Princeton University Press, 1992.

———. *Carnal Thoughts: Embodiment and Moving Image Culture*. Berkeley: University of California Press, 2004.

Soja, Edward W. *Postmodern Geographies: The Reassertion of Space in Critical Social Theory*. New York: Verso, 1989.

———. *Thirdspace: Journeys to Los Angeles and Other Real-and-Imagined Places*. Cambridge: Blackwell, 1996.

Stafford, Barbara. "Toward Romantic Landscape Perception: Illustrated Travel Accounts and the Rise of 'Singularity' as an Aesthetic Category." *Art Quarterly*, n.s., 1 (Autumn 1977): 89–124.

Stahl, Roger. *Through the Crosshairs: War, Visual Culture, and the Weaponized Gaze*. New Brunswick, N.J.: Rutgers University Press, 2018.
Staiger, Janet. "Hybrid or Inbred: The Purity Hypothesis and Hollywood Genre History." In *Film Genre Reader III*, edited by Barry Keith Grant, 185–299. 1997. Reprint, Austin: University of Texas Press, 2003.
Stam, Robert. "Mobilizing Fictions: The Media, the Gulf War, and the Recruitment of the Spectator." *Public Culture* 2 (1992): 102–103.
Stiasny, Philipp. *Das Kino und der Krieg, Deutschland 1914–1929*. Munich: edition text + kritik, 2009.
Stoler, Ann. *Race and the Education of Desire: Foucault's History of Sexuality and the Colonial Order of Things*. Durham, N.C.: Duke University Press, 1995.
Tan, Ed S. *Emotion and the Structure of Narrative Film*. Mahwah, N.J.: Lawrence, 1995.
Tegel, Susan. *Nazis and the Cinema*. London: Continuum, 2007.
Thrif, Nigel. *Non-representational Theory: Space, Politics, Affect*. London: Routledge, 2007.
Tignor, Robert L. *Egypt: A Short History*. Princeton, N.J.: Princeton University Press, 2010.
Tudor, Andrew. "Genre." In *Film Genre Reader III*, edited by Barry Keith Grant, 185–299. 1997. Reprint, Austin: University of Texas Press, 2003.
Turim, Maureen. *Flashbacks in Film: Memory and History*. New York: Routledge, 1989.
Tzanelli, Rodanthi. *The Cinematic Tourist*. New York: Routledge, 2007.
Urry, John. *Mobilities*. Cambridge: Polity, 2007.
———. *The Tourist Gaze*. 3rd ed. Los Angeles: SAGE, 2011.
Vajda, Ladislaus, Karl Otten, and Peter Martin Lampel, eds. *Kamerdschaft: Drehbuch Von Vajda/Otten/Lampel Zu G. W. Pabsts Film Von 1931*. Munich: edition text + kritik, 1997.
Vidler, Anthony. "Terres Inconnues: Cartographies of a Landscape to Be Invented." *October* 115 (Winter 2006): 13–30.
———. *Warped Space: Art, Architecture, and Anxiety in Modern Culture*. Cambridge, Mass.: MIT Press, 2000.
Virilio, Paul. *War and Cinema: The Logistics of Perception*. New York: Verso, 1991.
von Moltke, Johannes. *No Place like Home: Locations of Heimat in German Cinema*. Berkeley: University of California Press, 2005.
Wark, McKenzie. *Virtual Geographies: Living with Global Media Events*. Bloomington: Indiana University Press, 1994.
Watson, Alexander. *Enduring the Great War: Combat, Morale and Collapse in the German and British Armies, 1914–1918*. Cambridge: Cambridge University Press, 2008.
———. *Ring of Steel: German and Austria-Hungary in World War I*. New York: Basic Books, 2014.
Weber, Samuel. *Targets of Opportunity: On the Militarization of Thinking*. New York: Fordham, 2005.
Welch, David. *Propaganda and the German Cinema 1933–1945*. London: I. B. Tauris, 1983.
Winkel, Roel Vande, and David Welch, eds. *Cinema and the Swastika: The International Expansion of the Third Reich Cinema*. Basingstoke, U.K.: Palgrave Macmillan, 2007.
Williams, Linda. "Melodrama Revisited." In *Refiguring American Film Genres: History and Theory*, edited by Nick Browne, 42–88. Berkeley: University of California Press, 1998.
Winter, Jay. "Sites of Memory and the Shadow of War." In *Cultural Memory Studies: An International and Interdisciplinary Handbook*, edited by Astrid Erll and Ansgar Nünning, 61–76. Berlin: de Gruyter, 2008.
Wollenberg, Hans. "*Westfront 1918* (Vier von der Infantrie)." *Lichbildbühne* 124 (May 24, 1930).
Wöss, Fritz. *Hunde, wollt ihr ewig leben*. Hamburg: Zsolnay, 1958.
Yates, Frances A. *The Art of Memory*. 1966. Reprint, New York: Routledge, 2011.
Zabecki, David T. "Rethinking Rommel." *Military History* 32, no. 5 (2016): 24–28.

Index

Page numbers in *italics* refer to figures.

About the Author

JAIMEY FISHER is a professor of German and cinema and digital media at the University of California, Davis (UC Davis), where he is also director of the UC Davis Humanities Institute. He is the author of *Treme*, *Christian Petzold*, and *Disciplining Germany: Youth, Reeducation, and Reconstruction after the Second World War*. He is also the editor or coeditor of many volumes, including *The Berlin School and Its Global Contexts*, *Generic Histories of German Cinema: Genre and Its Deviations*, *Spatial Turns: Space, Place, and Mobility in German Literary and Visual Culture*, and *Critical Theory: Current State and Future Prospects*, among others.

Available titles in the War Culture series:

Tanine Allison, *Destructive Sublime: World War II in American Film and Media*
Ahmed Al-Rawi, *Cyberwars in the Middle East*
Brenda M. Boyle, *American War Stories*
Brenda M. Boyle and Jeehyun Lim, eds., *Looking Back on the Vietnam War: Twenty-First-Century Perspectives*
Katherine Chandler, *Unmanning: How Humans, Machines and Media Perform Drone Warfare*
Liz Clarke, *The American Girl Goes to War: Women and National Identity in U.S. Silent Film*
Martin A. Danahay, *War without Bodies: Framing Death from the Crimean to the Iraq War*
Jonna Eagle, *Imperial Affects: Sensational Melodrama and the Attractions of American Cinema*
Jaimey Fisher, *German Ways of War: The Affective Geographies and Generic Transformations of German War Films*
H. Bruce Franklin, *Crash Course: From the Good War to the Forever War*
Aaron Michael Kerner, *Torture Porn in the Wake of 9/11: Horror, Exploitation, and the Cinema of Sensation*
David Kieran and Edwin A. Martini, eds., *At War: The Military and American Culture in the Twentieth Century and Beyond*
Delia Malia Caparoso Konzett, *Hollywood's Hawaii: Race, Nation, and War*
Nan Levinson, *War Is Not a Game: The New Antiwar Soldiers and the Movement They Built*
Matt Sienkiewicz, *The Other Air Force: U.S. Efforts to Reshape Middle Eastern Media since 9/11*
Jon Simons and John Louis Lucaites, eds., *In/visible War: The Culture of War in Twenty-First-Century America*
Roger Stahl, *Through the Crosshairs: War, Visual Culture, and the Weaponized Gaze*
Mary Douglas Vavrus, *Postfeminist War: Women and the Media-Military-Industrial Complex*
Simon Wendt, ed., *Warring over Valor: How Race and Gender Shaped American Military Heroism in the Twentieth and Twenty-First Centuries*